THE
ILLUSTRATED
CONFEDERATE
READER

Other Random House Value Publishing Civil War Titles

The Civil War Society's Encyclopedia of the Civil War

History of the Confederate States Navy

Lee and His Generals

The Lost Cause

A Diary from Dixie (by Mary Chesnut)

Ambrose Bierce's Civil War

The Blue and the Gray

Images of the Civil War (by Mort Künstler)

Who Was Who in the Civil War

Secret Missions of the Civil War

The Official Military Atlas of the Civil War

Harper's Pictorial History of the Civil War

Hallowed Ground

The Civil War: Strange and Fascinating Facts

THE
ILLUSTRATED
CONFEDERATE
READER

Rod Gragg

GRAMERCY BOOKS
NEW YORK

This 1998 edition is published by Gramercy Books,
a division of Random House Value Publishing, Inc.,
201 East 50th Street, New York, New York 10022,
by agreement with HarperCollins Publishers, Inc.

Gramercy Books and design are registered trademarks of
Random House Value Publishing, Inc.

Random House
New York • Toronto • London • Sydney • Auckland
http://www.randomhouse.com/

Printed and bound in the United States of America

Library of Congress Cataloging-in-Publication Data
Gragg, Rod.
The Illustrated Confederate reader / Rod Gragg.
p.   cm.
Originally published: New York: Harper & Row, c1989.
Includes bibliographical references and index.
ISBN 0-517-20187-9
1. Confederate States of America—History. 2. United States—History—Civil War, 1861-1865.
3. Confederate States of America—History—Pictorial works. 4. United States—History—Civil War,
1861-1865—Pictorial works. I. Title.
[E487.G72 1998]
973.7´13—dc21   97-44186
                                                                                                                    CIP

8 7 6 5 4 3 2 1

For three sons of the South:
Bob, Charles, and Ted
And for a new generation:
Faith, Rachel, Elizabeth, Joni, and Penny

Contents

Preface

From Austin to Richmond, from Tallahassee to Frankfort, the story of the South's struggle for independence, 1861–1865, lies piecemeal in richly laden repositories, awaiting examination. From aged and yellowed letters, hastily scribbled diaries, century-old and dog-eared memoirs, and crisply formal official records, the voices of a generation of Southerners come forth at call to tell in evocative language the intimate details of a people at war.

In this book I've tried to assemble some of those voices and allow them to tell the story of the Southern people during the War Between the States. It is a story that bears telling and retelling, for—like their counterparts in the North—they were a remarkable people living in an equally remarkable era of American history.

In his classic account of the Confederate soldier, *The Life of Johnny Reb,* historian Bell Irvin Wiley aptly described the generation of Southerners caught up in the War Between the States. "Generally speaking," he wrote, "they were not the drab, improvident, depraved ignoramuses depicted in *Tobacco Road* and other fictional works. Many of them were deeply religious; most of those who had families repeatedly manifested concern for the education of their children; the overwhelming majority were generous in their impulses, wholesome in their reactions, and stalwart in their adversity."

The South's futile war for independence was an unprecedented American experience. Southerners of the 1860s endured a cataclysmic ordeal unmatched by any other region of the United States at any time in American history. The Southerners of the War Between the States were an exceptional body of Americans, deeply rooted in the life-style of the soil, and infused with the traditions and values of American agrarian society. Therefore, the Southern story of the war is told best, I believe, in the words of those who experienced it. I have attempted to present their words intact—spelling, grammar, and punctuation included—edited for clarity and brevity, and selected with the goal of presenting a historically accurate portrait of the Southern soldier and civilian.

It is my hope that this work captures in book-length detail the portrait effectively summarized in Professor Wiley's conclusion to *The Life of Johnny Reb,* which, although aimed at the Southern soldier, applies equally well to Southern civilians: "He was not immune to panic, nor even to cowardice, but few if any soldiers have had more than he of *élan,* of determination, of perseverance, and of the sheer courage which it takes to stand in the face of a withering fire. He was far from perfect, but his achievement against great odds in scores of desperate battles through four years of war is irrefutable evidence of his prowess and is an eternal monument to his greatness. . . ."

Rod Gragg

Conway, South Carolina

THE ILLUSTRATED CONFEDERATE READER

1

Soldiers of the South

They were the soldiers of the South—ordinary men drawn into an extraordinary war. They came from all over the South: from the piney woods of Alabama, the bayous of Louisiana, the mountains of North Carolina, the swampy flatlands of Florida. They hailed from Virginia's fertile Shenandoah, from the grassy prairie of Texas, from the red clay hills of Georgia, the moss-draped South Carolina Low Country, the rich farmland of Mississippi, the Ozark ridges of Arkansas, and the country hamlets of Tennessee.

Most were ordinary Southerners who, clad in Confederate gray and butternut, created what became one of the most acclaimed fighting forces in military history. Battling for Southern independence, they were eventually defeated. Yet, outnumbered, underfed, and poorly equipped, they withstood one of the world's most powerful military forces for four years of the bloodiest warfare ever waged in the Western Hemisphere. Today they are the one-dimensional figures of history, but in their day the Southern soldiers pictured on the following pages—and some 750,000 others—were the flesh-and-blood men at war who, under the Confederacy's Starry Cross, created the lasting legacy of Johnny Reb.

Splendidly attired in Confederate gray, Lt. Laurie M. Anderson, an officer in Company A of the 1st Florida Infantry, assumed a dignified pose for this early wartime photograph. Described by his troops as "brave and gallant . . . experienced and beloved," he rose in the ranks from private to lieutenant in just eight months. In April of 1862, he was mortally wounded at the Battle of Shiloh.

South Carolinian John Bagnel Brogdon was fifty years old when he volunteered for Confederate service in 1861. He became a private in Company I of the 7th South Carolina Cavalry, served through the war, and was present when Lee surrendered at Appomattox.

Within months of his enlistment in Company E of the 2nd Kentucky Mounted Infantry, Bugler John Washington Payne became a prisoner of war—captured at the Confederate surrender of Fort Donelson on February 16, 1862. After seven months in Indiana's Camp Morton prison, he was released in a prisoner exchange. He returned to his regiment and was promoted to regimental bugler—a post he held until war's end.

Three days after the surrender of Fort Sumter, Virginian Andrew F. Skidmore enlisted as a volunteer in the Mount Vernon Guards and posed for this photograph with shoulder epaulets in place and plumed shako in hand. A year later, as a private in Company E of the 17th Virginia Infantry, Skidmore was killed during a Federal artillery bombardment at Yorktown, Virginia.

David Grey Parker, a nineteen-year-old North Carolina farmer, enlisted in Confederate service in 1861, and became a sergeant in Company H of the 14th North Carolina Infantry. A year later he died in a Richmond hospital.

Lt. Andrew H. Ramsey of the 1st South Carolina Rifles stood erect and solemn for the photographer at war's beginning. In July of 1864, as a veteran captain serving near Richmond, he would take up an ax and chop off a toe—allegedly to avoid further duty. Faced with a court martial for "lack of courage," he would resign his officer's commission—an act his commanding officer would promptly approve "in the interest of the service."

In 1861, Texan Edward Currie volunteered for duty in Houston and was made captain in the Crockett Southrons—named in honor of one of the Southern heroes at the Alamo. Later, the Crockett Southrons would become Company I of the 1st Texas Infantry. With a saber in one hand and a cocked revolver in the other, Captain Currie presented a warlike appearance. When his regiment was transferred to Virginia, Currie failed to win reelection to captain and returned home to Texas.

Young John Rhodes was drafted into Confederate service at Richmond in April of 1864. He was assigned to the 5th Virginia Infantry and was made a provost guard. Six months later, he was captured at the Battle of Winchester and spent the remainder of the war in a Federal prisoner of war camp.

At the Battle of Sharpsburg in 1862, Lt. Thomas R. Love of the 8th Florida Infantry was promoted to captain on the field after the death of his commanding officer. At Gettysburg, he was seriously wounded while leading his troops in battle, and lay on the battlefield for several days. When he was finally brought to a field hospital, surgeons worked to save him, but he died of his wounds.

Drummer Charles E. Mosby was thirteen years old when he was mustered into Company I of the 6th Virginia Infantry in August of 1861. After serving a little more than half a year in the army, he went home and was declared AWOL. Soon afterward he was officially dismissed from the service by order of the Secretary of War, who declared Mosby a minor exempt from service.

When the war began, Georgia newspaper editor Benjamin G. Liddon left journalism and took up arms in Company D of the 3rd Georgia Infantry. He saw action at First Manassas, Sharpsburg, Fredericksburg, Gettysburg, and elsewhere. In 1864, he was mortally wounded in the Battle of the Crater at Petersburg.

South Carolinian James Parker Boswell left his mercantile business in 1862 and enlisted in Company G of the 3rd South Carolina Light Artillery, known as the Palmetto Battalion. Promoted to corporal, he spent most of the war defending Charleston, was sent to North Carolina to oppose Sherman's invasion in 1865, and eventually was surrendered with Gen. Joseph E. Johnston's Confederate army.

Capt. Amos Whitehead, a Florida planter who commanded Company M of the 2nd Florida Infantry, assumed a Napoleonic pose for the camera. He enlisted as a sergeant, rose through the ranks to captain, and saw extensive action in the war's Eastern Theater. He was wounded in action at the Battle of Sharpsburg and lost a foot. Undaunted, he returned to Florida to raise a troop of cavalry.

Confederate Navy officer W. F. Jones was third assistant engineer aboard the ironclad ram Chicora. In late 1863, Jones's vessel attacked and seriously damaged the U.S.S. Keystone State off Charleston. In February of 1865, when Charleston was evacuated by the Confederates, the Chicora was destroyed to prevent her capture by Federal forces.

Pvt. Ferdinand Berry was a member of Nashville's Rock City Guards, which became Company B of the 1st Tennessee Infantry in May of 1861. Berry's company saw action in the 1861 Cheat Mountain Campaign in West Virginia, accompanied Gen. Braxton Bragg on his 1862 invasion of Kentucky, and fought at Chaplin Hills, Murfreesboro, Chickamauga, and Missionary Ridge. In 1864, after his regiment had retreated to Dalton, Georgia, Berry's army service record was closed with a single notation: "died."

When he joined the Confederate army in 1862 at age eighteen, smooth-faced Hilliard Todd of Conwayboro, South Carolina, looked more like a schoolboy than a soldier. Even so, he enlisted for the duration, spent most of the war defending Charleston as a private in Manigault's Battalion of South Carolina Artillery, and was wounded in battle several times. One of five brothers who entered Confederate service during the war, he alone survived.

Second Lt. Robert Cunningham of the 4th Kentucky Cavalry rode with Confederate raider John Hunt Morgan. Cunningham was seriously wounded in action at Hartsville, Tennessee, in December of 1862, but was back in the saddle in time for Morgan's famous raids through Kentucky. Later, he was captured with 700 more of Morgan's men at Buffington Island, Ohio, during Morgan's ill-fated Ohio raid.

James Thomas Weaver, a thirty-three-year-old farmer from Buncombe County, North Carolina, was elected first lieutenant in Company A of the 60th North Carolina Infantry when the regiment was organized in 1862. Responsible and popular, he rose rapidly to lieutenant colonel. He survived some of the war's deadliest actions—at Murfreesboro, Missionary Ridge, and Chickamauga—and was cited for "gallantry and efficiency" under fire. On December 7, 1864, during the Franklin Campaign, Weaver and his regiment were detached to destroy a section of railroad near Columbia, Tennessee, and there Lt. Col. Weaver was killed by enemy fire.

Citadel cadet John Elias Boinest—his kepi decorated with a palmetto tree cockade—cradles a rifle and assumes a martial pose. Boinest spent much of the war defending the South Carolina coast with other cadets from The Citadel, the Charleston military academy whose cadets fired some of the war's opening shots against Fort Sumter.

In January of 1862, twenty-six-year-old John Scott Pickle enlisted in Company B of the 18th Texas Cavalry as a private. He furnished his own horse and two firearms, including a $75 revolver. A year later, he was among the 5,000 Confederates who surrendered at Arkansas Post. After a few months' imprisonment, Pickle managed to escape and returned to Confederate service.

Outfitted in an obviously new uniform, with his hat brim smartly bent back and a revolver stuck in his belt, Kentucky Confederate Alexander Macklin appeared ready for action. He went off to war in Beck's Partisan Rangers, rose to corporal in the 9th Kentucky Cavalry, and rode with Kentucky's famed Confederate raider, Gen. John Hunt Morgan.

With a bowie knife tucked in his belt and a pistol in his hand, Tennessean Robert Patterson went to war. He was a private in the 12th Tennessee Infantry and spent much of the war in his home state. In May of 1863, he died there in an army hospital.

Henry Laurens Benbow entered Confederate service as a captain in Hatch's Battalion of Coast Rangers, which later became the 23rd South Carolina Infantry. Just over a year later, Benbow was a full colonel—at age thirty-two. He was wounded at Second Manassas, recovered, and held command through the remainder of the war. In April of 1865, at the Battle of Five Forks, he was shot through both thighs and captured, ending the war as a Federal prisoner.

The identity of this well-armed Alabama teenager has been lost to history. Known to his descendants only as "Uncle Bud," he was killed in battle at age seventeen.

2

Johnny Reb in Camp and Field

His enemies called him Johnny Reb, Johnny, or just Reb. He was comfortable with any of those names, although he was officially a Confederate—a soldier of the Confederate States of America. Typically, he was eighteen to twenty-nine years old, although his ranks included the middle-aged and even old men. He was also most likely a farmer, but not a planter. Most soldiers in gray were small farmers and only a slim minority owned slaves or large amounts of land. Sprinkled among his ranks were teachers, laborers, artisans, politicians, lawyers, clerks, mechanics, merchants, and members of most nineteenth-century American professions. However, an estimated two thirds of Johnny Reb's ranks were filled by men of the soil—traditional Southern farmers.

Nobody knows how many Southerners wore the gray. Some authorities say as many as 1.4 million Confederates were in the field at one time or another during the course of the war. Others believe Confederate troops numbered as few as 600,000. The best estimate probably lies somewhere in between: probably some 750,000 Southerners were in Confederate service during the War Between the States.

Most of their time was not spent in battle. Fighting, although it was the ultimate goal of all soldierly activity, actually composed only a small portion of the Confederate soldier's life. Most of Johnny Reb's time was spent preparing for battle: training, drilling, waiting in camp, marching here and there.

From the excitement of the war's opening days, when Johnny Reb rushed to volunteer, to the sobering defeat at war's end, when the survivors trudged homeward, here, in his own words, is Johnny Reb's story of life in camp and field.

15

Johnny Rebs in camp near Pensacola, Florida.

"NO TWO KEPT THE SAME STEP"

They called themselves by a variety of colorful names—the Lone Star Rifles, the South Florida Bull Dogs, the Dixie Invincibles, the Charleston Light Dragoons, the Clayton Yellow Jackets. They were the young men of the South who rushed to arms in 1861. Most were eager to fight, but few were trained for war. However, they generally believed that whatever soldiering skills they lacked would be compensated for by their enthusiasm, the Southerner's natural military instincts, and the rightness of their cause.

Some had been reluctant secessionists, but most reservations about Southern independence had been washed away in a flood of sectional patriotism—a Southwide response to President Lincoln's call for 75,000 volunteers to crush "the insurrection" in the South. From Texas to Virginia, the men of the South organized themselves for war amid fervent celebration. Eventually, they would mature into one of the most highly regarded fighting forces in history, but in the war's early days most were equipped with an abundance of zeal and a shortage of experience.

Johnny Reb's first days were described by John B. Gordon, destined to become one of the Confederacy's prominent generals, who organized a company of troops from the mountains of Georgia, Alabama, and Tennessee. They called themselves the Raccoon Roughs.

My company did not wait for orders to move, but hastily bidding adieu to home and friends, was off for Milledgeville, then capital of Georgia. At Atlanta a telegram from the governor met us, telling us to go back home, and stay there until our services were needed. Our discomfiture can be better imagined than described. In fact, there broke out at once in my ranks a new rebellion. These rugged mountaineers resolved that they would not go home; that they had a right to go to the war, had started for the war, and were not going to be trifled with by the governor or anyone else. Finally, after much persuasion, and by the cautious exercise of the authority vested in me by my office of captain, I prevailed on them to get on board the home-bound train.

As the engine-bell and the whistle blew for the train to start, the rebellion broke loose again with double fury. The men rushed to the front of the train, uncoupled the cars from the engine, and gravely informed me that they intended to go to war, and that if Governor Brown would not accept them, some other governor would. They disembarked and left the empty cars on the track, with the trainmen looking on in utter amazement.

There was no course left me but to march them through the streets of Atlanta to a camp on the outskirts. The march, or rather straggle, through that city was a sight marvelous to behold and never to be forgotten. Totally undisciplined and undrilled, no two of these men marched abreast; no two kept the same step; no two wore the same colored coats or trousers. The only pretence at uniformity was the rough fur caps made of raccoon skins, with long, bushy, streaked raccoon tails hanging from behind them. The streets were packed with men, women and children eager to catch a glimpse of this grotesque company. Curiosity was on tip-toe, and from the crowded sidewalks there came to me the inquiry, "Are you the captain of that company, sir?" With a pride which I trust was pardonable, I indicated that I was. In a moment there came to me the second inquiry, "What company is that, sir?" Up to this time no name had been chosen—at least, none had been announced to the men. I had myself, however, selected a name which I considered both poetic and appropriate, and I replied to the question, "This company is the Mountain Rifles."

Instantly a tall mountaineer said in a tone not intended for his captain, but easily overheard by his companions and the bystanders: "Mountain hell! *We* are no Mountain Rifles; we are the Raccoon Roughs." It is scarcely necessary to say that my selected name was never heard of again. This towering Ajax had killed it by a single blow. The name he gave us clung to the company during all of its long and faithful service.

Once in camp, we kept the wires hot with telegrams to governors of other states, imploring them to give us a chance. Governor Moore of Alabama finally responded, graciously consenting to incorporate the captain of the "Raccoon Roughs" and his coon-capped company into one of the regiments soon to be organized. The reading of this telegram evoked from my men the first Rebel yell it was my fortune to hear. Even then it was weird and thrilling.

Alabama's governor had given us the coveted "chance," and with bounding hearts we joined the host of volunteers then rushing to Montgomery. The line of our travel was one unbroken scene of enthusiasm. Bonfires blazed from the hills at night and torch-light processions, with drums and fifes, paraded the streets of the towns. In the absence of real cannon, blacksmiths' anvils were made to thunder our welcome. Vast throngs gathered at the depots, filling the air with their shouting and bearing banners with all conceivable devices, proclaiming Southern independence and pledging the last dollar and man for the success of the cause. Staid matrons and gaily bedecked maidens rushed upon the cars, pinned upon our lapels the blue cockades, and cheered us by chanting in thrilling chorus:

> In Dixie-land I take my stand
> To live and die in Dixie.

At other points they sang "The Bonnie Blue Flag," and the Raccoon Roughs, as they were thenceforward known, joined in the transporting chorus:

> Hurrah, hurrah, for Southern rights hurrah!
> Hurrah for the Bonnie Blue Flag that bears a single star!

In the midst of this wild excitement and boundless enthusiasm, I was induced to make some promises which I afterward found inconvenient and even impossible to fulfill. A flag was presented bearing a most embarrassing motto. That motto consisted of two words: "No Retreat." I was compelled to accept it. There was, indeed, no retreat for me then; and in my speech accepting the flag I assured the fair donors that those coon-capped boys would make that motto ring with their cracking rifles on every battlefield. . . .

Youthful Confederates at Charleston's Castle Pinckney, in the war's early days.

"EVERY DAY IS VERY MUCH THE SAME"

The gray-clad recruits of '61 who sauntered off to war expecting a quick fight were no doubt dismayed when they found themselves facing a daily routine of camp chores and drill instead of the glories of battle. Yet such was the way of war for most Confederate recruits in 1861.

Although the South's many local militia companies at least knew how to march, most volunteers had a lot to learn before they would be turned loose on the Yankees. In a letter to his wife in the summer of 1861, James W. Morgan, an orderly sergeant in Company K of the 1st Kentucky Volunteers, described daily life for the Southern soldier in the war's early days.

Camp Bartow
Near Manassas Aug. 28th 1861

My Own Dear Wife,

After quite a hard day's work I am at leisure for a few hours or until 9½ o'clock, at which hour we "old sojer boys" are under the necessity of putting out lights and going to bed, and I know of no way of employing my time half so agreeably as in writing to you. . . .

You complain that I did not give you a picture of Camp life and as it was an oversight in me, I will do so now.

Well, at 5 A.M. reveille beats and in 5 minutes thereafter the boys fall into line to answer roll call. Everyone who has overslept himself or from any other cause except sickness who fails to answer to the call is marked for extra duty and has extra duty to perform.

The next thing is breakfast, after which comes company drill at 8 o'clock. Guard mounting begins at 9½ after company drill, which lasts until guard mounting. We or rather the company has no more drilling until 3½ P.M., at which hour Regimental drill commences and lasts two of the longest hours imaginable.

After Regimental drill is over we have a ½ hour rest before going on dress parade, which is only for a show and lasts only a few minutes. This ends the day's work with the exception of cooking supper, which is not an easy job by any means.

At 9½ o'clock P.M. comes the order, "lights out," and it must be obeyed. The time between supper and 9½ o'clock is spent outside the tents if the weather is fair and is the time for singing songs and indulging in merriment of various kinds. The above is a day in Camp and every day is very much the same. . . .

I must now close. I will write every opportunity and you must do likewise. Goodby for the present.

Yours Affectionaly,
Jas W. Morgan

"HUGH HAS GOT THE MEASLES"

Most Confederate recruits were country boys fresh from the farm. They had not been exposed to most diseases common to urban populations, and in the confined conditions of camp, contagious illnesses spread easily and rapidly. Further endangering the health of recruits were unsanitary camp practices, exposure to severe weather, the rigors of life in the field, poor diet, and bad water.

Soldiers who were ready and even eager to endure the hazards of battle had not reckoned on an inglorious death by measles, pneumonia, typhoid fever, or dysentery. Yet illness appears to have killed three times as many Southern soldiers as did combat. As volunteers assembled throughout the Southern states in 1861, scores sickened with camp diseases, and many did not recover.

A graphic description of camp illness was sent home in 1861 by D. C. Jones, a young Lone Star cavalryman in Terry's Texas Rangers.

Camp Johnson Nov. 21, 1861
Dear Father and Friends,

I write you a few lines to inform you of the times. Hugh has got the measles. He has been complaining two or three days. I have just returned from the hospital where I have been to carry him—distance from camp is half mile. He is not complaining very much, yet he would be knocking about if he was not afeared. He has a very bad cold and cough. The measles have not broken out on him yet.

We carried two from our mess today. There was twelve of us at first. There is but six now able for duty. Four has the measles, one has the chils, one the typhoid newmonia. . . .

I am pretty well fatigued, somewhat from the loss of sleep. Hugh is doing pretty well. His bowels run most too free though they appear to be easy controld. One dose of powders will check them for six or eight hours, then they will run off two or three times in the course of eight or ten hours. He says he feels pretty well. He coughs some and spits up right smart fleam. His stools smell very bad, which I expect is the case with all who have the measles.

I will have to close this letter as I have the opportunity of sending it to the office immediately.

My throat is nearly well. None of our boys have died yet as I have heard of. Some of them in the hospital are very low.

Write soon. I will write you a few lines again soon if I am spared. My letters will be short for a while until I have more time. I am too much engaged to learn much news.

your son,
D. C. Jones

"WENT OFF LAUGHING"

Military discipline was a novelty to most Confederate volunteers. Many took to soldiering readily, but others resented authority and did not hesitate to argue with officers. Eventually, most volunteers acquired an adequate martial attitude, although Confederate troops displayed a distinctive casualness throughout the war.

In the war's opening months, the Southern soldier's independent spirit was particularly evident—as is illustrated by this 1861 entry in the diary of Samuel Edward Burges, a South Carolinian in the Moultrie Guards, posted to a camp near Charleston.

Sunday, February 2

Quarrel with Capt about breakfast. Said if I got none it would be my fault. replied it would be his fault, that he never troubled himself to see that the men were properly provided. On inspection said my rifle was dirty. replied it was clean, having cleaned it three days ago and had not used it since. gave me an hour to clean it in. replied I would think of it and laughed at him. ordered Lieut to report me. I finally went to him for things to clean it if the State furnished. said it did not. would lend me an oiled rag. I did not borrow. However I soaped over the rust and carried it to him. said rifle was in first rate order. I replied that it was no cleaner than before, only soaped over. Went off laughing at him.

Southern recruit Samuel Edward Burges.

"WE'LL PROUDLY BEAR THIS BANNER"

Across the Confederacy, in county seats and sprawling camps, the soldiers of the South ceremoniously assembled to observe an early wartime ritual: the official presentation of the company or regimental battle flag. Often the banner was made and presented by a patriotic band of local maidens. After dramatic speeches and boisterous cheers, the troops might depart for the war, presumably inspired for the glory that lay ahead.

The ornate oratory of one Confederate flag presentation was preserved by an unlikely source—a Yankee soldier who found the speech on the battlefield at Fredericksburg. The unknown author apparently delivered this dramatic, eloquent oration upon accepting a battle flag presented to the Mississippi College Rifles, a volunteer company afterward absorbed into the 18th Mississippi Infantry.

Ladies of Clinton and vicinity—

With high beating hearts and breasts full of emotion, we receive from your hands this handsome flag; proud emblem of our young Republic: which, though but a few months this since, was first unfurled to the breeze, now has millions of freemen nobly rallying around it, and that too with no idle fancy but with a devotion unconquerable, a call unearthly and a love undying.

We prize this flag, ladies, not so much for its intrinsic worth, but for the sake of those who gave it, and while it floats o're us, fauned by the passing breeze, its every fold shall tell, in terms more eloquent than tongues can speak, of the fair form that bent over it and the bright eyes that followed the fingers as they plied the very stitch; and its every thread shall be a tongue to chant the praise of woman's virtue and woman's worth. . . .

Again, ladies, allow me to acknowledge the honor you have done us and assure you that whether in peace or war your gift shall ever be cherished and guarded, that it never shall trail in the dust disgraced, dishonored. I give you the sacred pledge of our company. Hear it ye gallant few and redeem the pledge as becomes a Mississippian. Today shall long be remembered to those of us whose fate it may be to die a soldier's death, it will recall your kindness and sympathy, and we will include you in the prayer for the loved ones we leave behind and bless you in that trying hour. If our country be invaded and your homes endangered, with your gift streaming o're us and the fond memories and associations of this day inspiring our hearts and nerving our arms, we'll bare our bosoms for the glorious strife and at our country's call we'll proudly bear this banner to the battlefield. And in that dark and trying hour, in the breaking forth of power, in the rush of steeds and men, May God's right hand protect it then. . . .

Their battle flag waving atop a boxcar, Confederate troops leave for the front in 1861.

"WE MUST RECONCILE OURSELVES TO HIS WILL"

The men in gray had more to worry about than camp life, combat, and their next meal. They fretted about wives and children left behind, mulled over unfinished business back home, and pondered the chances of an end to what had quickly become a very deadly war.

A sick child . . . uncollected bills . . . underfed hogs . . . camp gossip—such were the subjects troubling Thomas J. Rankin, soon to be elected lieutenant of Company F, 7th Mississippi Infantry, when he wrote home from camp on the Mississippi coast.

Camp Goode November 27th 1861

Dear Sarah,

I received your letter of the 24th tonight which found me as well as usual. I am really sorry to hear that Henry gets no better. I was in hopes that I would hear that he was getting better, but alas, I was mistaken.

It was a hard trial for me to give up our other little boy and now to lose Henry would nearly kill me, but the will of the Lord must be done and we must reconcile ourselves to his will the best we can. I know our little boy is now in Heaven and if I and you never meet again in this world, my prayer is that we may meet him there.

It is reported here that we will leave this place before many more days for Columbus, Kentucky or some other place. I don't know how true the statement is but one thing is certain—great preparations are being made in Kentucky for a big battle which, if it proves victorious on our side, will probably bring about peace. A part of this Brigade is in Kentucky by this time and we may follow them shortly. I would hate to go there very bad now unless I could see you and Henry once more, then I wouldn't care much about going. But as I am in the service of my country, I am willing to go where I am needed most, and if I fall in defence of it, may my fall be Heavenward. I know it would be very hard for me to go where probably I would never see my family again, but rather than submit to Lincolnism I would rather die. . . .

I send enclosed a note for L. Warren which I want you to send to him. If he pays you any money send it to me. Look among my papers and get his account and send it to him with the note. If he don't pay it I want you to keep the account, if he does give him a receipt for the money. . . .

Our election for Lieutenant hasn't come off yet and it will be rather doubtful who is elected, but one thing is very certain—the Captain's favorite will not get the office. . . . I understand he is opposed to my running for Lieutenant, but I am going to run this time if I don't get three votes. . . .

If you need any salt and lard send to Joe's and get it. Joe is to let me have two sacks of salt and some lard. . . .

Mississippi troops in camp on the Gulf coast.

You must make those hogs fat before you kill them. Kill some of those wild ones over the river when you get out of meat.

You and Sarah Ann had better give up coming down here unless the health of this country gets better.

Nothing more. Give my respects to everybody.
Your affectionate husband,
T. J. Rankin

Lieutenant Rankin was elected captain by his company in May of 1862, but before he could be commissioned, he caught the fever and died.

FROM CIVILIAN TO SOLDIER

A native of East Tennessee, twenty-six-year-old Robertson Gaston Freeman left the family farm in the mountains near Asheville, North Carolina, in April of 1862 and joined Company A of the newly formed 60th North Carolina Infantry. Above left, he posed for the photographer as a civilian in his Sunday finery, and, right, he was later photographed in Confederate gray. Freeman was made fourth sergeant upon enlisting, but was reduced in rank after deserting in December of 1862. He returned to duty a few weeks later, after his regiment fought the bloody Battle of Murfreesboro, and on April 22, 1863, he died of pneumonia in winter camp at Tullahoma, Tennessee.

"NO SOLDIERS EVER MARCHED WITH LESS"

In the field, they became real soldiers. They responded to the demands of the military and adapted to the conditions of war. The innocence and ignorance of the recruit were gradually replaced by the savvy experience and field wisdom of the veteran.

Pvt. Carlton McCarthy of the Richmond Howitzers witnessed the transformation.

The volunteer of 1861 made extensive preparations for the field. Boots, he thought, were an absolute necessity, and the heavier the soles and longer the tops the better. His pants were stuffed inside the tops of his boots, of course. A double breasted coat, heavily wadded, with two rows of big brass buttons and a long skirt, was considered comfortable. A small stiff cap, with a narrow brim, took the place of the comfortable "felt" or the shining and towering tile worn in civil life.

Then over all was a huge overcoat, long and heavy, with a cape reaching nearly to the waist. On his back he strapped a knapsack containing a full stock of underwear, soap, towels, comb, brush, looking-glass, toothbrush, paper and envelopes, pens, ink, pencils, blacking, photographs, smoking and chewing tobacco, pipes, twine string and cotton strips for wounds and other emergencies, needles and thread, buttons, knife, fork and spoon, and many other things as each man's idea of what he was to encounter varied. On the outside of the knapsack, solidly folded, were two great blankets and a rubber or oilcloth. This knapsack, etc., weighed from fifteen to twenty-five pounds, and sometimes even more.

In addition to the knapsack, each man had a haversack, more or less costly, some of cloth and some of fine morocco, and stored with provisions always, as though he expected any moment to receive orders to march across the great desert, and supply his own wants on the way. A canteen was thought indispensible, and at the outset it was thought very prudent to keep it full of water. Many, expecting terrific hand to hand encounters,

carried revolvers, and even bowie-knives.

Experience soon demonstrated that boots were not agreeable on a long march. And so good, strong, broad-bottomed and big flat-heeled brogans or brogues succeeded the boots, and were found much more comfortable and agreeable, easier put on and off, and altogether the most sensible.

A seasoned Johnny Reb halts for dinner beside a cornfield.

A short-waisted, single-breasted jacket usurped the place of the long tail coat, and became universal. The enemy noticed this peculiarity, and called the Confederates gray jackets, a name which was immediately transferred to [body lice], those lively creatures, which were the constant admirers and inseparable companions of the boys in gray and blue.

Caps were destined to hold out longer than some other uncomfortable things, but they finally yielded to the demands of comfort and common sense, and a soft felt hat was worn instead.

Overcoats an inexperienced man would think an absolute necessity for men exposed to the rigors of a Northern Virginia winter, but they grew scarcer and scarcer. They were found a great inconvenience and burden. The men came to the conclusion that the trouble of carrying them hot days outweighed the comfort of having them when the cold days arrived. Besides they found that life in the open air hardened them to such an extent that the changes in the temperature were not felt to any degree.

The knapsack vanished early in the struggle. It was found that it was inconvenient to "change" the underwear too often, and the disposition not to change grew, as the knapsack was found to gall the back and shoulders, and weary the man before half the march was accomplished. Certainly it did not pay to carry around clean clothes while waiting for the time to use them.

Very little washing was done, as a matter of course. Clothes once given up were parted with forever. There were good reasons for this. Cold water would not cleanse them or destroy the vermin, and hot water was not always to be had. One blanket to each man was found to be as much as could be carried, and amply sufficient for the severest weather. This was carried generally by rolling it lengthwise, with the rubber cloth outside, tying the ends of the roll together, and throwing the loop thus made over the left shoulder with the ends fastened together hanging under the right arm.

The haversack held its own to the last, and was found practical and useful. It very seldom, however, contained rations, but was used to carry all the articles generally carried in the knapsack; of course the stock was small. Somehow or other, many men managed to do without the haversack, and carried absolutely nothing but what they wore and had in their pockets. The infantry threw away their heavy cap-boxes and cartridge-boxes, and carried their caps and cartridges in their pockets. Canteens were very useful at times, but they were as a general thing discarded. They were not much use to carry water, but were found useful when the men were driven to the necessity of foraging, for conveying buttermilk, cider, sorghum, etc., to camp. A good strong tin cup was found better than a canteen, as it was easier to fill at a well or spring, and was serviceable as a boiler for making coffee when the column halted for the night.

Revolvers were found to be about as useless and heavy lumber as a private soldier could carry, and early in the war were sent home to be used by the women and children in protecting themselves from insult and violence at the hands of the ruffians who prowled about the country shirking duty.

Tents were rarely seen. All the poetry about the "tented field" died. Two men slept together, each had a blanket and an oilcloth. One oilcloth went next to the ground. The two laid on this, covered themselves with two blankets, protected from the rain with the second oilcloth on top, and slept very comfortably through rain, snow or hail, as it might be.

Reduced to the minimum, the private soldier consisted of one man, one hat, one jacket, one shirt, one pair of pants, one pair of drawers, one pair of socks, and one pair of shoes. His baggage was one blanket, one rubber blanket, and one haversack. The haversack generally contained smoking tobacco and a pipe and generally a small piece of soap, with temporary additions of apples, persimmons, blackberries, and such other commodities as he could pick up on the march.

The company property consisted of two or three skillets and frying pans, which were sometimes carried in the wagon, but oftener in the hands of the soldiers. The infantrymen generally preferred to stick the handle of the frying pan in the barrel of a musket, and to so carry it.

The infantry found out that bayonets were not much use, and did not hesitate to throw them, with the scabbard, away.

The artillerymen, who started out with heavy sabers hanging to their belts, stuck them in the mud as they marched, and left them for the ordnance officers to pick up and turn over to the cavalry.

The cavalrymen found the sabers very tiresome when swung to the belt, and adopted the plan of fastening them to the saddle on the left side, with the hilt in front and in reach of the hand. Finally sabers got very scarce even among the cavalrymen, who relied more and more on their short rifles.

No soldiers ever marched with less to encumber them, and none marched faster or held out longer.

"MARCHING ALONG AT A BRISK RATE"

Most Confederate troops were infantry, and that meant marching. They marched in all seasons, under a multitude of conditions, and in almost all kinds of weather. The most famous Confederate foot soldiers were the men of "Jackson's Foot Cavalry," the hard-marching, hard-fighting troops led by Gen. Thomas J. ("Stonewall") Jackson. His soldiers could cover an estimated twenty-five miles a day and were said to be the fastest-marching infantry of the war.

Sgt. John H. Worsham, a veteran of Old Jack's Foot Cavalry, described roadwise Confederates on the march.

No one who has not had the experience knows what a soldier undergoes on a march. We start off on a march some beautiful morning in spring; at midday slight clouds are seen floating about, which thicken with the appearance of a heavy storm soon to come; the instinct of home comes over us, and, instead of the merry chatter of the morning, stillness pervades the ranks. Each man is thinking of home and some place to shelter himself from the storm. The command "Close up!" awakens him from his reverie, and he is made to think of his place in ranks. A flash of lightning and a loud peal of thunder cause him to realize his position all the more, and now the rain commences and soon pours down!

Poor fellow! He pulls down his hat, buttons up his jacket, pulls up his collar, and tries to protect his gun. In a short while he feels the water running down his arms and legs, but he is defiant yet, and the same good old Confederate! Now the water is slowly feeling its way down his back, and, as it gradually covers him, the courage goes out, and when his back gets completely wet, he, for a few minutes, forgets that he is a Confederate soldier. The thought only lasts a few minutes, but the storm within him breaks loose, resulting in his cursing the Confederacy, the generals, and everything in the army, including himself! Then, with a new inspiration he commences on the Yankees, is himself carried away, and is once more the good old Confederate soldier, marching along at a brisk rate in the pelting rain! He is all right now, conversation commences, and when he reaches camp he builds his fire, and has something to eat. It makes very little difference when he lies down to rest whether it is raining or not!

March-hardened Confederates on the move.

We went through equal trials in very dusty marches; when our eyes, our noses, our mouths, our ears, and, in fact, our whole person became soiled with dirt, and dust finding its way all over one. Besides, we had muddy days to march in! We soon got our shoes full, our pants wet to the knees, and some comrade, stepping into a mud hole, would throw it all over one!

Then think of the marches in hot weather, when we became so hot and tired that we could hardly put one foot before the other, but on we went, the words "Close up!" being always in our ears! In winter too, amid sleet and snow, and sometimes when it was so cold that with an overcoat on we could not keep warm. Indeed, any season makes no difference to the soldier; when he is ordered to fall in, he takes his place in ranks, ready to face whatever may come!

At the commencement of the war, soon after starting on a march we were given the route step; on passing a village or town we were called to attention and marched through with military precision; but towards the close of the war we generally kept the route step throughout the march, as all had learned that the men got along so much better and could march much farther by being allowed to carry their guns as they chose and take their natural step.

"THIS HORDE OF RAGAMUFFINS"

By the time Robert E. Lee's Army of Northern Virginia waded across the Potomac in the 1862 invasion of the North, the green recruits of '61 had become seasoned Confederates.

A memorable description of veteran Confederate soldiers on the march was recorded as Lee's army passed through Frederick, Maryland, bound unknowingly for the Battle of Sharpsburg. It was penned with grudging admiration by one of Frederick's Unionists.

Frederick City, Maryland
September 13th, 1862

I wish my dear Minnie, you could have witnessed the transit of the Rebel army through our streets a day or two ago.

Their coming was unheralded by any pomp and pageant whatever. No burst of martial music greeted your ear, no thundering sound of cannon, no brilliant staff, no glittering cortege dashed through the streets, instead came three long dirty columns, that kept on in an unceasing flow. I could scarcely believe my eyes. Was this body of men moving so smoothly along, with no order, their guns carried in every fashion, no two dressed alike, their officers hardly distinguishable from the privates—were these, I asked myself in amazement, were these dirty, lank, ugly specimens of humanity, with shocks of hair sticking through the holes in their hats, and the dust thick on their dirty faces, the men that had coped and encountered successfully, and driven back again and again our splendid legions with their fine discipline, their martial show and color, their solid battalions keeping such perfect time to the inspiring bands of music?

I must confess, Minnie, that I felt humiliated at the thought that this horde of ragamuffins could set our grand army of the Union at defence. Why it seems as if a single regiment of our gallant boys in blue could drive that dirty crew in the river without any trouble.

And then, too, I wish you could see how they behaved—a crowd of boys on holiday don't seem happier. They are on the broad grin all the time. Oh! they are so dirty! I don't think the Potomac river could wash them clean; and ragged!—there is not a scarecrow in the corn-fields that would not scorn to exchange clothes with them; and so tattered!—there isn't a decently dressed soldier in their whole army. I saw some strikingly handsome faces though; or, rather, they would have been so if they had had a good scrubbing.

They were very polite, I must confess, and always asked for a drink of water, or anything else,

Veteran Johnny Rebs: "no two dressed alike."

and never think of coming inside a door without an invitation.

Many of them were bare-footed. Indeed I felt sorry for the poor, misguided wretches, for some were limping along painfully, trying hard to keep with their comrades. But I must stop. I send this by Robert, and hope it will reach you safely. Write to me as soon as the route is open.

Kate

"THE INCENTIVES TO PIETY WERE ABUNDANT"

As a rule, Johnny Reb was religious. The Judeo-Christian ethic was the dominant world view of nineteenth-century America, especially in the South, and was reflected in the attitude and conduct of the Southern soldier.

A biblical perspective was frequently and casually expressed in Confederate letters and diaries, and even in official military dispatches. Religious services were officially encouraged and routinely held. Spontaneous hymn singing, Bible reading, and revival services were common in camp.

Undeniably, all Southern armies contained a measure of thieves, liars, carousers, and scoundrels. Yet, there also existed well-defined morality and self-restraint, molded and reinforced by a general Southern acceptance of biblical authority. As the War Between the States edged toward a Southern defeat, a religious revival swept the Confederate armies, from the officer corps to the ranks of the enlisted man. An Alabama officer and lay preacher left an account of the spiritual perspective distinctive to the South and its soldiers.

Among Southern soldiers there was religion, pure and undefiled, and a great deal of it. The manifestations of it were abundant in all parts of our army, as perfectly competent witnesses attest, and in my own heart the love of God was realized and enjoyed in very great measure. There came to our soldiery, from the Lord, seasons of refreshing, which were inexpressibly glorious, and the work of grace moved on while the war lasted.

All the soldiers of our command were not Christians, to be sure, and some there were who had backslidden after they had joined the army, but there were many who were devout followers of Christ. Among those who were Christians were those who came into the army as such and those who professed religion during the progress of the war. To me it was always a matter of surprise that a soldier, of all men, could be satisfied to live in sin; and it was passing strange that one would throw away his religion in the midst of the dangers of warfare. There was nothing in the soldier life to suggest to me the benefit or propriety of being a sinner, but everything to suggest the importance of being a Christian.

Death was staring us in the face all the time, a perpetual reminder of the final judgement in the presence of God; and we were away from the unholy allurements of society life. There were some drinking and gambling at times among the soldiers, but these were not in such form nor to such extent as to carry with them the attractive force of a temptation. Few and uninviting were the forms of sin in the army; while, on the other hand, the incentives to piety were abundant and the methods of grace were alluring.

As to special revival services, we simply engaged in them whenever and wherever we could, and in connection with whomsoever they might

General Lee and troops at a prayer meeting.

be begun or conducted. In our regular prayer meetings we would go from company to company, having them in one company one night, and in another company the next night, and so on until we met with all the companies of the regiment. Sometimes, however, our facilities would be better for holding them at some particular place, say near the center of the regiment, and we would meet there from night to night.

Congregations assembled for preaching wherever the best arrangements could be made to accommodate the greatest number of men, and sometimes we could get the use of a church near which we chanced to stop. In the camp, on the march, and along the lines of fortifications we continued throughout all our campaigns to hold our religious services of one kind or another.

Those of us who conducted the services from time to time lost no opportunity nor occasion of warning our sinful comrades of the dangers that constantly threatened them, and of presenting the blessed Savior to them as their only refuge and security. And I am sure there were many who were so impressed with the importance of becoming Christians that they did in reality begin religious lives. . . .

"THE GRAYBACK WAS AN UNDISPUTED SUCCESS"

Confederate service introduced Southern soldiers to a variety of new experiences, including some that most Johnny Rebs gladly would have avoided if possible. Lt. Albert T. Goodloe of Company D, 35th Alabama Infantry, survived the war and later reminisced about one creature of army life encountered by almost every soldier in the ranks—the grayback.

The army louse, or grayback, was an army appendage of which honorable mention need not particularly be made, but which fidelity to the facts of army life demands that a record at least be made. The grayback was never here until Lincoln's soldiers came, and the easy presumption is that they brought him along with them and turned him loose on us. Did not the Yankees bring the chicken cholera, the hog cholera, women-in-breeches, and various other pests and plagues?

For size, the army louse was a success. As to locomotion he seemed not to be brisk, but moved from place to place with leisurely dignity, always, however, coming in time to locate himself in such quarters as suited his comfort and convenience. He was a quiet, easy bloodsucker, and so took up his lodging where his business would be convenient to him. Unlike the flea and the seed tick and the chigoe, he did not mean to worry you when his suction pump for blood was in operation and really he would sometimes be nearly through with the performance before you knew he had begun, and then you would only experience a slight local warmth and itching sensation, making it a veritable luxury to scratch. Any soldier would at anytime have traded off a flea or a chigoe for a grayback. I can vividly recall an occasion when our command, in stopping to rest where there were very many rotten logs, was liberally supplied with chigoes from the logs upon which they seated themselves; and there was a universal desire to trade off chigoes for graybacks, some of the soldiers offering as many as ten chigoes for one grayback, if the other party would catch the chigoes.

My first palpable personal experience with the grayback was Monday morning, April 27, 1863. I had slept in a covered bridge near Enterprise, Mississippi, the night before with a number of our regiment, to protect us against rain, and all night I was troubled with an inordinate propensity to scratch. Before breakfast I went up the river a short distance above the bridge for a bath.

Having made the necessary preparations to go into the river, it occurred to me to examine the inside of my undergarments, and upon turning them inside out I found them literally specked with graybacks. To the inevitable I most reluctantly surrendered; and from that day . . . I have held that no soldier is to be accredited with perfect fidelity to all his duties who did not have the companionship, in liberal measure, of the grayback.

The habitation, by preference, of the grayback was the inner seams of the garments next to the skin, whether they were drawers or pants, shirts or jackets; for sometimes the veteran of the Stars and Bars could afford no undergarments, his only wearing apparel being breeches and jacket, wearing them therefore, of course, next to his skin. To be sure the grayback would not stay in the seams all the time; for he must live by foraging, and so would travel about over the body and limbs of the one who carried him, in quest of a tender place in the skin into which to introduce his suction pump. He often had the honorable title of "Body Guard" bestowed upon him, so vigilant was he in his attentions to the person of the soldier, over which he quietly and watchfully glided.

Capturing graybacks, when one was so cruel as to do so, was a careful and systematic procedure. This was the only method by which the soldier could get rid of them to any extent, for boiling water is no exterminator of them, as many witnesses who have tried it most emphatically declare.

When embarking seriously in an expedition against graybacks, the soldier would take his seat on a log some distance from camp and proceed about as follows: First he removes his jacket and carefully inspects it within and without, and then

Confederates in the field: At home with graybacks?

hangs it on a bush in the sun. This sunning process is to allure any grayback from his hiding place, by its genial warmth, that may have been overlooked. The shoes are then taken off and thoroughly jarred with the open side downward and put to one side. The socks are removed, one at a time, slowly and cautiously, with the eyes fixed intently on every inner stitch within and without; they are then well shaken and hung in the sun wrong side out. Next the pants are slipped off easily, and the outside carefully examined; then by degrees the inside of each leg is turned out until the pants as a whole are turned, while with increasing eagerness the wearer examines every seam and wrinkle. This garment is also hung in the sun inside out. Now for the shirt. A like inspection and sunning is undergone with that, while the soldier is no less watchful but much more busy than he had heretofore been.

Lastly the drawers come off as the pants did and are likewise inspected and hung in the sun. The removal of these is done with greater care and closer inspection, if possible, than was the case heretofore with the other garment, and the graybacks and nits that are popped between the nails of the thumbs need not be guessed at. A corporal inspection is then undergone, a bunch of penny-royal is rubbed on the surface, if any is at hand, and the soldier puts on his clothes again. He dresses slowly, carefully reinspecting each garment before putting it on and then goes whistling ''Dixie'' back to camp.

As to the general contour of the grayback, my memory does not serve me sufficiently to state more than to say what has already been said: that the grayback was, as a louse, an undisputed success.

"I ASSURE YOU I AM LONELY AND SAD"

Among the most painful hardships of the soldier's life was separation from loved ones at home. Left behind were wives, children, parents, relatives, and sweethearts. Ever present too was the knowledge that reunion might never occur. The deep anguish of a disrupted family life is obvious in the letter Maj. Patrick A. McGriff of the 12th Georgia Infantry wrote to his wife from the Atlanta front in 1864.

Baker's Ferry on the Chattahoochee
Picket Post July 1st, 1864

My Dear Susan,

I received your letter of the 23rd June on the 28th at night, after I had laid me down on my blanket to try and while away the lonely hours of the night. It may seem strange to you that I say *lonely hours* when I am in camp surrounded by a crowd of noisy men but, I assure you I am lonely and sad. I cannot sleep at night but little. I feel the responsibility of my position and then most of all I realize the fact that I am separated from my dear, dear family. I roll from side to side on the damp ground (for this is my bed) and view the starry

decked heaven (for this is my covering since I have been on this post) and I think of you my dear wife and children. I imagine in those lonely night watches you too are awake lonely and sad. I strive then to turn my thoughts beyond the confines of Earth and in all sincerity of heart try to lift my prayers to our Heavenly Father to spare us to meet again. And oh how earnestly I pray that death may not intervene to prevent our meeting— with my darling children around our own hearth stone.

The song is "When this cruel war is over we shall meet again." Oh cruel indeed is this war. I never knew or had any conception approximating

Major Patrick A. ("Pat") McGriff.

the cruelty of this contest until I got here. I wrote you the day before I got your letter of the scenes and daily happenings, of women and children being driven from their homes. Those, who a few days ago were blessed with a complement of this world's goods to make them comfortable, today are homeless wanderers begging meat. I saw in our camp yesterday four little boys begging bread and meat. They stated that their father is in the war and their mother has been driven from home by the merciless foe. As I looked at them the tears trickled down my cheeks. We could give them bread but we had not the meat. We get only ⅓ of a pound a day and draw every five days and generally on the last day we have none.

We were sent to picket this ferry for five days and we have been here now eight. I cannot tell when we will be relieved. Our regiment has gone on to the front and as soon as we are relieved we will go to it. The regt. is within two miles of the Yankee lines. I gave you in my last letter an account of my feelings on Monday the day of the big fight. I could see the smoke of the battle, and the roar of artillery and rattle of musketry was awful to listen to. The words of the song—"I see the death shafts gleaming from the cannons fiery breath and ranks upon ranks of fallen lie"—was virtualy depicted before me in my imagination. I *may realize it in fact before many days,* "but let not your heart be troubled neither let it be afraid." Put your trust in God and trust him for his mercies sake. No good thing will he withhold from them who love him. Ask in faith nothing doubting and we shall receive. Trust in all dangers the Lord will provide.

You will see by the papers that all the Militia troops have been ordered to the front. Sherman has made his boast that he would take Atlanta on the 4th and celebrate it as Grant did Vicksburg—but in this he will be disappointed. He may eventually take Atlanta but not by the 4th. Sherman is making desperate efforts now—he is firing on our men night and day. The boom of his cannon is heard all hours of the day and night. He advanced with seven lines of battle on our breastworks last Monday and some of his men got into our ditches but we succeeded in driving them out and repulsing them with heavy loss. We are getting too close now to the Army to give you any news more than you can see in the papers. . . .

Now my dear wife I do not want you to grieve and fret because I am going to the front. I thank God that I feel no hesitation in going. I know that he is able to bring me through safe. My whole trust is in him and he will hear your prayers and answer them . . . pray to be enabled by his grace to say in all sincerity, "not *our will* but *thine oh God be done.*"

You wrote my dear that we had a great deal of rain and that the crop was injured and the land badly mashed. I am sorry to hear it, but I know and feel that all has been done that could possibly be done. . . .

I can not give you an idea of when I will have an opportunity of coming home. No furloughs are allowed except in *extreme cases*. We will not be mustered out of service until the big fight takes place less that be long or short. . . .

My paper is out and I must close. Oh it is hard to say farewell, but such is my lot. I feel like I have been talking with my precious Susan, but alas, recollections at hand remind me it is all a delusion. May the God of Heaven bless you and my dear children is the sincere prayer of your affectionate.

Pat

Major McGriff survived the war and returned to his wife and children. On December 20, 1877, he was killed in a hunting accident.

"BOTH MEN WERE COOL"

Johnny Reb sometimes ran afoul of military authority and at times paid dearly for his transgressions. Drunkenness was a common infraction. So was fighting. Soldiers were also disciplined for disobedience, stealing, being absent without leave, cowardice, sleeping on guard duty, insubordination to officers, desertion in the face of the enemy and other violations of military order.

The usual punishment for misbehavior was a stint in the guardhouse. Extra guard duty was also a common penalty. Some wayward Rebs had to perform additional camp chores, while others had to endure public censure or wear a ball and chain. Some were ordered to wear the "barrel jacket"—to parade around camp attired in a tight-fitting barrel. Other punishments included reduction of pay, time in the stocks, banishment from the regiment, and reduction of rations. Less frequently, soldiers were hanged by their thumbs, "bucked and gagged," or branded.

Capital crimes could result in the death sentence, although such punishment was infrequent. Murder was rare, rape even rarer. Most executions appear to have been punishment for desertion, although deserters usually received some other form of discipline if caught. Even those convicted of desertion and scheduled for execution frequently were paroled or received reduced sentences.

An unfortunate minority, however, faced the firing squad. Execution of deserters seems to have occurred most often when desertion was committed in the face of the enemy or when the discipline and morale of the army seemed imperiled by the act. In such cases execution was apparently deemed necessary as a deterrent.

An account of a double execution was recorded by Col. William Lamb, the commander of Fort Fisher, the huge Confederate fort that guarded the entrance to the Cape Fear River near Wilmington, North Carolina. In his diary, Lamb detailed the execution of privates Vincent Allen and Dempsey Watts, soldiers in the 36th North Carolina Artillery.

Thursday Nov 24th, 1864 25 min. after 11 o'clk, the prisoners left Maj. Stevenson's office in the ambulance accompanied by Chaplain McKinnon. They were guarded by

Wartime victim of a firing squad.

the reserve of eight men under a corporal. The officer of Guard & Surgeons accompainied the guard. The battalion was drawn up in two lines facing the prisoners. Light Artillery & Scouts [on the] right. Infantry battalion under Capt. Munn [on the] left.

Prisoners arriving at stakes, a prayer was offered by Chaplain. They declined making any remarks and requested not to be tied. They knelt down facing the guard & were blindfolded. There were nine men for each condemned man, one squad under the sergeant and the other under Officer Guard.

At the command "aim," one file fired. The officer of the Guard immediately followed with command "fire," but the discharge was irregular.

Allen, who was at the old stake, was instantly killed. Watts was only wounded, but mortally. He groaned distressingly, "Lord have mercy on me," when I immediately ordered up the reserve of four to within two paces of him & he received two shots through the head, & died. Both men were cool, Watts as calm as if he had been on parade, the last thing he did before being blindfolded, was to turn and look at Allen & adjust his arms & hands like his. Allen stood during the Chaplain's prayer & seemed a little affected but as if in prayer. He was praying while shot.

After execution, the troops were broke into columns & marched around the bodies to the dead march. The bodies were carried to Camp Wyatt where a *post mortem* was held under

Vincent H. Allen was 38 years old, 5 ft 5½ in. high, gray eyes, dark hair & florid complexion. Born in Gaston Co., N.C., a farmer by occupation & was married. Dempsey Watts was 37 years old, 5 ft 4 in. high, grey eyes, black hair, & dark complexion. Born in Horry Dist., S.C., a farmer by occupation & was married. Allen received seven shots. Watts rec'd seven shots, three the first time and four the last. A *post mortem* examination was held by Surgeon Singleton.

"THE YOUNG LADIES WERE LOOKING THEIR PRETTIEST"

Beards were the fashion of the day, so in their photographs many Confederates look older than their years. Yet, despite a fair sampling of fatherly figures and gray-headed Rebels, most Southern soldiers were young men. J. E. B. Stuart died at thirty-one. John Singleton Mosby organized his Partisan Rangers at twenty-nine. Joseph Wheeler was a major general commanding all the cavalry of the Army of Tennessee at age twenty-six.

As typical of young men, Johnny Reb spent some of his time thinking about the young ladies. Despite the inconvenience of war, the Southern soldier sometimes managed to pursue youthful romance. Four decades after the fighting ended, Charles O'Ferrall, a young colonel in the Army of Northern Virginia, recalled a romantic expedition he undertook with a comrade in 1864.

Two or three days before the battle of Winchester I invited Sergeant-Major Trent Traylor to go with me to visit two charming young ladies who lived in the neighborhood of our camp. He accepted the invitation, and when the appointed evening came we prepared ourselves as best we could and rode to the fine old country home. The young ladies were looking their prettiest, and it was not long before I could see one of them had captured Trent, and could feel that I was fast surrendering to the other. After tea we returned to the parlor, and soon the strains of the piano and guitar, and the sweet voices of the young ladies, were adding fuel to the flames in the breast of both of us. Time flew, minutes passed like seconds, and two hours after tea glided by so swiftly that not a thought of leaving had entered our minds. Suddenly the father came into the parlor, and after conversing for a few minutes he said, "Gentlemen, you will of course spend the night with us." We thanked him and said no, that we must return to camp. He bade us goodnight and left the parlor. We looked at our watches, and it was only a few minutes after nine o'clock. We settled ourselves deeper in the seat with the thought of at least another hour, perhaps two, of ecstasy—but we knew not what was just ahead of us.

Directly the parlor door opened and in walked the father again. We had supposed he had retired for the night. He said, "Gentlemen, we are Presbyterians here; our bed time is nine o'clock and we must close up the house; you had better spend the night." We then realized how dull we had been not to take the hint before, but we had not. We again thanked him and apologized for staying so long and forcing him to break his rule for retiring. He said, "That's all right; come and see us again; we will always be glad to see you," and left the parlor.

The young ladies were embarrassed, assured us that their father had made no exception of us, and reproached themselves for not letting us know of

A romantic interruption of duty.

the inexorable rule.

We took our departure immediately, the ladies declaring that they had enjoyed the evening and inviting us to call again. Neither Trent nor I, after mounting our horses, spoke a word until we had ridden a hundred yards or more, then he said: "Colonel, didn't that beat thunder. I was never so pleased in my life as I was with Miss L., and Miss N. was just charming, and to be cut off at nine o'clock is too bad. Why, the chickens hadn't more than gone to sleep. Didn't Mr. B. say that they were Presbyterians?"

I said, "Yes."

"Well, is that a regular Presbyterian rule? If it is, I would like to know what time a fellow has to court a Presbyterian girl. He must do it by daylight, or put in his licks mighty fast at night."

Poor Trent was killed a day or two after this visit, at the Yellow House, about two miles from Mr. B.'s. I have never seen the ladies since, but that visit saved Trent from a burial on the field— a trench burial, a burial with the countless "unknown." Hearing that he had been killed, Misses L. and N. went in search of his body. They found it and had it interred in a neighborhood church-yard, and planted roses upon his grave. . . .

"GIVE MY LOVE TO ALL THE CHILDREN"

More than 286,000 Confederate soldiers perished in the War Between the States. An estimated 192,000 died of illness and approximately 94,000 were killed or mortally wounded in combat. History reduces the carnage to impersonal numbers. Yet each was a son, a father, a brother, a husband, or a boyfriend—each with personal hopes and worries, plans and priorities, desires and fears. War struck them down prematurely and reduced their lives to an impersonal statistic on a printed page.

In their day, however, their lives were held precious, and to those who knew them and loved them, the death of each soldier was heartrending tragedy. Typical, perhaps, was the family disruption caused by the death of Abram M. Glazener, a common soldier in the 18th Alabama Infantry. Glazener performed no recorded heroics, achieved no dramatic rise in rank, and did nothing to attract the attention of historians. But his children remembered him. Fifty years after he was killed at Chickamauga, they still viewed his death as a sad milestone in their own lives.

Here are his last letters to his family—and a letter from a son who, a half century later, still felt the loss of his father.

Tyner Station, Tennesie
July 31st 1863

My dear son,

Well, Henry, I have many things I could tell you if I was with you, but as I have to write it to you I cannot tell you much. We are campt in the woods at the same place we have been for two weeks. We have but very few shelters. We stretch our blankets for our shelters. It rained very hard here yesterday. Most of us got wet as the wind blew and our blankets did not turn the rain. We may stay here some time or we may not stay long. It is uncertain. We get more to eat than we did a few days ago, still it is scarce.

Well, son, I often think of you and wish that you was large enough to make a suport for your Ma and sisters. I want you to learn to be industrious and good to your Ma. It seems a long time since I saw you and it may be still longer. You and William must take care of everything that you can and study your books so you can write to me. I want you to have me a good letter wrote.

Let me know how Fannie and Billy looks and what the old mare is doing; how all the cows, hogs and corn and potatoes and everything is doing. How often you and William goes to see Dick Shuford and all the nuse, whether you have any apples, peaches, watermilions. So I will close. Give my love to all the rest of the children.

Your father,
A. M. Glazener

My dear daughter,

It is with pleasure I write to you to inform you that I am well. We have hard times here. A grate many is sick. It seems like providence provides for the soldiers or they would all be sick. I know I would never have went through the exposure that I have here at home without being sick. I took the rain, mud, lay on the wet ground for 10 days without a blanket or anything to shelter with. I was wet 4 days and I never was dry. I cannot tell you half what we did do.

I feel thankful that I came through as well as I did. If I had bin taken prisner you would have never have known what had went with me until I would have got back. I hope never to see such a time again.

My daughter I want you to do all you can to make a support as I know that times will be hard and provisions scarce. I want to know whether you all have bacon to do you. I have just finished eating my dinner. It was cooked without any grease and but very little salt in it. I feel well satisfied that I had that.

I have bin looking for a letter from home for some time. I want you to write to me and give me all the nuse, everything you may think. It would be foolish to write little things, still it would interest me. So I will close. Give my love to your Ma and all the children. Keep that sweet balm for me.

Your Father as ever,
A. M. Glazener

Childersburg, Ala.
September 10, 1913

Dear sister,

I received your card a few days ago. I should have written sooner. I was glad to hear from you. I did not know what had become of you.

Lee spent the night with me last fall. He did not know where you was.

Bamma is at Panama, Okla. Tulitha is I think at Ida, Okla. Henry is at Blackspring, Ark. We are all well at present.

I am farming this year. There is a fine corn crop.

Chickamauga: Among the dead was Pvt. Abram Glazener.

I think I will make a thousand bushels and lots of hay. . . .

Well, I can't realize that we are so old as we are. Time is passing fast. Just to think it has been 50 years September the 19th that father was kild.

Well, we will all soon pass away and be forgotten. . . .

Your brother,
W. P. Glazener

A SOLDIER'S VIEW OF ARMY LIFE

Val C. Giles enlisted in Company B of the 4th Texas Infantry at Camp Clark, Texas, in July of 1861. During his four years of service, he saw action in both the Eastern and Western Theaters of the war as a soldier in Hood's Texas Brigade and rose from private to sergeant. He was wounded in action during the Seven Days Campaign in Virginia, fought with the Texans at Gettysburg, and was captured during fighting at Chattanooga in October of 1863. He was imprisoned at Indiana's Camp Morton for a year and a half, but successfully escaped from the prison hospital in February of 1865 and returned to Dixie. An amateur artist with a keen eye for detail, Sergeant Giles left these simple but perceptive sketches of Johnny Reb's life in the ranks.

Perched on a rock beneath the Starry Cross, a soggy Johnny Reb dries his wet feet in winter camp.

On the second day at Gettysburg, soldier-artist Val Giles saw a hapless Confederate soldier named Haynes killed by enemy artillery fire as he lay wounded on a stretcher.

Their campaign hats left behind in a tent, unruly Johnny Rebs undergo the discipline of the "barrel jacket" as a watchful guard oversees their punishment.

In a moment of off-duty jubilation, roughhousing Johnny Rebs empty a couple of jugs.

Led by Gen. Robert E. Lee, the battle-weary soldiers of the Army of Northern Virginia prepare to cross the Potomac as they head back south after Gettysburg. Sergeant Giles was among them.

" ONE DAY WITHOUT ANYTHING TO EAT WAS COMMON"

The typical Southern soldier could never be sure where he would find his next meal. Attempts by Confederate authorities to match the rations of the Federal army ended early in the war. The Confederacy lacked the efficient delivery system necessary to provision the Southern armies adequately.

Unlike the well-supplied Federal troops, Confederate forces endured recurring shortages and inconsistent rations. Food supplies ranged from an overabundance, as when a Federal commissary camp was captured, to nonexistent, as on the retreat toward Appomattox, when some troops were forced to consume the grain stocked for artillery horses.

For most of the war, however, troops in the field were issued rations that were barely adequate for survival. Hunger was frequent, and soldiers were often left to forage for themselves. Yet, as one veteran of the Army of Northern Virginia recalled in his memoirs, the soldiers of the Confederacy could display appropriate ingenuity and remarkable perseverance when left with an empty stomach.

Sometimes there was an abundant issue of bread and no meat; then meat in any quantity and no flour or meal. Sugar in abundance and no coffee to be had for "love or money," and then coffee plenteously without a grain of sugar. For months nothing but flour for bread and then nothing but meal, till all hands longed for a biscuit, or fresh meat until it was nauseating; and then salt pork without intermission.

To be one day without anything to eat was common. Two days fasting, marching and fighting was not uncommon, and there were times when no rations were issued for three or four days.

A soldier in the Army of Northern Virginia was fortunate when he had his flour, meat, sugar, and coffee all at the same time and in proper quantity. Having these, the most skillful axeman of the mess hewed down a fine hickory or oak, and cut it into "lengths." All hands helped to "tote it" to the fire. When the wood was convenient, the fire was large and the red coals abundant.

The man most gifted in the use of the skillet was the one most highly appreciated about the fire,

and as tyrannical as a Turk; but when he raised the lid of the oven and exposed the brown, crusted tops of the biscuit, animosity subsided. The frying pan, full of "grease," then became the center of attraction. As the hollow-cheeked boy "sopped" his biscuit, his poor, pinched countenance wrinkled into a smile and his sunken eyes glistened with delight.

And the coffee, too—how delicious the aroma of it, and how readily each man disposes of a quart.

And now the last biscuit is gone, the last drop of coffee, and the frying pan is "wiped" clean. The tobacco bag is pulled wide open, pipes are scraped, knocked out and filled, the red coal is applied, and the blue smoke rises in wreaths and curls from the mouths of the no longer hungry, but happy and contented soldiers.

Songs rise on the still night air, the merry laugh resounds, the woods are bright with the rising flame of the fire, story after story is told, song after song is sung, and at midnight the soldiers steal away one by one to their blankets on the ground and sleep till reveille. Such was a meal when the mess was fortunate. How different when the wagons had not been heard from for forty-eight hours, and the remnants of stock on hand had to do. Now, the meat is too little to cook alone, and the flour will scarcely make six biscuits. The result is that "slosh" or "coosh" must do. So the bacon is fried out until the pan is half full of boiling grease. The flour is mixed with water until it flows like milk, poured into the grease and rapidly stirred till the whole is a dirty brown mixture. It is now ready to be served. Perhaps some dainty fellow prefers the more imposing "slap jack." If so, the flour is mixed with less water, the grease reduced, and the paste poured in until it covers the bottom of the pan, and, when brown on the underside, is by a nimble twist of the pan turned and browned again. If there is any sugar in camp it makes a delicious addition.

A large proportion of the eating of the army was done in the houses and at the tables of the people—not by the use of force, but by the wish and invitation of the people. It was at times necessary that whole towns should help to sustain the army of defence, and when this was the case, it was done voluntarily and cheerfully. The soldiers—all who conducted themselves properly—were received as honored guests and given the best in the house. There was a wonderful absence of stealing or plundering, and even when the people suffered from depredation, they attributed the cause to terrible necessity rather than to wanton disregard of the rights of property. And when armed guards were placed over the smoke-houses and barns, it was not so much because the Commanding General doubted the honesty as he knew the necessities of his troops. But even pinching hunger was not held to be an excuse for marauding expeditions.

The inability of the government to furnish supplies forced the men to depend largely upon their own energy and ingenuity to obtain them. The officers knowing this, relaxed discipline to an extent which would seem, to an European officer

Outside winter quarters in Virginia, Texans bake bread and do their wash.

for instance, ruinous.

It was no uncommon sight to see a brigade or division, which was but a moment before marching in solid column along the road, scattered over an immense field searching for luscious blackberries. And it was wonderful to see how promptly and cheerfully all returned to the ranks when the field was gleaned. In the fall of the year a persimmon tree on the roadside would halt a column and detain it till the last persimmon disappeared.

The sutler's wagon, loaded with luxuries, which was so common in the Federal Army, was unknown in the Army of Northern Virginia; and for two reasons, the men had no money to buy sutlers' stores and the country no men to spare for sutlers. The nearest approach to the sutler's wagon was the "cider cart" of some old darkey or a basket of pies and cakes displayed on the roadside for sale.

The Confederate soldier relied greatly upon the abundant supplies of eatables which the enemy was kind enough to bring him, and he cheerfully risked his life for the accomplishment of the two-fold purpose of whipping the enemy and getting what he called "a square meal." After a battle there was general feasting on the Confederate side. Good things, scarcely ever seen at other times, filled the haversacks and the stomachs of "Boys in Gray." Imagine the feelings of men half famished when they rush into a camp at one side, while the enemy flees the other, and find the coffee on the fire, sugar at hand ready to be dropped in the coffee, bread in the oven, crackers by the box, fine beef ready cooked, desiccated vegetables by the bushel, canned peaches, lobsters, tomatoes, milk, barrels of ground and toasted coffee, soda, salt, and in short everything a hungry soldier craves. Then add the liquors, wines, cigars and tobacco found in the tents of the officers and the wagons of the sutlers, and remembering the conditon of the victorious party, hungry, thirsty and weary, say if it did not require wonderful devotion to duty and great self denial to push on, trampling under foot the plunder of the camp, and pursuing the enemy till the sun went down.

When it was allowable to halt, what a glorious time it was! Men who but a moment before would have been delighted with a pone of corn-bread and a piece of fat meat now discuss the comparative merits of peaches and milk and fresh tomatoes, lobster and roast beef, and forgetting the briar-root pipe, faithful companion of the vicissitudes of the soldier's life, snuff the aroma of imported Havanas.

Crackers, or "hard tack" as they were called, are notoriously poor eating, but in the hands of the Confederate soldier were made to do good duty. When on the march and pressed for time, a piece of solid fat pork and a dry cracker was passable or luscious, as the time was long or short since the last meal. When there was leisure to do it, hard tack was soaked well and then fried in bacon grease. Prepared thus it was a dish which no Confederate had the weakness or the strength to refuse.

The most melancholy eating a soldier was ever forced to do, was when pinched with hunger, cold, wet and dejected, he wandered over the deserted field of battle and satisfied his cravings with the contents of the haversacks of the dead. If there is anything which will overcome the natural abhorrence which a man feels for the enemy, the loathing of the bloated dead, solitude and silence, it is hunger. Impelled by its clamoring, men of high principle and tenderest humanity become for the time void of sensibility and condescend to acts which, though justified by their extremity, seem afterwards, even to the doers, too shameless to mention.

Roasting-ear time was a trying time for the hungry privates. Having been fed during the whole of the winter on salt-meat and coarse bread, his system craved the fresh, luscious juice of the corn, and at times his honesty gave way under the pressure. How could he resist?—he didn't—he took some roasting ears! Sometimes the farmer grumbled, sometimes he quarreled and sometimes he complained to the officers of the depredations of "the men." The officers apologized, ate what corn they had on hand and sent their "boys" for some more.

The Confederate soldier knows the elements of his success—courage, endurance and devotion. He knows also by whom he was defeated—sickness, starvation, death. He fought not men only, but food, raiment, pay, glory, fame and fanaticism. He endured privation, toil and contempt. He won, and despite the cold indifference of all and the hearty hatred of some, he will have for all time, in all places where generosity is, a fame untarnished.

"THE LADY WEPT AND THE CHILDREN SOBBED"

For some soldiers, the ability to procure the next meal became a polished talent. Yet even the most gifted Confederate forager sometimes encountered the unexpected when searching for a supplement to his rations—as illustrated by this account from an unidentified Johnny Reb.

We had a deep sense of our sacrifices and often used them to stir the soul of pity in some good woman, so as to add to our rough and scanty rations. Very seldom was a prosperous farmhouse visited by a soldier who had eaten anything in three days and the look of gaunt, hollow-eyed hunger he could assume would melt the heart of a graven image, and has brought forth many a good dinner.

After a hard day's march, we went into our camp a little before sundown, and three days rations of cornbread and bacon were issued to us and stowed away in our haversacks. Near our camp there flowed a beautiful stream, and on its banks were fine farms that seemed to have an abundance of things good to eat. The instinct and the appetite of the men at once told them that it was a good place to replenish rations, and a number of them, with or without permission, started out to forage, not wanting to lay aside or empty their haversacks.

Pretty soon they came to a farmhouse in which the family were just sitting down to supper. They sent in one of their number to see what could be gotten. This one was very skillful in gaining the good will of anyone that sympathized with the "poor soldier." He found the family to consist of a mother, evidently a woman of refinement, and three or four children, while there were plenty of servants. As the farm was rather out of the line of the army, it had not been visited before by hungry soldiers, and they were glad to see a Confederate. After an extraordinary meal—for our boy was long and "hollow to his heels"—he told the lady that this was his first meal in three days, and asked

if she would have three dozen biscuits made for him, with a slice of boiled ham in each. He wanted them for himself and his two messmates, and would pay well for them. The good and guileless woman told him that she would gladly do what she could for a Southern soldier, and would not think of taking pay—which was well, as he had "forgotten" his purse. The cook was ordered to prepare the biscuits and ham.

Meanwhile he laid himself out to entertain the lady with the story of our privations. With touching pathos he described the pangs of hunger and emphasized his own sufferings in contrast with the abundance he had left at home. He painted the weary march and the long and lonely vigil of the sentinel, almost exhausted by his lack of food. So moving was the story that the lady wept and the children sobbed in sympathy. At last the soldier himself was so carried away by the pity of it that he shed tears freely over the mournful memory.

Confederate foragers return with food and stories.

Right in the midst of the sad scene the cook came in, bringing the great dish of ham and biscuits, and set it down before the sorrowing soldier. He at once began to take care of it, and picking up his haversack from his side, he took out pone after pone of cornbread, and then a big "hunk" of bacon, laying them on the table, while their place in his haversack was taken by the more toothsome viands. All the while he went on with the tale of his sufferings.

Directly he noticed that the sobbing had ceased and there was a strange stillness with his weeping auditors. Looking up, he saw the lady gazing at him with an expression of wonder and amuse-ment, while the tears still glistened on her cheeks, and it flashed on him that he had forgotten in his anguish of spirit how his fat haversack would discredit his own story.

As he waited for her reproaches she broke into the merriest laugh, in which he could only join, a self-revealed fraud. She said he was welcome to the rations, for she had not enjoyed so good a cry in a long time; it was such a relief for her. But she begged that in the future he should not give way to his grief, but try to bear up under his sufferings. Then she bundled up his bacon and cornbread for him to take with him, for she knew such an appetite would need all it could get.

"WE UNS CALLS IT STONE SOUP"

When Johnny Reb couldn't beg or charm a meal from a civilian, he at times would stoop to making "stone soup"—as described by Pvt. Alexander Hunter.

A hungry-looking, lank, angular specimen of the genus Reb appeared at the farm house of a widow lady—not far from Gordonsville—who was noted for her niggardliness and parsimony. Indeed, so close and mean was she that a placard was nailed on her gate with the inscription: "No soldiers fed or housed here."

The best foragers and piraters of the brigade met their match in this old woman and returned defeated from the field, and at last she was left in undisturbed possession of her place and no hungry soldiers were fed at her table.

So when [a lone, hungry Confederate soldier] stalked into her yard, the old lady was prepared for hostilities immediately.

The sad-faced defender of the soil asked in a humble way:

"Please marm, lend me your iron pot?"

"Man, I haven't no iron pot for you!"

"Please marm, I won't hurt it."

"You don't s'pose I am agwine to lend you my pot to carry it to camp, do you? I would never see it again. Go over there where Mrs. Hanger lives, she will lend hers to you."

"Marm, I will bring your pot back, hope I may die if I don't. I won't take it out of the yard and will kindle the fire here."

"What do you want with it?" said the old lady.

"I want to bile some stone soup," answered the soldier, looking plaintively at the questioner.

"Stone soup! What's stone soup?" and the old lady's curiosity began to rise. "How do you make it and what for?"

"Marm," replied the sad-faced infantryman, "ever since the war began, the rations have become scarcer and scarcer, until they have stopped entirely, and we uns have to live on stone soup to keep from starving."

"Stone soup, how do you make it?"

"Please marm, you get a pot with some water, and I will show you. We bile the stone."

The ancient dame trotted off, full of wonder and inquisitiveness, to get the article, and by the time she returned the soldier had kindled a fire, and setting the kettle on the pile, waited for the water to boil, taking a rock about the size of his head, he

A cold night in camp with nothing but coffee.

washed it clean and put it in the pot, and then said to the old woman who was peering in the pot:

"Marm, please get me a small piece of bacon, about the size of your hand, to gin the soup a relish."

The old lady again trotted off and got it for him. Another five minutes passed by.

"Is it done?" inquired the woman.

"It's most done; but please marm, give me half a head of cabbage just to make it taste right." The cabbage was brought. Ten minutes came and went.

"Is it done, now?" asked the wondering daughter of Eve.

"Mos' done; but please marm, give me half dozen potatoes, just to gin it a final flavor." "All right," answered the widow, who by this time had become deeply absorbed in the operation. The potatoes followed the meat and cabbage. Another ten minutes was numbered in the cycle of eternity.

"Isn't it done yet? 'Pears to me that it's a long time a cooking," remarked the antique mother, who was getting impatient.

"Mos' done; just get me a handful of flour, some salt and pepper, one or two termatusses, and it will be alright."

These things were brought, and after bubbling in the pot awhile, the utensil was lifted off the fire, the soldier pulled his knife with spoon attachment, and commenced to eat. The economical widow went in, got a plate, came out, and filled it, the first spoonful she tasted she exclaimed:

"Why, man, this is nothing but common vegetable soup."

"So it is, marm," responded the soldier, who was making the best time he could: "but we uns calls it stone soup."

"WE STOOD THERE WITHIN A FEW MINUTES OF ETERNITY"

"This will inform you that it will be impossible for me to come home," wrote a frustrated Johnny Reb after his request for furlough was refused. "I hope I may live these twelve months out, I want to be on an equality once more with these cursed officers."

The disgruntled Confederate who penned these lines expressed a complaint familiar to the soldier of the South. More often than not, a request for furlough was denied. Southern manpower was too sparse to allow a liberal furlough policy.

The happy soldiers who received furloughs often waited months for approval. Even then the inadequate Southern transportation system prevented many troops from reaching distant homes or consumed precious days of furlough en route. A furlough was commonly offered as a reenlistment aid, but when a soldier reenlisted, the promised leave time sometimes failed to materialize. Many soldiers simply went home without permission, willing to face the consequences when they returned to their regiments.

Even an official pass home did not necessarily provide Johnny Reb with a reprieve from the horrors of war. C. L. Hardcastle, an Alabama Confederate home on leave, was exposed to the possible dangers of a wartime furlough when confronted by a notorious gang of bushwhackers.

On the 21st of December, 1863, I was at home on furlough. My people were living in Marshall County, Ala., on the northern side of the Tennessee River. About ten days before the expiration of my leave of absence we were alarmed by the sudden appearance in our neighborhood of the notorious Ben Harris and his gang of marauders. Knowing that if we were caught we would in all probability share the same fate of many others who had been killed by this murderer, I, with James M., F. M., and Porter Roden and others, sought refuge on Buck Island. There Roden had already driven his cattle and constructed a rude cabin for himself and his family in case of neces-

sity, and in order to prevent his cattle from being stolen by various parties of foragers. At this place of concealment we were joined by old Mr. Ben Roden.

We remained in supposed security until the morning of December 27, when, about two o'clock, we were aroused from our sleep by a knocking at the door and a demand for our surrender. To our dismay we found that we were in the hands of Ben Harris. He demanded to know the place where we had concealed our boat, and we were promised our lives if we would aid him and his men in raising the boat, which we had sunk after ferrying the stock from the island to the

Bushwhackers exact a toll.

eternal Judge of man that ever fell from mortal lips. When he had finished we faced them, and as we stood in line it so happened that I was the last one at the end of the line. Harris and his men began shooting from the head of the line, and shot them all from two to four times each with their pistols. I, being at the foot of the line, was the last one, and at the flash of the first pistol shot aimed at me at close range I fell to the ground as if dead. I turned sideways to them as they shot, and the ball passed through my right arm, cutting the artery.

When they were dragging our bodies to throw them into the river they stopped to feel my pulse, but, fortunately for me, the pulsation of the wrist was absent, and they threw me into the river with the others like so many hogs. As I was plunged into the water, unfortunately I became slightly strangled and coughed. Some one said, "Stick your saber into his d——d body," but I had floated out from the bank, beyond reach of their weapon. They shot at me again, but missed me. As they fired I held my breath and sank under the water, and they turned and left me for dead.

I floated under some driftwood which had caught in the trees on the bank of the river, and under this brush I succeeded in concealing myself where I could get air until they left. I was so greatly weakened from the cold (for this was winter) and from loss of blood that I was scarcely able to reach the bank and crawl up out of the water. How long I remained upon the ground I scarcely know, but it seemed like a long time before I was able to travel about one mile to the house of my brother-in-law, Mr. J. H. Stearns, and there got some stimulants, food, and dry clothes. My friends then ferried me to the other side.

north bank of the river. He was accompanied by a squadron of men in the uniform of the United States Cavalry, but they were not enlisted in the Union Army. After we had accomplished this work we were taken a few hundred yards down the river bank, and were then informed that we had to be shot.

It so happened that old Mr. Roden had long been acquainted with Capt. Harris, and he asked him to step aside that he might speak with him privately; but his plea for our lives was in vain. When he returned he told us that our case was hopeless, and that we were condemned to be shot. We realized that the object of Harris in shooting us was to prevent it being known afterwards that he had taken cattle and property belonging to Mr. Roden. Harris stated that if any of us wanted to pray we could do so.

In looking back over this horrible experience, it still seems to me that the prayer Porter Roden made for himself and for all of us as we stood there within a few minutes of eternity was one of the most earnest appeals to the mercy of the

"I WAS IN BED WITH A DEAD MAN"

Furloughs were sometimes granted to wounded soldiers so they could recuperate at home. In 1864, Confederate E. I. Killie, a nineteen-year-old Texas

cavalryman in the Army of Tennessee, was furloughed to escort a wounded comrade back home to Georgia. After a leisurely visit with his friend's family, Killie left for the front, traveling with another soldier and relying on the hospitality of fellow Southerners. Stopping at one Georgia farmhouse, where a funeral wake was in progress, the young Confederate unintentionally provided some exciting after-dinner entertainment.

As dark approached we saw a large two-story house some distance back from the road and concluded to try our luck in getting to spend the night there. We rode up to the gate, and soon a gentleman came out, to whom we explained our plight. When he found out that we were going to the army, he invited us to get down, saying that he would gladly take care of us and adding: "Come right in. I'll have your horses cared for."

He took us through the house and out into the dining room, which was detached from the house. Seating us at a table full of good old Georgia victuals, he called a negro woman and told her to wait on us, excusing himself to go see about our horses. He soon came back and conversed with us about the war and its outcome until we were through eating. "I will show you where to sleep, young man," he said to me, designating a room.

On arriving at the top of the stairs I saw a door open and a candle burning on a table in the corner. A Confederate candle was a poor affair for giving light. However, I supposed that the room was intended for me. The bed was in the far corner, and I went over to it and saw there was someone in it; but, it not being uncommon to put two soldiers in a bed, I thought nothing about it and, taking off my jacket and pants and shoes, blew out the candle and rolled in. In getting into the bed I rolled against the other fellow on purpose, thinking I would wake him and let him know I was there also. He didn't move, however, and I turned over and went to sleep.

How long I had been asleep, I have no idea; it might have been but a few minutes or an hour; but I woke up suddenly, hearing voices in the room. Someone said: "Why, who put out the candle?" The candle was relit and a man and a woman took seats at the table, the woman facing me. I could not go to sleep, and kept watching them as well as I could from my position and wished they would get out. Finally the lady said in rather an indignant voice: "You ought to be ashamed to be talking about love in the presence of the dead."

In less time than I can tell it I realized that my bedfellow was dead; that I had got into the wrong room. I knew I was in bed with a dead man, and I didn't intend to stay. Without thinking anything about the consequences, I sat up and looked toward them.

The lady saw me first, and with a scream that, it seemed, would take the roof off the house, she jumped clean out of the room. The man looked toward the bed and with a yell and a leap he kicked over the table, and those two people got down those stairs in a hurry. I got out and, gathering up my duds, scampered across the hall into another room (the one intended for me I guess) and, fastening the door, rolled into bed.

The commotion that was going on downstairs soon had everybody, negroes and all, aroused. I could hear the women call for camphor and all manner of restoratives, and the men were running about to beat the band. It took some time to find out what was the cause of all the trouble; but finally I heard them coming up the stairs.

I played off so sleepy that I couldn't understand that a dead man had come to life in the room opposite. They were all apparently afraid to go in, until [one man] said, "Give me the candle. If he's not dead he needs attention," and in he went. He went up to the bed and found the sheet turned down as I had left it, and said: "Why, the man is dead. The wind just blew the sheet off."

A furloughed soldier's war stories mesmerize an audience.

"No, sir, that man rose and was sitting up looking at me," exclaimed the man who was in the room when I got up. He doubtless thought so.

There was no sleep for me the balance of that night, and as soon as the chickens began crowing for the day I went and saddled up.

"THAT BANNER WAS CONQUERED"

By 1865, discerning soldiers knew the Cause was doomed. Even so, Lee's surrender and the collapse of the Confederacy sent a shock wave of despair through the Southern ranks. Four years of fighting and suffering had ended in failure. Cessation of the bloodshed brought relief, but the dream of Southern independence and nationhood was forever shattered.

In camp and field from Virginia to Texas, arms were stacked and flags were furled. Johnny Reb went home defeated—to face a devastated homeland, a destroyed economy, and a world turned upside down: Brother Bobby was dead, killed back in '62 at Malvern Hill. Cousin Milton, dead of pneumonia, lay in an unmarked grave in Tennessee. Uncle Alfred had disappeared in battle at the Wilderness. Young George, who had grown up just one farm over, had died in a Yankee prison camp. All the livestock was gone. The barn was in ashes, and an occupation army was camped on the courthouse lawn.

The armies of the South, which had seemed so invincible, were down at last, never to rise again. Yet, already the legacy of the Southern soldier was being preserved for future generations in a poem written as the Confederacy perished. The author of the verse was a Confederate chaplain, a Catholic priest named Abram Joseph Ryan, who had ministered in camp and combat throughout the war. His poem, "The Conquered Banner," was printed and reprinted in newspapers across the stricken South, and was embraced by the defeated Confederates as a faithful, moving tribute to the soldiers of the Lost Cause.

Here is Father Ryan's account of how he wrote the celebrated poem, followed by the complete set of verses.

When the news came that General Lee had surrendered at Appomattox Court-House, it was night, and I was sitting in my room in a house where many of the regiment of which I was chaplain were quartered. An old comrade came in and said to me: "All is lost; General Lee has surrendered." I looked at him. I knew by his whitened face that the news was too true. I simply said, "Leave me," and he went out of the room.

I bowed my head upon the table and wept long and bitterly. Then a thousand thoughts came rushing through my brain. I could not control them. That banner was conquered; its folds must be furled, but its story had to be told. I looked around for a piece of paper to give expression to the thoughts that cried out within me. All that I could find was a piece of brown wrapping paper that lay on the table about an old pair of shoes that a friend sent me. I seized this piece of paper and wrote the "Conquered Banner." Then I went to bed, leaving the lines there upon the table.

The next morning the regiment was ordered away, and I thought no more of the lines written in such sorrow and desolation of spirit on that fateful night. What was my astonishment a few weeks later to see them appear above my name in a Louisville paper! The poor woman who kept the house had gone, as she afterward told me, into the room to throw the piece of paper into the fire, when she saw that there was something written upon it. She said that she sat down and cried, and, copying the lines, she sent them to a newspaper in Louisville. And that was how the "Conquered Banner" got into print.

Father Abram Joseph Ryan, Confederate chaplain.

THE CONQUERED BANNER

Furl that banner! for 'tis weary
Round its staff 'tis drooping, dreary;
  Furl it, fold it, it is best;
For there's not a man to wave it,
And there's not a sword to save it,
And there's not one left to lave it,
In the blood which heroes gave it,
And its foes now scorn and brave it;
  Furl it, hide it, let it rest.

Take that banner down! 'tis tattered;
Broken is its staff and shattered,
And the valiant hosts are scattered
  Over whom it floated high.
O, 'tis hard for us to fold it,
Hard to think there's none to hold it,
Hard that those who once unrolled it
  Now must furl it with a sigh.

Furl that banner! furl it sadly;
Once ten thousands hailed it gladly,
And ten thousands wildly, madly,
  Swore it should forever wave;
Swore that foeman's sword could never
Hearts like theirs entwined dissever,
Till that flag would float forever
  O'er their freedom or their grave.

Furl it! for the hands that grasped it,
And the hearts that fondly clasped it,
  Cold and dead are lying low;
And the banner, it is trailing,
While around it sounds the wailing
  Of its people in their woe,
For, though conquered, they adore it.
Love the cold, dead hands that bore it.
Weep for those who fell before it,
Pardon those who trailed and tore it,
And, O, wildly they deplore it,
  Now to furl and fold it so.

Furl that banner! true 'tis gory,
Yet 'tis wreathed around with glory,
And 'twill live in song and story,
  Though its folds are in the dust;
For its fame on brightest pages,
Penned by poets and by sages,
Shall go sounding down the ages,
  Furl its folds though now we must.
Furl that banner! softly, slowly,
Treat it gently—it is holy—
  For it droops above the dead;
Touch it not, unfold it never,
Let it droop there furled forever.
  For its people's hopes are dead.

3

Down Home in Dixie

In many ways, the War Between the States was just as much an ordeal for Southerners at home as for those in uniform. During four years of warfare, the women, the children, and the elderly of the South had to cope with a multitude of challenges, face a host of fears, and deal with a variety of threats.

Serious food shortages affected the Confederate home front. Basic necessities were often unobtainable. Most luxury items and many common conveniences disappeared completely. Familiar routines were forcibly altered; business was disrupted or destroyed; education was interrupted; and for many, daily life was a previously unimagined ordeal. Those on the home front faced the fury of the invader and the grief of families forever split asunder.

Yet, somehow, most learned to cope and endured to the end. When the awful conflict was finally over, a generation of Southerners could tell their youngsters with justifiable pride how they had learned to live with the war—back home in Dixie.

February 18, 1861: The inauguration of President Jefferson Davis.

"MR. DAVIS CAME FORWARD AMID A STORM OF APPLAUSE"

Although remembered mainly for the actions of its armies, the Confederate States of America was a civilian creation. The War for Southern Independence was waged by men at arms, but oversight of the conflict and all other official acts of the short-lived nation was conducted primarily by a government of civilians.

On February 18, 1861, Confederate President Jefferson Davis, a former U.S. senator and secretary of war, was inaugurated on the front portico of the state capitol in Montgomery, Alabama. Three months later, after Virginia seceded, the Confederate capital would be transferred to larger, more influential Richmond, but on this day Montgomery was the seat of power for the world's newest democracy.

Present at the creation was South Carolinian Henry D. Capers, soon to become a chief aide to the new Confederate secretary of the treasury. On horseback at the edge of the inaugural crowd, Capers witnessed Davis' inauguration as president. Until the end of his days, he would remember the birth of the nation and the installation of its only president. His account of the event:

Early on the morning of the 18th, the good people of Montgomery were astir preparing for the ceremonies of the day. The weather could not have been more auspicious. Brightly the sun shone, while the soft, southwesterly winds had brought out the first smiles of spring to gladden the many warm hearts that were waiting to greet the first President of the new-born government. The ringing noise of the hammer had ceased, while busy fingers and the strong arms of noble women and gallant men had transformed the front of the stately capitol building into a grand amphitheater, whose huge columns were wreathed with festoons of laurel and of magnolia.

Promptly at 10 o'clock, Col. H. P. Watson of Montgomery, as chief marshal, appeared in front of the Exchange Hotel, accompanied by the fol-lowing aids, appointed by the convention to represent the several States: Florida—Hamilton Wright; Georgia—Daniel S. Printup; South Carolina—Henry D. Capers; Louisiana—Robert C. Wood; Mississippi—Joseph P. Billups; Texas—Preston H. Roberts; The procession was formed on Montgomery street, the right, or escort, being composed of military companies.

Following the military came the special committees from the convention of delegates, the state legislature, and the city council, in open carriages. The President-elect followed in an open carriage drawn by six beautiful gray horses. To the left of Mr. Davis sat the Vice-President, Mr. Stephens, and in his front Rev. Dr. Basil Manly, of Montgomery. Next came the members of the Provisional Congress, governors of the several seceded states, and other distinguished citizens in carriages, followed by a division of civic societies and many hundreds who had left their homes and varied business occupations to do honor to the occasion.

At the capitol, Mr. Davis ascended the steps of the portico with Mr. Cobb, followed by Mr. Stephens and the Rev. Dr. Manly. The spacious platform in their front was occupied by the delegates and members of the Alabama convention, and other distinguished persons, while on either side there were thousands eagerly securing every available spot to see and hear what was to take place.

As the last gun from a section of artillery finished a salute, the ceremony of the inauguration was begun with an impressive prayer from the venerable Doctor Manly. Never can I forget the scene that at that moment presented itself, and while my mind retains its faculties, I will recall the pleading eloquence of the aged man as he invoked the blessing of God upon the President-elect and upon the cause he was chosen to maintain. The great concourse of people seemed to have been similarly impressed, and were awed into silence so complete that, seated on horseback near the outskirts of the assembly, I heard with great distinctness, nearly every word of this most impressive prayer. At its close, Mr. Cobb formerly announced that the President-elect, Mr. Davis, had arrived and was now ready to take the oath of office. Mr. Davis came forward amid a storm of applause. As soon as it was quieted, in a clear and measured tone of voice, he gave a distinct utterance to his inaugural address.

At the close of his address, turning to Mr. Cobb, Mr. Davis declared his readiness to take the oath of office as President of the Confederacy, which was accordingly administered by Mr. Cobb.

In uttering the words, "So help me God!" Mr. Davis, turning his eyes toward Heaven, in a most impressive manner repeated, "So help me God," in a tone so loud and clear that he could have been heard by everyone present.

Thus ended the ceremony of this historic occasion, an occasion never to be forgotten by those who were present. At night there was a reception followed by a brilliant ball at Estell Hall. Here, the beauty and chivalry of the South, from Texas to Carolina, was assembled, and amid a wealth of flowers, rich draperies, emblematic decorations, and all that a cultivated taste could flourish, the first hours of the new-born government was ushered in.

"THERE WAS NO SLEEP IN RICHMOND"

It was a tense and sorrowful scene: civilians waiting anxiously for news from the battlefield. The mournful ritual would be repeated throughout the South during the next four years, but it was first enacted in Richmond, the new Confederate capital, on the evening of July 21, 1861, following the Battle of First Manassas. Although soon to be dwarfed in size and carnage by battles to come, First Manassas was the South's initial exposure to the reality of war, and it yielded what seemed to be an awful harvest of Southern casualties. Almost 2,000 Confederate troops had fallen dead or wounded on the field of battle, and throughout the South the cheers of victory were tempered by grief.

Years later, one who was there could still recall Richmond's reaction to the reality of war.

There was no sleep in Richmond that night. Men and women gathered in knots and huddled into groups on the corners and doorsteps, and the black shadow of some dreadful calamity seemed

Richmond residents aid Confederate combat casualties.

brooding over every rooftop. Each splashed and weary-looking man was stopped and surrounded by crowds, who poured varied and anxious questions upon him. The weak tremble of gray-haired old men besought news of son, or grandson; and on the edge of every group, pale, beseeching faces mutely pleaded with sad, tearless eyes for tidings of brother, husband or lover.

But there was no dispairing weakness, and everyone went sadly but steadily to work to give what aid they might. Rare stores of old wines were freely given; baskets of cordials and rolls of lint were brought; and often that night, as the women leaned over their baskets they so carefully packed, bitter tears rolled from their pale cheeks and fell noiselessly on bandages and lint. For who could tell but that very piece of linen might bind the sore wound of one far dearer than life.

Slowly the night wore on, trains coming in occasionally only to disappoint the crowds that rushed to surround them. No one came who had seen the battle—all had heard what they related. Next day the news was more full, and the details of the fight came in with some lists of the wounded. The victory was dearly bought. Bee, Bartow, Johnson, and others equally valuable were dead. Some of the best and bravest from every state had sealed their devotion to the flag with their blood. Still, so immense were the consequences of the victory now judged to be, that even the wildest rumors of the day before had not told one half.

At night the President returned; and on the train with him were the bodies of the dead generals, with their *garde d'honneur.* These proceeded to the Capitol, while Mr. Davis went to the Spotswood [Hotel] and addressed a vast crowd that had collected before it. He told them in simple but glowing language that the first blow for liberty had been struck and struck home; that the host of the North had been scattered like chaff before Southern might and Southern right; that the cause was just and must prevail. Then he spoke words of consolation to the stricken city: Many of her noblest were spared; the wounded had reaped a glory far beyond the scars they bore; the dead were honored far beyond the living, and future generations would twine the laurel for their crown.

The great crowd listened with breathless interest to his lightest word. Old men, resting on their staves, erected themselves; reckless boys were quiet and still; and the pale faces of the women, furrowed with tears, looked up at him till the color came back to their cheeks and their eyes dried. Of a truth, he was still their idol. As yet they hung upon his lightest word, and believed that what he did was best.

Then the crowd dispersed, many mournfully winding their way to the Capitol where the dead officers lay in state, wrapped in the flag of the new victory. An hour later, the rain descending in torrents, the first ambulance train arrived.

First came forth the slightly wounded, with bandaged heads, arms in slings, or with painful limps. Then came the ugly, narrow boxes of rough plank. These were tenderly handled, and the soldiers who bore them upon their shoulders carried sad faces, too; for happily as yet the death of friends in the South was not made, by familiarity, a thing of course. And lastly—lifted so gently, and suffering so patiently—came the ghastly burdens of the stretchers. Strong men, maimed and torn, their muscular hands straining the handles of the litter with the bitter effort to repress complaint, the horrid crimson ooze marking the rough cloths thrown over them; delicate, fair-browed boys, who had gone forth a few days back so full of life and hope, now gory and livid, with clenched teeth and matted hair, and eyeballs straining for the loved faces that must be there to meet them.

It was a strange crowd that stood in the driving storm, lit up by the fitful flashes of the moving lanterns.

The whole city was there—the rich merchant, the rough laborer, the heavy features of the sturdy serving-women, the dusky but loving faces of the negro, the delicate profile of the petted belle—all strained forward in the same intent gaze, as car after car was emptied of its ghastly freight. There, under the pitiless storm, they stood silent and still, careless of its fury—not a sound breaking the perfect hush, in which the measured tramp of the carriers, or the half-repressed groan of the wounded, sounded painfully distinct.

Now and then, as a limping soldier was recognized, would come a rush and a cry of joy—strong arms were given to support him—tender hands were laid upon his hair—and warm lips were pressed to his blanched cheek, drenched with the storm.

Here some wife or sister dropped bitter tears on the unconscious face of the household darling, as she walked by the stretcher where he withered in fevered agony . . . or the wild, wordless wail of sudden widowhood was torn from the inmost heart of some stricken creature who had hoped in vain!

There was a vague, unconscious feeling of joy in those who had found their darlings—even shattered and maimed; an unbearable and leaden weight of agonizing suspense and dread hung over those who could hear nothing.

Day after day the ambulance trains came in, bearing their sad burdens, and the same scene was ever enacted. Strangers miles from home met the same care as the brothers and husbands of Richmond; and the meanest private as much a hero as the tinseled officer.

It is strange how soon even the gentlest natures gain a familiarity with suffering and death. The awfulness and solemnity of the unaccustomed sight loses rapidly by daily contact with it; even though the sentiments of sympathy and pity may not grow callous as well. But as yet Richmond was new to such scenes; and a shudder went through the whole social fabric at the shattering and tearing of the fair forms so well known and dear.

Gradually, very gradually, the echoes of the fight rolled into the distance; the wildest wailing settled to the steady sob of suffering and Rich- mond went her way—only here and there a wreck of manhood or pale-faced woman in deepest mourning to recall the fever of that fearful night.

"THERE IS NO END TO THESE HORRORS"

Southern nurses quickly learned the awful lessons of war—long before other civilians in the South. Kate Cumming, a resident of Alabama, began nursing Southern troops in April of 1862, following the Battle of Shiloh, and remained at the bedside of the wounded and ill until war's end. In a carefully penned diary kept throughout the war, she recorded a vivid account of her first exposure to the victims of battle—the casualties from Shiloh. It was an unforgettable experience shared by countless military nurses throughout the embattled Confederacy.

April 12. I sat up all night, bathing the men's wounds and giving them water. Everyone attending to them seemed completely worn out. Some of the doctors told me that they had scarcely slept since the battle. As far as I have seen, the surgeons are very kind to the wounded, and nurse as well as doctor them.

The men are lying all over the house on their blankets, just as they were brought from the battlefield. They are in the hall, on the gallery, and crowded into very small rooms. The foul air from this mass of human beings at first made me giddy and sick, but I soon got over it. We have to walk and, when we give the men anything, kneel in blood and water; but we think nothing of it at all. There was much suffering among the patients last night; one old man groaned all the time. He was about sixty years of age and had lost a leg.

Another, a very young man, was wounded through the leg and through the lungs, had a most excruciating cough, and seemed to suffer awfully. One fine-looking man had a dreadful wound in the shoulder. Every time I bathed it he thanked me, and seemed grateful. He died this morning before breakfast.

I have been busy all day, and I can scarcely tell what I have been doing; I have not taken time even to eat, and certainly not time to sit down. There seems to be no order. All do as they please. We have men for nurses, and the doctors complain very much at the manner in which they are appointed; they are detailed from different regiments, like guards. We have a new set every few hours. I can not see how it is possible for them to take proper care of the men, as nursing is a thing that has to be learned, and we should select our best men for it.

Sunday, April 13. Enjoyed a very good night's rest upon some boxes. I slept so soundly that I did not even dream, as I was completely worn out with the labor of the day.

I have been told by a friend that the night of the first day's battle he passed by a wounded Federal, who requested him to bring him some water from a spring nearby. On going to it, he was much shocked to see three Federals with their heads lying in it. They had dragged themselves to the spring to slack their thirst, and there they had breathed their last. There is no end to the tales of horror related about the battle-field. They filled me with dismay.

I have conversed with some of the wounded prisoners. One of them, quite a young man, named Nott, is very talkative. He says that he

A Confederate field hospital after battle.

dislikes Lincoln and abolitionism as much as we do; declares that he is fighting to save the Union, and nothing more. All of them say the same thing. Seeing an enemy wounded and helpless is a different thing from seeing him in health and power. The first time I saw one in this condition every feeling of enmity vanished at once.

As I was passing one of the rooms, a man called to me and begged me to do something for him and others who were with him. No one had been to see them that morning and they had had no breakfast. I gave them something to eat, and got a nurse to take care of them. About eight were in the room, among them Mr. Regan of Alabama and Mr. Eli Wasson of Texas, both of whom had lost a leg. I paid these special attention, as they were worse than the others. They were very grateful, and thanked me all the time. Mr. W. said that he knew he would get well now. They were both unmarried, and talked much of their mothers and sisters, as all men do now.

April 17. I was going round as usual this morning, washing the faces of the men, and had got half through with one before I found out that he was dead. He was lying on the gallery by himself, and he had died with no one near him. I thought that my patients were all doing well. Mr. Wasson felt better, and knew that he would soon go home. I asked the surgeon who was attending him about his condition, and was much shocked when I learned that neither he nor Mr. Regan would live to see another day. This was a sad trial for me. I had seen many die, but none of them who I had attended so closely as these two.

About dark a strange doctor was visiting the patients. When he came to Mr. Wasson I was sitting by his bedside. Mr. Wasson looked at him and said, "Doctor, I wish you might tell me if I am going to die." The doctor felt his pulse and replied, "Young man, you will never see another day in this world." A pallor passed over his countenance, and for a little while he could not speak. When he did, he looked at me and said, "Sister, I want to meet you in Heaven," and then requested me to get a clergyman to visit him. There happened to be one in the hospital. I sent for him, and he prayed and talked with him for some time. Mr. W. then asked me if I could not let his brothers know his condition. He then asked me to write to his mother, who lived in Grimes County, Texas. He desired me to inform her that he had made his peace with God, and hoped to meet her in that land where all is peace and happiness.

April 18. I remained with Mr. Wasson all night. A child could not have been more composed. He told me how good the Lord was in giving him such peace and strength at the last hour. About 4 o'clock A.M. he insisted that I should leave him, as I required rest. He begged so hard that I left him for a little while. When I returned he had breathed his last. One of his companions was with him, and was very attentive—told me that he died as if going to sleep.

Mr. Regan died this morning; was out of his mind to the last.

April 23. A young man whom I have been attending is going to have his arm cut off. Poor fellow! I am doing all that I can to cheer him. He says that he knows that he will die, as all who have had limbs amputated in this hospital have died. It is but too true; such is the case.

April 24. Mr. Isaac Fuquet, the young man who had his arm cut off, died today. He lived only a few hours after the amputation.

The amputating table for this ward is at the end of the hall, near the landing of the stairs. When an operation is to be performed, I keep as far away from it as possible. Today, just as they had got through Mr. Fuquet, I was compelled to pass the place, and the sight I there beheld made me shudder and sick at heart. A stream of blood ran from the table into a tub in which was the arm. It had been taken off at the socket, and the hand, which but a short time before grasped the musket and battled for the right, was hanging over the edge of the tub, a lifeless thing. I often wish I could become as callous as many seem to be, for there is no end to these horrors.

"I WISH YOU COULD HAVE SEEN MA"

For Southern families with men in uniform, one of the war's worst ordeals was the agony of not knowing. First would come news of a battle, then would come the awful suspense of waiting for word from loved ones involved in the fighting. When it finally came, good news meant relief and rejoicing—as revealed by this letter from an Arkansas girl to her brothers, who had survived the Battle of Helena.

Little Rock July 20, 1863

Dear Brothers,

. . . You must imagine how we felt when we heard of the Helena battle and that Fagan's brigade was in the engagement. It was on Monday night that we heard it. Captain Simpson told us.

Pa, as he always does when troubled, resorted to his Psalm book. Ma did not know what to do.

Willie and Jenkins were as still as mice. After prayers, Pa went to bed groaning. Ma was walking the floor.

I was in my room, when we heard someone say, "Mrs. Brantly, Anna, I have good news."

Pa jumped out of bed. Ma ran to the door. . . .

It was Mrs. Cook. She said that you both were safe. I wish you could have seen Ma. She put her arms around her neck and kissed her.

Pa is calling me to get my letter. Margaret says she hopes to see you soon. You must write to me. I must close.

Sister Mary A. Brantly

A Southern belle shows her support for the menfolks at war.

"I WANT TO SEE YOU . . . THE WORST I EVER DID"

The long-awaited letter to home did not always produce joy. Sometimes it revealed only the suffering and misery of the loved one those at home so longed to see. Such were the contents of this letter, sent home to North Carolina by one of Atlanta's Confederate defenders.

Covington Hospital, Georgia
June 20th 1864

dear wife and children,

Seat myself this day to drop you a line which will inform you that i am not well. i have got shot thru the hand in the fight on Saturday the 18th.

Hit has hurt me very bad. i shall have one of my fingers taken off. Today i am suffering very bad at this time. i expect i shall lose my hand.

i do not no whether they will let me come home or not. i will not be able to come home under two weeks if i get the chance.

i hope this will come safe to hand and find you all well. . . . We have bin fighting hear near Mary-iter for more than a week. ther has bin a grat many kild on both sides. We lay in our brest works six dayes and nights in mud and water to our knees.

i never new what hard times was till now. But the hard fight has not come off yet. Thear will be hundreds and thousands of lives lost at this place.

i want to see you and the children the worst i ever did in my life. . . .

Harvey Bailey

"OUR CIRCLE HAS BEEN BROKEN"

It was the letter every Southern family feared—the death notice. Delivered with little or no warning, it was usually penned by a relative in the ranks, a fellow soldier, or a commanding officer. Sometimes it arrived during a major campaign or following an important battle, but often it reported an obscure death in a remote location during an action of minor importance.

Sometime during the war, almost every family in the South received "the heartrending tidings," or knew someone who did. Invariably, the writer tried to lessen the shock and heartache with expressions of comfort and sympathy, but, undoubtedly, few words could mute the suffering ignited by letters like this one, received in 1864 by an Arkansas family.

Field Infirmary
D. H. Reynolds Brigade
Aug. 19, 1864

My dear Pa and Ma,

How shall I prepare you for the sad and heart-rending tidings? Our family, heretofore so fortunate during this struggle, must now mourn the loss of a "loved one": Brother Jester is no more. He now "sleeps the sleep that knows no waking," beneath Georgia's bloodstained soil, a glorious martyr to the cause of liberty. He was killed near Marietta, Georgia, June 22, while on skirmish. Our skirmishers were ordered to attack the enemy's line for the purpose of a demonstration and accordingly had charged them three times, each time driving them to their entrenchments. At the beginning of the third charge he was wounded slightly, but he would not retire from the field, and as our skirmishers were falling back, the "Yanks" pursuing them, he stopped and turned to look back—just as he turned, the fatal ball popped through his chest, killing him almost instantly. The Litter Bearers rushed forward, under a very heavy fire, and brought off his body. Oh, it is difficult to realize that the dark gloomy portal of the tomb encloses the beloved form of our dear Jester who was but a few weeks since in the vigor and bloom of manhood, with all the bright hopes which illuminate the pathway of the young.

I had not seen him for more than twelve months, being in different departments. When our corps were thrown together May 14, at Resaca, I was wounded before seeing him and I returned to the command a few days before he was killed and had no opportunity of seeing him. I went to see him the morning of the 23rd but instead of

Bad news from the front.

meeting my Dear Brother, was told by his comrades that they had just buried him—had given him a soldier's burial. His lieutenant met me with tears streaming down his cheeks and told me that his best friend and bravest soldier was gone. He was the beloved of his company and the general favorite with his regiment. All spoke of his piety—he died a Christian soldier. He has left us a bright example. We can meet him again—it is a glorious thought—our only consolation. He has only gone before, soon we shall follow. Our family circle has been broken, may it be unbroken in heaven. Mysterious are the ways of God and meekly must we submit to His decrees. Weep not, dear sorrow-stricken Parents. "He who tempers the wind to the shorn lamb" will pour the healing balm upon your wounded hearts. May He bless us in our affliction and enable us to say in the spirit language of Job, "The Lord giveth and the Lord taketh away, blessed be the name of the Lord." Despond not, we will meet him again. . . .

Cousin John Ben Cooke was killed in the Saline River fight in April. He was colonel of a Regiment. Cousin Tom Davis died at Dalton in March last. Cousin Allen was wounded July 22, near Atlanta, a severe flesh wound.

The last news I had from Nannie was through a letter from Mr. Dial dated April 18. All were well then. Sallie and the baby had measles; the baby died. Sallie got well.

Confederate pickets fall back under fire.

Brother Allen . . . was struck May 6 with four balls, the skin being broken in two places. He did not retire from the field. He has indeed been fortunate.

I was severely wounded through my left hand with a Schrapnel shot at Resaca May 14. The bones being badly broken. I was fortunate, however, in extracting all pieces. Consequently it healed rapidly and has left but little deformity. I can use my hand almost as well as ever I could. It is still regaining strength and I think I will soon have good use of it as ever, notwithstanding the deformity. . . .

My Regiment and Brigade have lost more than half our number in killed and wounded. We have been in six engagements, besides daily skirmishing. Major Noles was killed June 27. Tul Smith wounded, not severely. My Col. was killed July 28. In fact we have but one field officer in our Brigade—4 Regiments are commanded by Captains. Oh, I am so tired of this long exhausting campaign. Three days excepted, we have been in line of battle for more than 100 days. We feel confident of success, let the issue come when it will. The troops are in fine spirits and eager for the final moment. We believe that somewhere and sometime we must make a final stand in this great struggle. If we are brave men entitled to independence, and resolved to win it or perish, any time or any place Gen. Hood chooses will suit us—and in the language of Gen. Stewart (our corps commander) we will take no more steps backward, but here and now will stand or fall. I believe this campaign will close the war and I care not how soon it may end.

Should you receive this I will write again soon.

Your Son, Affectionately,
Milton [Walls]
    25th Regt. Ark. Vols.
    D. H. Reynolds Brig.
    Walthal Division,
    Stewart Corps
    Army of Tenn.

"WE BORE BRAVELY EVERY REVERSE OF FORTUNE"

"The contrast between Southern women and their Northern sisters was striking. The Northern woman was never called upon to endure. She lived far from the seat of war and carnage; the sword did not cross her threshold; the smoke of battle did not dim her sight; the foe did not trample her heritage, burn her barns, rob her orchards, devastate her firesides, pillage her altars and drive her forth a homeless wanderer on the face of mother earth. One throe they shared in common—the loss of their sons and brothers."

So observed Rose W. Frye, a Kentucky homemaker who left a memoir of wartime life in the Confederacy. She recalled the drastic changes in the Southern life-style. Husbands, sons, brothers, and fathers marched away—and many would never return. Basic commodities disappeared. Inflation ravaged the Confederate economy. Something as common as a sewing needle became a treasure. A pound of coffee, if it could be found at all, sold for more than two days' wages. Life in the Confederacy was hard, and it became harder as the war progressed.

Yet, as Rose Frye observed, somehow the women of the South made do.

The great difficulty lay in the fact that we had always looked to the North for everything, from a hair-pin to a shoestring, and from a cradle to a coffin. The South was agricultural and not inventive. But with the war came the blockade, a stoppage of all commercial intercourse between the two sections.

The merchants' counters were quickly depleted, and wares which had been laid on the shelf for years as useless now met with a ready sale. We were often in need of a needle to patch our clothes. The blockade runners imported what they could, but far from sufficient to supply our ever-growing needs.

Prices rose steadily from 1861 to 1865. The first year we paid 50 cents in Virginia currency for English calicoes; the second, $1 in Confederate script per yard, and so on up to ten and twenty dollars per yard! I went through the war on four calicoes, and when I close my eyes I can see those precious calicoes yet! We cut up the household linen. We wore calico bedgowns. We quilted winter petticoats. We dyed our faded merinos. We knitted cotton hose. We borrowed of each other. We hemstitched linen collars and kerchiefs. We braided straw for hats, dyed and varnished them, and twisted a gay ribbon around the crown.

Our fingers were never idle, nor did they stop at the adornment of self. We stitched incessantly. What a precious thing a needle was in those days! We picked cotton and wool, carded and twisted it, and where there were no mills, spun the yarn and wove the fabric. Cotton and woolen yarn was used for a hundred different purposes. It was knitted into gloves, caps, jackets, comforters, socks, shirts and skirts. The click of the needle was heard in every household. My mother knit on an average three pairs of socks per week for the boys in the field, whenever the material could be obtained.

Sheepskin made a soft but stretchable shoe. I remember having a pair which were two inches too long! But what did that matter? They were shoes! We gave as high as $125 for a pair of kid boots!

A wartime sewing circle in Virginia.

We formed ourselves in cooperative societies. I have seen the most delicate fingers toiling over a coarse fly tent, coarse jean trousers or jacket, heavy woolen shirt, cloth cap and cloth overcoat. We quilted comforts. We pieced quilts. We made carpets. We utilized every stray rag or paper which came our way.

To sum up all in a word, we bore bravely every reverse of fortune, penury, want and privation, for were not our boys in the field? We spurned soft living when their pillow might be the cold ground, their fare a crust.

My first mourning was very simple. A black calico, a black ribbon twisted around my leghorn hat, a dyed merino—that was all—but oh! the horror of it, the unutterable sadness of that first shadow. Long, long did it last.

Yet there was marrying and giving in marriage in those disturbed days. A friend of mine was married in the winter of 1862. Her mother's household linen, consisting of sheets and pillow slips, furnished her underwear, which was trimmed with handmade embroidery. The wedding gown, a brown silk, shot with gold, came from Richmond. It cost five hundred dollars.

Wheat, rye, corn and chestnuts were used as substitutes for Java and Mocha. Sassafras and other herbs were infused as teas. These were sweetened with brown or maple sugar. Molasses and strained honey were in demand for putting up fruit and manufacturing preserves. Sorghum, made from the Chinese sugarcane, was an acid syrup in high favor at the table and for making black and ginger cakes. Molasses and apple pies formed our great rallying point wherever the question of dessert presented itself to our vexed minds. Doughnuts were great favorites with the soldiers, and the best our boards afforded were always set before them. Buttermilk was a favorite draught, corn bread pones baked in a dutch oven took the place of sweetened puddings. Eggs and butter were often scarce, and impossible to buy in the winter season.

Medicines were scarce and hard to obtain, so we fell back upon nature and old ladies' simples— horehound, mint, catnip tea and other decoctions, roots and extracts. Turpentine gotten in the forests of North Carolina was our most valuable remedy. It was used in fevers, colds, sore-throats, bruises, sprains, aches, etc.

In summer we lived upon a vegetable and fruit diet, but in winter corn bread and pork formed the bulk of our living. The country people fared better than those living in the cities, and who were dependent upon the market. A roast potato or bowl of mush and milk often formed our bill of fare for supper in the hard season.

Home manufactured tables, chairs and stools, covered in chintz, replaced broken furniture. Paper blinds covered our windows, and oiled paper patched our broken panes! Walls were lined with this useful material. It was used whenever paste could be applied. In short, it served a hundred useful purposes.

We proved the truth of the old adage, that woman's wit never fails, and that woman's ingenuity will surmount all obstacles.

"WE EXPECTED TO MAKE OUR DASH"

Practically everything imported into the Confederacy during the war had to run the Federal naval blockade, which eventually bottled up the Southern coastline. A few Southern businessmen and numerous British shipping firms reaped immense profits from blockade running, but it could be a hazardous profession. By 1864, when the blockade runner Lillian *tried to slip into the Cape Fear River near Wilmington, the risk of capture was nearing a wartime high. James M. Morgan, one of several Confederate naval officers aboard the* Lillian, *recorded this account of the blockade runner's harrowing dash to port.*

The Lillian was a very small paddlewheel steamer whose deck was not more than three or four feet above the water line, and she drew only between seven and eight feet of water. In heavy seas she labored so that she spent about as much time under the water as she did on top of it.

We floundered across the Gulf Stream, and on the afternoon of the night we expected to make our dash through the blockading fleet—and while we were still distant some fifty miles from the Cape Fear River—a big, bark-rigged, steam sloop-of-war, which we afterwards learned was the U.S.S. *Shenandoah,* caught sight of us and gave chase.

The captain, when in his cups, would swear by all the gods of the sea that the little Lillian could run seventeen knots an hour; but we were to witness the phenomenon of a heavy man-of-war, that could not make more than nine or ten knots at most, gain rapidly on us, as our fool captain persisted in steering a course which permitted the man-of-war to carry all of her immense spread of sail. Our captain went below and stowed several big drinks of brandy under his vest and then, coming on deck, in a spirit of braggadocio, hoisted the Confederate flag. Mr. Campbell ordered us to go below and put on our uniforms and side arms, as we wished to be captured, if captured we had to be, as officers of the Confederate Navy.

Returning to the quarter-deck, we awaited developments. The warship still steadily gained on us. Within an hour from the time she sighted us she fired a shot. We naval officers knew that she was only trying to get the range, as we saw the projectile fall short several hundred yards from us; but our captain thought that was the best she could do, and with his habitual swagger he mounted to the bridge which reached from one little paddlebox to the other. From that point of vantage he looked down on us and in the most dramatic manner said, "I want you naval officers to know that I am captain of her as long as a plank will float!" Just then the *Shenandoah,* having got the range, sent a screaming rifled projectile through both paddleboxes, the shot passing only a foot or two under the bridge on which the captain was standing. With a yell of dismay he threw up his hands and came scampering down the ladder, screaming, "Haul that flag down. I will not have any more lives sacrificed!" Nothing besides the paddleboxes had as yet been

The Lillian *runs the blockade under pursuit.*

touched—except the captain's yellow streak.

Lieutenant Campbell took up a position alongside the little flagstaff from which the Confederate colors were fluttering. Laying his hand on the flag halyards, he quietly said: "Captain, if you want to give up this boat, turn her over to me. I will not allow you to surrender her. These officers are branded as pirates; and according to President Lincoln's proclamation may be hung if captured." Just then the man-of-war yawed and let fly her whole broadside, cutting the *Lillian* up considerably.

The captain looked dazed for a moment, but was brought out of his mental stupor by a shot from a rifled gun which grazed the top of one of the boilers, letting the steam out with a roar. The engine-room force rushed on deck and gathered around us. The captain bolted for the booby hatch leading down into the cabin, stopping only long enough to say: "I told the agent in Bermuda how it would be if he forced me to take a lot of pirates on board. If you are going to take my ship away from me, take her!"—and disappeared below. Mr. Campbell, as cool as though nothing extraordinary was taking place, turned to us and said, "Kill the first man who touches those flag halyards."

All this time the *Shenandoah* was yawing first to starboard and then to port, apparently so certain that she had us that she was amusing her crew at target practice. Mr. Campbell went into the pilot house and took command of the *Lillian*. The first order he gave changed our course so that the man-of-war had to take in her sails, and after that we appeared to be holding our own in the contest of speed. Shots continued to fly over and around us, occasionally one striking the frail sides, causing the splinters to fly as it passed through. The shells were bursting and their fragments whistling all around us. We were dripping wet from the spray thrown up by projectiles which hit the water alongside. In the midst of it all Mr. Campbell ordered me to go down into the cabin and report to him what the captain was doing. I reported:

"Captain in his berth dead drunk with an empty bottle of brandy beside him."

All this time Lieutenant Campbell was edging the *Lillian* in toward land, which we sighted between sundown and dark, and how we did pray that night would come soon. With our light draft we continued the "edging-in" maneuver until the heavy man-of-war, drawing some eighteen or twenty feet of water, had to change her course for fear of striking the bottom. She hauled to the southward with the object of heading us off from Wilmington, from which port we were far northward by this time. We had to change our course to the southward, giving the broadside of the *Shenandoah* a fine target as we streamed in parallel lines down the coast, the *Lillian* being so close into the beach that she was rolling on the curlers of the outer line of surf. Night at last came to our relief.

We had hopes of reaching the bar before daylight, and thus elude the vigilance of the blockading fleet, but luck and the speed of the *Lillian* were against us. Day broke when we were still a couple of miles away and the fleet at once saw us and opened fire. We had no choice but to go on, as the last few shovelfuls of coal on board were then being tossed into the furnaces. Fortunately none of the shots touched our remaining boiler or machinery. There was one small gunboat right in our path, inside of the bar, and very close to Fort Fisher. The people in the fort and on the gunboat must have been asleep. Lieutenant Campbell ordered the man at the wheel to steer for her, saying that she was so near the fort that she would not dare fire, as Fort Fisher would blow her out of the water if she did. He was right, for when she saw us coming she slipped her cable and scampered off without firing a shot and a few minutes afterwards we dropped our anchor in safety under the sheltering guns of the famous fortress.

The rattling of the chain cable when the anchor was dropped had awakened our captain from his drunken sleep and he shortly appeared on deck looking very sheepish, but the arrival of several officers from the fort soon caused him to resume his swaggering air. Resuming his role as captain, he received them at the gangway, and the first one who stepped on the deck seized his hand and exclaimed, "Well done, captain! That was the most daring dash through the blockade we have yet witnessed!" The captain modestly replied, "Oh, it is nothing; we have to take some chances in our business, you know!" And Lieutenant Campbell, standing a few feet away, never said a word.

"AN INDIAN GRABBED LITTLE BETTY"

When the men of the family left for war, Southern women and children on the Texas frontier faced a threat unimagined by other Southerners—Indian raids. Most feared were the Comanches, whose swift, deadly raids produced a bloody harvest among the frontier families of wartime Texas.

Her father was away in Confederate service the day twelve-year-old Jane Brown saw the Comanche war party galloping toward the family farm in West Texas. Three quarters of a century later, she vividly recalled the personal horror she experienced that day in 1863.

It was August 10, 1863, about 8 o'clock in the morning. We had started down to a nearby field to gather some pumpkins for dinner. We heard the Indians had stolen a neighbor's horse the night before and Ma warned us to be on the lookout. Just before we left home for the field, she sent Betty, my sister, down to the creek a little way from the house to ask Mr. Welch, a neighbor, to keep watch for the Indians. Mr. Welch and two negro slave boys were at the creek washing wool. He heard the warwhoop of the Indians as they came down the creek and had just sent his womenfolks to hide. He started to warn us, but before he could reach Betty the howling Comanches cut in between him and our home. An Indian grabbed little Betty and slung her across his horse. Then they came toward our house. Of course, we other children had heard screams and warwhoops and were running as fast as we could to the nearest hiding place. Sister Sarah grabbed one of ma's twins and I grabbed the other one. The other children were old enough to follow us as we struck out for the creek bottom.

Ma heard the commotion, saw the Indians and came running back toward the house screaming: "My babies! My babies!" As she passed me she saw I had one of the babies. Sister Sarah, who was some distance from ma, ran toward her, holding up the other baby, but ma was excited and we could not stop her. She ran right between the Indians and on toward the house. But she never reached the house. Three Indian arrows brought her down dead a few feet from the front door.

Sister Sarah, who had halted a few seconds while trying to show ma that she had the other baby, came within range of the Indians' arrows and was shot three times, twice beneath one shoulder and once in the spine. Although badly wounded, she kept on running until she escaped in the brush on Spring Creek.

The rest of us finally ran on to the creek and hid in the brush. The Indians didn't chase us; they were more bent on plundering our home before Mr. Welch could return with help and with guns.

It was this desire to steal and plunder that enabled sister Betty to escape. She told us how she watched for an opening. As more Indians went inside our home to plunder only a few were left outside to guard her and pack away the loot. The Indian who held Betty captive loosed his hold on her a moment to grab something thrown to

One of the perils of life in wartime Texas: Indians stalk a homesteader.

him by another Indian from inside the house. Betty saw her chance, slid from the horse and ran toward the creek. She was shot with arrows several times during her run for freedom but not as severely as Sister Sarah.

We children stayed hidden in the underbrush along the creek until the last Indian had left. We could hear them whoop as they galloped away, their horses loaded down with all the earthly possessions of our little home.

Kindly neighbors came at last to our rescue, but did not pursue the Indians because they had been gone for hours and it was too late to try to overtake and fight them.

Sister Sarah died in a few days from wounds, and the twin baby she rescued died a little later from exposure.

Father soon learned the fate of his family, but

could not immediately get leave of absence from the army. Finally he returned, made arrangements for us children to live with neighbors and was off again to war. For almost two years I had no permanent home—just drifted from neighbor to neighbor. The family with whom I was first placed could not continue to keep me. A home was hard to find because all able-bodied men were in the Southern armies and the womenfolks could hardly provide for their own children. I did domestic work for various families who would keep me. There was one generous family who took pity on me and gave me a home. It was the Pickard family—an old couple—with just one child, a son who was in the war.

I remained with the Pickards and was kindly treated until the fall of the Confederacy.

"EACH BOMB CALLED FORTH WAILS AND SHRIEKS OF TERROR"

The violence of war could strike the Southern home front suddenly and unexpectedly. In August of 1862, for instance, the battle for Baton Rouge, Louisiana's capital, spilled over into the city's streets, forcing many of the city's civilians to flee in panic.

Eliza Ripley, a planter's wife living on the outskirts of Baton Rouge, watched Confederate soldiers march off to battle one morning, then afterwards witnessed the terrorized flight of the city's residents.

In the gray of early morning there assembled a rough, stalwart set of men. I do not know how many fought the next day, nor how many ran, but they were quietly and soberly enthusiastic. We furnished a hearty breakfast by candlelight, filled their tin cans with coffee, and, as they were not burdened with arms or accoutrements, a substantial lunch was put into their pockets. They marched off in the early dawn, toward the rear of the plantation, and no more earnest prayer was ever offered to the God of battles than ascended from our lips as, with dimmed eyes and beating hearts, we watched them vanish in the veil of mist which at that hour rises from the river.

Knowing that the assault was planned for the following morning, we felt anxious and excited all day; and at evening my husband mounted his horse, followed by an attendant, both loaded down with hastily prepared lint, linen sheets for bandages, and all the medicines we had. They also vanished amid the descending shades of night, and I was left alone with two little children and a few house-servants.

The next morning, at the first blush of dawn, firing was distinctly heard from the direction of town. Now, while the town was distant four miles by the road winding with the river, it was not half that far as the crow flies.

I sprung from my bed, and flew half dressed to the windows commanding a view of the scene. The roar of cannon was distinctly heard, and the house seemed to tremble and shake with the unusual noise; the rattle of musketry, the flying of bursting bombs from the Federal boats, the incessant smoke and the rumble of nameless battle-sounds, kept us in suspense and excitement, pride and fear, alarm and enthusiasm, that were painful.

My thoughts turned from these exultant channels, to see what at first seemed to be stampeded sheep, emerging from the foggy mist in the far-away bend of the road, swelling and surging and rushing in the wildest hurry and flight, through a volume of dust made ten times more stifling by the fierce heat. These were not sheep, but human beings, running pell-mell, under intense excitement, as fast as their legs could carry them.

That morning, standing alone at my window, watching through the dim mist what seemed to be the ebb and flow of battle, hearing in the distance the booming, hissing, and rattling sounds of conflict, I never once thought of the homes of that besieged city, of the women and children, the old men and the sick—never once thought of them, so swallowed up the destiny of the day every other consideration. But when that struggling mass was revealed to me—pouring, panting, rushing tumultuously down the hot, dusty road, hatless, bonnetless, some with wrappers hastily thrown over nightgowns; now and then a coatless man on a bare-back horse holding a helpless child in his arms before him, and a terrified woman clinging on behind; men trundling children too young to run in dirty wheelbarrows, while other little half-clad, barefoot ones ran beside, weary and crying; an old man, who could scarcely totter along, bearing a baby in his trembling arms, while the distracted mother carried an older child with wounded and bleeding feet; occasionally could be decried a battered umbrella held over some delicate woman to temper the rays of what was fast becoming a blazing August sun.

Some ran, some stumbled along, others faltered and almost gave out; but before I could hurry on my clothes, they poured into our gates and invaded the house, a small army of them, about five hundred tired, exhausted, broken down, sick, frightened, terrified human beings—all roused from their beds by firing and fighting in the very streets; rushing half-clad from houses being riddled with shot and shell; rushing through streets filled with men fighting hand to hand; wildly running they scarce knew whither, being separated from children and wives and mothers in the midst of the roar of battle, and no time to look for them; no turning back; on—on—through yards over fences and down narrow, dusty lanes—anywhere to get away from the clash of steel and the bursting of countless bombs!

Once on the open road and away from the very midst of battle, they ran as though demons pursued them, never turning back or branching off. There was but the one hot, dusty road to run, and that led straight to our ever-open gates and to other gates beyond; but when they gained the first, by common consent they turned in.

The battle roared and surged, but there was a roaring and surging battle for bread in that house which for the moment silenced every other. Our store-closets were thrown wide open; but how the crowd managed that day I never knew. Before

Their possessions piled high atop a wagon, Southern refugees flee the fighting.

noon news came of our defeat. I lay down beside my half starved babe, whose nourishment was cut short by the excitements of the morning, and while I wept the bitterest tears I ever shed, told the little unconscious child it did not matter much whether we lived or died; we were beaten—beaten!

Long before noon the twelve pounds of tea from the store-closets had entirely disappeared. We had immense iron kettles "set" in the laundry room where soap had been made by the barrel for plantation use, fires were kindled under them and tea made but it could not be furnished fast enough to meet the demands of the parched and thirsty crowd. Many became alarmed and took up their weary march, some going down to neighboring plantations on the riverbank and others going back into the woods and swamps. Enough remained, however, to overflow the house—every stairstep had its reclining form, every inch of sofa, bed, and the floor was occupied by tired, sleepy humanity. There were two very large oak trees in front of our house with wide spreading branches and luxuriant foliage. In those sturdy trees a whole colony of boys roosted, congratulating themselves that nobody could turn them out.

A hissing noise rent the air, and a bomb exploded in front of the house; then another, and another; and a fourth went whizzing over our heads, exploding with loud reports back of the house, and on this side and on that. A gunboat anchored in the river was sending its deadly missiles far and wide. The boys tumbled out of those trees like overripe fruit in a gale, like a great shake to a tree of ripe persimmons, all fell at once. Each bomb called forth wails and shrieks of terror from the thoroughly alarmed and nervously excited people. After having accomplished their purpose, the boat moved off.

The first slanting rays of the rising sun saw a good many tired fathers and mothers march off with their little half-clad families in various directions. Others wandered back to their demolished and desecrated homes, or to homes of friends in the country; and by noon none were left to our hospitable care, except the mothers with the new babies.

Several days after the Federal Army evacuated Baton Rouge we ventured to enter the gates of our sweet little city, on errands of mercy, mingled with no little curiosity to see the condition in which it had been left by its unwelcome and turbulent visitors. The tall, broad-spreading shade trees that lined the streets had been felled and thrown across all the leading thoroughfares, impeding travel so that our landau made many ineffectual attempts to thread its way. At last I descended and walked the dusty, littered, shadeless streets from square to square. Seeing the front door of the late Judge Morgan's house thrown wide open, I entered.

No words can tell the scene that those deserted rooms presented. The grand portraits, heirlooms of that aristocratic family, men of the Revolutionary period, high bred dames of a long past generation in short bodices, puffed sleeves, towering headdresses, and quaint golden chains—ancestors long since dead, not only valuable as likenesses that could not be duplicated, but acknowledged works of art—these portraits hung upon the walls, slashed by swords clear across from side to side, stabbed and mutilated in every brutal way! The contents of closets had been poured over the floors; molasses and vinegar and everything that defaces and stains had been smeared over the walls and furniture. Upstairs, *armoires* with mirror doors had been smashed in with heavy axes or hammers, and the dainty dresses of the young ladies torn and crushed with studied, painstaking malignity, while china, toilet articles, and bits of glass were thrown upon the beds and broken and ground into a mass of fragments; desks were wrenched open, and the contents scattered not only through the house, but out upon the streets, to be wafted in all directions; parts of their private letters as well as letters from the desks of other violated homes, and family records torn from numerous Bibles, were found on the sidewalks of the town, and even on the public roads beyond town limits!

Our experience before and after the battle was so painful and harassing as to lead to the determination never again to be placed under the arbitrary rule of an army of occupation. . . .

"SISTER DEALT HIM A SEVERE STROKE WITH THE CORN KNIFE"

Many Southern women, left alone or in the company of none but children, the elderly and the infirm, faced dangerous, sometimes deadly threats, and often reacted with bold courage and fearsome tenacity. Nineteen-year-old Mary Bedichek, for example, stranded with her aged father behind the Federal lines in strife-torn Missouri, somehow mustered the courage necessary single-handedly to fight off a gang of renegade Union soldiers. Her story was later recorded by her brother.

It was on the night of the 6th of June, while the most cruel phase of a horrible war was seen nightly in ghastly murders and lurid flames, that a band of soldiers was seen in father's yard seven miles northwest of Warrensburg, in Johnson County, Missouri.

Soon a knock was heard at the door. My sister Mary Bedicheck, then nineteen years old, asked, "Who is there?"

"Friends," said a voice outside.

"What do you want?"

"We want to come in to warm."

"You have guns?"

"Yes."

"If you leave your guns outside, you may."

"Oh! Well, if that will please you we will." Whereupon the leader came in. No other seemed to care to enter. Sister closed the door and locked it. The soldier asked if there were any bushwhackers in the house.

"There is no one but father and me."

"Your two brothers are in the Rebel army, eh?"

"Yes."

When the militiaman was satisfied that none but father and sister were in the house, he said, "Old man, I've come to kill you," drawing his pistol at the same instant. Father grabbed the pistol and a most terrible scuffle ensued. The assailant having the advantage of the hold on the pistol, wrenched it out of Father's hand and began beating him over the head with it.

Sister ran to the kitchen, seized a very large and sharp corn knife and soon directed an effectual blow at the up lifted arm. The arm fell. She then with strong and rapid blows chopped his head until he hallooed, "Help! Help! For God's sake let me out!" Whereupon one of the party on the outside ran to the north side of the house, opened the door, gun in hand, and tried to see which one to shoot. Sister, hearing the door slam against the wall, turned in time and leaping toward him, caught the gun with her left hand and dealt him a severe stroke on his head with the corn knife. He jerked the gun from her, but on giving him another cut on the arm she rushed him out the door. Then she shut the door on him and locked it, turning the window shade so he could not see whom to shoot.

Those on the south of the house opened fire into the window and door and with a beam burst the door down. Sister rushed to the door to defend it. No one attempted to come in, but the wounded man staggered to the door and down the steps. His comrades asked him if he was hurt. He replied, "I am a dead man." He fell within ten steps of the door and his comrades carried him off.

Northern troops raid a rural Southern home.

Father sent word to Warrensburg that his house had been attacked. Colonel Thomas T. Crittenden of the Federal Army, later Democratic governor of Missouri, sent out a Federal scouting party under Captain Box, who soon approached the house. As his company was about to enter our yard he bade them keep back for a minute.

Sister saw them coming. She thought they were coming for revenge, hence, she took a long dagger and holding it in the folds of her dress, waited at the door the approach of the Captain.

"Well," said the Captain, "you have had a battle here, I understand. I can well believe it from the looks of the room." There were blood, hair, a cut-up hat, gloves, etc., strewn around. "Well, tell me how it happened and all about it." As sister was telling her story the Federals soon became so interested by an occasional word which came to their ears that they drew nearer and formed a semicircle close around the door. One said, "I wish she had killed the other one too." Another said, "I wish she had killed the whole outfit."

Sister, seeing they meant no harm, turned and placed the dagger in the dresser drawer, whereupon one of the soldiers said, "Don't you see, she would have fought the whole company."

"YOUNG GENTLEMAN, YOU SEEM TO BE A LITTLE EXCITED"

Although most Southern civilians understandably tried to avoid hostile fire, some adapted surprisingly well to the dangers of a war on their doorsteps. In early May of 1863, during the Second Battle of Fredericksburg, the old Virginia city again suffered a damaging Federal bombardment.

During the battle, Confederate Maj. Robert Stiles dodged enemy artillery fire to deliver a dispatch to Brig. Gen. William Barksdale—and thus encountered a resolute Fredericksburg resident who endured the dangers of war with casual disdain.

During the bombardment I was sent into Fredericksburg with a message for General Barksdale. As I was riding down the street that led to his headquarters it appeared to be so fearfully swept by artillery fire that I started to ride across it, with a view of finding some safer way of getting to my destination, when, happening to glance beyond that point, I saw a lone woman walking quietly and unconcernedly along the same street I was on, and approaching General Barksdale's headquarters from the opposite direction. She apparently found the projectiles which were screaming and exploding in the air, striking and crashing through the houses, and tearing up the streets, very interesting—stepping a little aside to inspect a great, gaping hole one had just gouged out in the sidewalk, then turning her head to note a fearful explosion in the air.

I felt as if it really would not do to avoid a fire which was merely interesting and not at all appall-

Battered by the Federal bombardment, Fredericksburg smolders in ruins.

ing to a woman; so I stiffened my spinal column as well as I could and rode straight down the street toward headquarters and the self-possessed lady. Having reached the house, I rode around back of it to put my horse where he would at least be safer than in the front.

As I returned on foot to the front, the lady had gone up on the porch and was knocking at the door. One of the staff came to hearken, and on seeing a lady held up his hands, exclaiming in amazement: "What on earth, madam, are you doing here? Do go to some safe place if you can find one."

She smiled and said with some little tartness: "Young gentleman, you seem to be a little excited. Won't you please say to General Barksdale that a lady at the door wishes to see him?"

The young man assured her General Barksdale could not possibly see her just now; but she persisted. "General Barksdale is a Southern gentleman, sir, and will not refuse to see a lady who has called upon him."

Seeing that he could not otherwise get rid of her, the General did come to the door, actually wringing his hands in excitement and annoyance. "For God's sake, madam, go and seek some place of safety!" he said. "I'll send a member of my staff to help find you one."

She again smiled gently—while old Barksdale fumed and almost swore—and then she said quietly: "General Barksdale, my cow has just been killed in my stable by a shell. She is very fat and I don't want the Yankees to get her. If you will send some one down to butcher her, you are welcome to the meat."

"TERROR STRICKEN, WE REMAINED CROUCHED IN THE CAVE"

For the residents of Vicksburg, Mississippi, the war produced a unique ordeal. The Federal campaign to seize Vicksburg, strategically located on the Mississippi, evolved into a six-week siege before the city's defenders were compelled to surrender. An extended Federal artillery bombardment pounded the city relentlessly and forced many residents into hastily dug caves.

A young Vicksburg mother separated from her soldier husband at the time of the siege, Mary Ann Loughborough, took her child underground to escape the bombardment. She survived to record her experiences as a cave dweller in the beleaguered city.

The caves were plainly becoming a necessity, as some persons had been killed on the streets by fragments of shells. The room that I had so lately slept in had been struck by a fragment of a shell during the first night, and a large hole made in the ceiling. I shall never forget my extreme fear during the first night, and my utter hopelessness of ever seeing the morning light. Terror stricken, we remained crouched in the cave, while shell after shell followed each other in quick succession. I endeavored by constant prayer to prepare myself for the sudden death I was almost certain awaited me. My heart stood still as we would hear the report from the guns, and the rushing and fearful sound of the shell as it came toward us. As it neared, the noise became more deafening; the air was full of the rushing sound; pains darted through my temples; my ears were full of the confusing noise; and as it exploded, the report flashed through my head like an electric shock, leaving me in a quiet state of terror—the most painful that I can imagine—cowering in a corner, holding my child to my heart, rendered almost breathless.

Our new habitation was an excavation made in the earth, a cave in the shape of a T. In one of the wings my bed fitted; the other I used as a kind of a dressing room. In this the earth had been cut down a foor or two below the floor of the main cave. I could stand erect here and when tired of

sitting in other portions of my residence, I bowed myself into it and stood impassively resting at full height. Our quarters were close indeed, yet I was more comfortable than I expected I could have been under the earth.

We were safe at least from fragments of shell—and they were flying in all directions—though no one seemed to think our cave any protection should a mortar shell happen to fall directly on top of the ground above us.

About four o'clock one Wednesday morning—the shelling during the day had gone on about as usual—I was reading in safety, I imagined, when the unmistakable whirring of Parrott shells told us that the battery we so much feared had opened from the entrenchments. I ran to the entrance to call the servants in; and immediately after they entered, a shell struck the earth a few feet from the entrance, burying itself without exploding. I ran to the little dressing room, and could hear them striking around us on all sides. I crouched closely against the wall, for I did not know at what moment one might strike within the cave. A man came in much frightened and asked to remain until the danger was over. The servants stood in the little niche by the bed, and the man took refuge in the small ell where I was stationed. He had been there but a short time, standing in front of me and near the wall, when a Parrott shell came whirling in at the entrance and fell in the center of the cave before us all, lying there smoking. Our eyes were fastened upon it, while we expected every moment the terrific explosion would ensue. I pressed my child closer to my heart and drew nearer to the wall. Our fate seemed almost certain; and thus we remained for a moment with our eyes fixed in terror on the missile of death, when George the servant boy rushed forward, siezed the shell, and threw it into the street, running swiftly in the opposite direction. Fortunately, the fuse had become nearly extinguished, and the shell fell harmless near the mouth of the cave, as a trophy of the fearlessness of the servant and our remarkable escape.

Sitting in the cave one evening, I heard the most heartrending screams and moans. I was told that a mother had taken a child into a cave about a hundred yards from us and having laid it on its little bed, as the poor woman believed, in safety, she took her seat near the entrance of the cave. A mortar shell came rushing through the air and fell with much force, entering the earth above the sleeping child—cutting through into the cave— oh! most horrible sight to the mother—crushing in the upper part of the little sleeping head, and taking away the young innocent life without a look or word of passing love to be treasured in the mother's heart.

I sat near the square of moonlight, silent and sorrowful, hearing the sobs and cries—hearing the moans of a mother for her dead child.

That evening some friends sat with me. One took up my guitar and played some pretty little airs for us; yet, the noise of the shells threw a discord among the harmonies. To me it seemed like the crushing and bitter spirit of hate near the light and grace of happiness. How could we sing and laugh amid our suffering fellow beings—amid the shriek of death itself?

This only breaking the daily monotony of our lives! This thrilling knowledge of sudden and horrible death occurring near us, told tonight and forgotten in tomorrow's renewal! This sad news of

a Vicksburg day! A little negro child, playing in the yard, had found a shell; in rolling and turning it, had innocently pounded the fuse. The terrible explosion followed, showing, as the white cloud of smoke floated away, the mangled remains of a life that to the mother's heart had possessed all of beauty and joy.

A young girl, becoming weary in the confinement of the cave, hastily ran to the house in the interval that elapsed between the slowly falling shells. On returning, an explosion sounded near her—one wild scream and she ran into her mother's presence, sinking like a wounded dove, the life blood flowing over the light summer dress in crimson ripples from a death-wound in her side

Vicksburg cave dwellers cower before a live Federal shell.

caused by the shell fragment.

A fragment had also struck and broken the arm of a little boy playing near the mouth of his mother's cave. This is one day's account.

I told my friends of my little girl's distress when the shells fell thickly near us—how she ran to me breathless, hiding her head in my dress without a word; then cautiously looking out, with her anxious face questioning. She would say: "Oh! mamma, was it a mortar shell?" Poor children, that their little hearts should suffer and quail amid these daily horrors of war!

"MARSTER WAS GOOD AN' KIND BUT I LIKE TO BE FREE"

Among the Southern families who endured the war back home in Dixie were almost four million slaves. Although slavery existed throughout the South and in some parts of the North, the largest slave populations were located where the climate, soil, and geography favored the plantation system. In South Carolina's coastal rice country, for instance, almost 90 percent of the resident population was composed of slaves, while among the small farmers living in the mountains of western North Carolina, slaves composed only about four percent of the local population.

Most Southerners did not own slaves; those who did usually owned fewer than five. The great majority of slaves was held by a relatively small number of very affluent plantation owners. In the 1850 census, for example, there were 347,525 slaveholders in a total white population of approximately six million, meaning approximately six percent of Southerners at that time were slaveholders. However, practically all Southerners were affected by slavery, which was an integral part of the Southern economy.

Slaves made important contributions to the Southern war effort. They constructed fortifications, produced much of the food issued to Confederate troops, provided the labor that allowed slaveholders to go off to war, and—in the dying moments of the Confederacy—a futile attempt was made to induct slaves into the Confederate Army in exchange for freedom.

Many Southern officers and some enlisted men went to war accompanied by their body servants, and in several cases slaves picked up weapons and fought alongside their masters in combat. Most slaves remained at home, however, and freedom, when it came, was generally celebrated. Still, many slaves were fearful and suspicious of Yankee troops; many looked indignantly upon the thieving and destruction committed by the invaders, and many remained loyal to their owners—especially to those who had treated their slaves humanely.

Melvin Smith was a slave who weathered the war as a field hand on a coastal plantation in South Carolina. In 1937, at age ninety-seven, he reminisced about the war years in Dixie during an interview with journalist Elizabeth Watson, a writer employed by the WPA Federal Writer's Project. Like most of the Project interviewers, Watson tried to preserve dialect as she heard it. Here is her interview with former slave Melvin Smith.

I was twenty-four years ole when th' war was over. I was born in 1841. My white folks lived in Beaufort, South Carolina, an' that's whar I was born.

Old Marster was name Jim Farrell an' his wife was Miss Mary. They had three chillun name Mary, Jim an' Martha. They lived in a big white house sot off from th' road 'bout two an' a half mile from Beaufort. Marster was rich I reckon, 'cause he had 'bout a sixteen horse farm an' a whole hoodle of niggers. If you measured 'em it would a-been several cowpens full.

Marster was good to his niggers, but he had a overseer that was a mean man. He beat th' niggers so bad that Marster showed him th' road an' told him to git. Then th' Boss an' his son looked after th' hands theyselves 'till they could get another one. That overseer's name was Jimmy.

Ever' mornin' at four clock th' overseer blowed a conch shell an' all us niggers knowed it was time to git up an' go to work. Sometimes he blowed a bugle that'd wake up the nation. Ever'body worked from sunup 'till sundown.

We never worked on Christmas or the Fourth of July. Marster always give us big sacks of fruit an' candy on Christmas an' a barbecue the Fourth of July. We never worked none New Year's Day, neither. We just sot around an' et chicken, fish an' biscuit. Durin' the week on Wednesday an' Thursday night we had dances an' then they was a lot of fiddlin' an' banjo playin'. We was glad to see days when we never had to work 'cause then we could sleep. It seem like the niggers had to git up soon's they lay down. Marster was good to us but the overseer was mean.

The niggers had a church right thar on the place. Preacher Sam Bell came ever' Sunday mornin' at ten clock an' we sot thar an' listened to him 'till 'leven thirty. Then we tear home an' eat our dinner an' lie round till four-thirty. We'd go back to church an' stay 'bout hour an' come home for supper. The preacher was the onliest one that could read the Bible. When a nigger joined the church he was baptized in the creek.

Did you ever hear how the niggers was sold? They was put on a stage on the courthouse square an' sold kinder like they was stock. The prettiest one got the biggest bid. They said that they was a market in North Ca'lina but I never see'd it. The ones I saw was jest sold like I told you. Then they went home with they marsters. If they tried to run away they sont the hounds after them. Them dogs would sniff around an' first news you knowed they caught them niggers. Marster's niggers run away some, but they always come back. They'd hear that they could have a better time up North so they think they try it. But they found out that they wasn't no easy way to live away from Marster. He always took 'em back, didn't beat 'em nor nothin'. I run away once myself but I never went nowhere.

I see'd the Yankee soldiers drill right thar in front of our house. They'd be marchin' 'long this way an' the cap'n say, "Right" an' they turn back this here way. Cap'n say, "Fire" an' they fire. I see'd 'em most ever' day. Ol' Marster was a cap'n in *our* army. I hear big guns a-boomin' all a-time an' the sights I did see! Streets jest runnin' with blood jest like it was water. Here lay a man on this side with his legs shot off; on that thar side they was a man with his arms shot off. Some of them never had no head. It was a terrible sight. I wasn't scared 'cause I knowed they wouldn't hurt me. Them Yankees never bothered nothin' we had. I hear some folks say that they stole they vittles but they never bothered ours 'cause they had plenty of they own. After the war Marster called us together an' say, "You is free an' can go if you want to," an' I left, so that's all I know.

In a sense the niggers is better off since freedom come. Ol' Marster was good an' kind but I like to be free to go whar I please. Back then we couldn't go nowhar 'less we had a pass. We don't have no overseer to bother us now. It ain't that I didn't love my Marster, but I jest likes to be free.

While Southern slaves generally yearned for

freedom, their desire for liberty did not necessarily eliminate respect and, in many cases, genuine affection for their owners. In 1937, when ninety-year-old Sarah Debro, once a young house servant on a large plantation in central North Carolina, reminisced about her life to WPA interviewer Travis Jordan, she candidly expressed an undiminished affection that transcended both time and bondage. Her account:

I was bawn in Orange County way back sometime in de fifties. Mis' Polly White Cain an' Marse Doctor Cain was my white folks. Marse Cain's plantation joined Mister Paul Cannon's land. Marse Cain owned so many niggers dat he didn' know his own slaves when he met dem in de road. Sometimes he would stop dem an' say: "Whose nigger am you?" Dey'd say, "We's Marse Cain's niggers." Den he would say, "I'se Marse Cain," and drive on.

Marse Cain was good to his niggers. He didn' whip dem like some owners did, but if dey done mean he sole dem. Dey knew dis so dey minded him. One day gran'pappy sassed Mis' Polly White an' she told him dat if he didn' behave hesself dat she would put him in her pocket. Gran'pappy wuz er big man an' I ax him how Mis' Polly could do dat. He said she meant dat she would sell him den put de money in her pocket. He never did sass Mis' Polly no more.

I was kept at de big house to wait on Mis' Polly, to tote her basket of keys an' such as dat. Whenever she seed a chile down in de quarters dat she wanted to raise by hand, she took dem up to de big house an' trained dem. I wuz to be a house maid. De day she took me my mammy cried kaze she knew I would never be 'lowed to live at de cabin wid her no more. Mis' Polly was big an' fat an' she made us niggers mind an' we had to keep clean. My dresses an' aprons was starched stiff. I had a clean apron every day. We had white sheets on de beds an' we niggers had plenty to eat too, even ham. When Mis' Polly went to ride she took me in de carriage wid her.

Former slaves face the new challenges of freedom.

De driver set way up high an' Mis' Polly set way down low. Dey was two hosses with shiney harness. I toted Mis' Polly's bags an' bundles, an' if she dropped her hank'chief I picked it up. I loved Mis' Polly an' loved stayin' at de big house.

I was 'bout wais' high when de sojers mustered. I went wid Mis' Polly down to de musterin' fiel' whare dey was marchin'. I can see dey feets now when dey flung dem up an' down, sayin', "hep, hep." When dey was all ready to go an' fight, de women folks fixed a big dinner. Aunt Charity an' Pete cooked two or three days for Mis' Polly. De table was piled wid chicken, ham, shoat, barbecue, young ham, an' all sorts of pies, cakes an' things, but nobody eat nothin much. Mis' Polly an' de ladies got to cryin'. De vittles got cold. I was so sad dat I got over in de corner an' cried too. De men folks all had on dey new sojer clothes, an' dey didn' eat nothin neither. Young Marse Jim went up an' put his arm 'roun' Mis' Polly, his mammy, but dat made her cry harder. Marse Jim was a cavalry. He rode a big hoss, an' my Uncle Dave went wid him to de fiel' as his body guard. He had a hoss too so if Marse Jim's hoss got shot dare would be another one for him to ride. Mis'

Polly had another son but he was too drunk to hold a gun. He stayed drunk.

De first cannon I heard skeered me near 'bout to death. We could hear dem goin' boom, boom. I thought it was thunder, Mis' Polly say, "Lissen, Sarah, hear dem cannons? Dey's killin' our mens." Den she 'gun to cry. I run in de kitchen whare Aunt Charity was cookin' an' tole her Mis' Polly was cryin'. She said: "She ain't cryin' kaze de Yankees killin' de mens; she's doin' all dat cryin' kaze she skeered we's goin' to be sot free." Den I got mad an' tole her Mis' Polly wuzn' like dat.

I 'members when [some soldiers from] Wheelers Cavalry come through. Dey was 'Federates but dey was mean as de Yankees. Dey stold everything dey could find an' killed a pile of niggers. Dey come 'roun' checkin'. Dey ax de niggers if dey wanted to be free. If dey say yeh, den dey shot dem down, but if dey say no, dey let dem alone. Dey took three of my uncles out in de woods an' shot dey faces off.

I 'members de first time de Yankees come. Dey come gallupin' down de road, jumpin' over de palin's, tromplin' down de rose bushes an' messin' up de flower beds. Dey stomped all over de house, in de kitchen, pantries, smokehouse, an' everywhare, but dey didn' find much, kaze near 'bout everything done been hid. I was settin' on de steps when a big Yankee come up. He had on a cap an' his eyes was mean.

"Whare did dey hide duh gold an' silver, nigger?" he yelled at me. I was so skeered my hands was ashy, but I tole him I didn' know nothin' 'bout nothin'; dat if anybody done hid things dey hid it while I was asleep.

"Go ax dat ole white-headed devil," he said to me. I got mad den kaze he was tawkin' 'bout Mis' Polly, so I didn' say nothin'. I jus' set. Den he pushed me off de step an' say if I didn' dance he gwine shoot my toes off. Skeered as I was, I sho dons some shufflin'. Den he give me five dollars an' told me to go buy jim cracks, but dat piece of paper won't no good. 'Twuzn nothin' but a shin plaster like all dat war money, you couldn' spend it.

Dat Yankee kept callin' Mis' Polly a white-headed devil an' said she done ram-shacked 'til dey wuzn' nothin' left, but he made his mens tote off meat, flour, pigs, an' chickens. After dat Mis' Polly got mighty stingy wid de vittles an' we didn' have no more ham.

When de war was over de Yankees was all 'roun' de place tellin' de niggers what to do. Dey tole dem dey was free, dat dey didn' have to slave for de white folks no more. My folks all left Marse Cain an' went to live in houses dat de Yankees built. Dey wuz like poor white folks houses, little shacks made out of sticks an' mud wid stick an' mud chimneys. Dey wuzn' like Marse Cain's cabins, planked up and warm, dey was full of cracks, an' dey wuzn' no lamps an' oil. All de light come from de lightwood knots burnin' in de fireplace.

One day my mammy come to de big house after me. I didn' want to go, I wanted to stay wid Mis' Polly. I 'gun to cry an' Mammy caught hold of me. I grabbed Mis' Polly an' held so tight dat I tore her skirt bindin' loose an' her skirt fell down 'bout her feets.

"Let her stay wid me," Mis' Polly said to Mammy. But Mammy shook her head. "You took her away from me an' didn' pay no mind to my cryin', so now I'se takin' her back home. We's free now, Mis' Polly, we ain't gwine be slaves no more to nobody." She dragged me away. I can see how Mis' Polly looked now. She didn' say nothin' but she looked hard at Mammy an' her face was white.

Mammy took me to de stick an' mud house de Yankees done give her. It was smoky an' dark kaze dey wuzn' no windows. We didn't have no sheets an' no towels, so when I cried an' said I didn' want to live in no Yankee house, Mammy beat me an' made me go to bed. I laid on de straw tick lookin' up through de cracks in de roof. I could see de stars, an' de sky shinin' through de cracks and it looked like long blue splinters stretched 'cross de rafters. I lay dare an' cried kaze I wanted to go back to Mis' Polly.

I wuz never hungry til we wuz free an' de Yankees fed us. We didn' have nothin' to eat 'cept hardtack an' middlin' meat. I never saw such meat. It was thin an' tough wid a thick skin. You could boil it all day an' all night an' it wouldn't cook done. I wouldn't eat it. I thought 'twuz mule meat; mules dat done been shot on da battlefield den dried. I still believe 'twuz mule meat. . . .

Dem was bad days. I'd rather have been a slave den to been hired out like I wuz, kaze I wuzn' no fiel' hand, I was a hand maid, trained to wait on de ladies. Den too, I wuz hungry most of de time an' had to keep fightin' off dem Yankee mens. Dem Yankees was mean folks.

I looks back now an' thinks. I ain't never forgot dem slavery days, an' I ain't never forgot Mis' Polly. . . .

"THE MANLY AND UPRIGHT WILL BRAND YOUR NAME INFAMY"

In late May of 1864, following the Federal defeat at the Battle of New Market, Gen. David Hunter led almost 19,000 Federal troops on a sweeping, destructive raid through Virginia's lush Shenandoah Valley. A few weeks later, he was driven away by a seasoned Confederate force under Gen. Jubal A. Early. By then, however, Hunter's Federals had burned the town of Lexington, ripped up miles of Southern railroad, torched the Virginia Military Institute, destroyed numerous mills and factories, and looted and burned a multitude of private dwellings.

Among the many homes Hunter's troops destroyed that summer was the residence of Edmund J. Lee, a prominent Virginian and a relative of Robert E. Lee. The day after her house was burned down, Edmund J. Lee's wife, Henrietta, penned this bold letter to General Hunter—the man who had destroyed her home.

Shepherdstown, Va., July 20, 1864
General Hunter:

Yesterday your underling, Captain Martindale, of the First New York Cavalry, executed your infamous order and burned my house. You have had the satisfaction ere this of receiving from him the information that your orders were fulfilled to the letter, the dwelling and every outbuilding, seven in number, with their contents, being burned. I, therefore, a helpless woman whom you have cruelly wronged, address you, a Major-General of the United States Army, and demand why this was done? What was my offence? My husband was absent—an exile. He has never been a politician or in any way engaged in the struggle now going on, his age preventing. This fact your chief-of-staff, David Strother, would have told you.

The house was built by my father, a Revolutionary soldier, who served the whole seven years for your independence. There was I born; there the sacred dead repose. It was my house and my home, and there has your niece, Miss Griffith, who lived among us all this horrid war up to the present moment, met with all kindness and hospitality at my hands. Was it for this that you turned me, my young daughter, and little son out upon the world without shelter? Or was it because my husband is the grandson of the Revolutionary patriot and "rebel," Richard Henry Lee, and the near kinsmen of the noblest of Christian warriors, and greatest of generals, Robert E. Lee? Heaven's blessings be upon his head forever! You and your Government have failed to conquer, subdue or match him; and disappointed rage and malice find vent on the helpless and inoffensive.

Hyena-like, you have torn my heart to pieces! For all hallowed memories clustered around that homestead; and demonlike, you have done it without even the pretext of revenge, for I never saw or harmed you. Your office is not to lead, like a brave man and soldier, your men to fight in the ranks of war, but your work has been to separate yourself from all danger, and with your incendiary band steal unaware upon helpless women and children, to insult and destroy. Two fair homes did you yesterday ruthlessly lay in ashes, giving not a moment's warning to the startled inmates of your wicked purpose; turning mothers and children out of doors, your very name is execrated by your own men for the cruel work you give them to do.

Northern troops fire a Virginia mill.

In the case of Mr. A. R. Boteler, both father and mother were far away. Any heart but that of Captain Martindale (and yours) would have been touched by that little circle, comprising a widowed daughter just risen from her bed of illness, her three fatherless babies—the eldest five years old— and her heroic sister. I repeat, any man would have been touched at that sight but Captain Martindale! One might as well hope to find mercy and feeling in the heart of a wolf bent on his prey of young lambs, as to search for such qualities in his bosom. You have chosen well your agent for such deeds, and doubtless will promote him.

A colonel of the Federal Army has stated that you deprived forty of your officers of their commands because they refused to carry out your malignant mischief. All honor to their names for this, at least! They are men, and have human hearts and blush for such a commander! I ask who that does not wish infamy and disgrace attached to him forever would serve under you? Your name will stand on history's pages as the Hunter of weak women, and innocent children: the Hunter to destroy defenceless villages and beautiful homes—to torture afresh the agonized hearts of widows; The Hunter of Africa's poor sons and daughters, to lure them on to ruin and death of soul and body; the Hunter with the relentless heart of a wild beast, the face of a fiend, and the form of a man. Oh, Earth, behold the monster! Can I say "God forgive you"? No prayer can be offered for you! Were it possible for human lips to raise your name heavenward, angels would thrust the foul thing back again, and demons claim their own. The curse of thousands, the scorn of the manly and upright, and the hatred of the true and honorable, will follow you and yours through all time, and brand your name infamy! infamy!

Again, I demand why you have burned my house; Answer as you must answer before the Searcher of all hearts; why have you added this cruel, wicked deed to your many crimes?

Henrietta E. Lee

"THE ROOMS SWARMED WITH ARMED MEN"

At war's end, as Federal armies swept across the Confederacy, some Southern families living on likely invasion routes fled from home to escape confrontation with the enemy. Ironically, such flights sometimes brought families face to face with the very forces they were trying so desperately to avoid.

South Carolinian Helen Clifford and her family evacuated their comfortable house in Charleston, which they feared would be invaded and sacked by Sherman's army, and retreated to an isolated farmhouse in the foothills of the Blue Ridge Mountains. There, in April of 1865, they received a terrorizing visit from Gen. George Stoneman's Federal raiders, who looted the family residence in search of booty.

At home with Helen the day the blue-clad horsemen arrived were a fifteen-year-old brother, a sister-in-law named Iris, and her husband Earle—Helen's brother—who was home recovering from a serious battle wound. Years later, Helen Clifford still remembered the day Stoneman's raiders arrived.

All glorious shone the sunlight of the happy springtime. Earle was improving in health, and this fact alone lent a brighter hue to life and its duties. Feeling stronger than usual, he determined to ride to the nearest town, ten miles distant, where he had some important business to transact.

He had been absent several hours when suddenly, the cry rang out—unmistakable and fearful—uttered in half frantic, half jubilant tones, by the negroes on the place. "Yonder dey come! De Yankees! De Yankees!"

We sprang to the door and saw an armed band, whose numbers seemed legion, clad in the uniform of the Federal army, riding rapidly toward the house. They were a hard-looking set, and our hearts sank as we beheld Earle bound and helpless in their power.

In a second of time the room swarmed with armed men intent on finding "the treasure." Fearful oaths and threats were heard as they explored the house from cellar to garret; succeeded by shouts of savage exultation as the heavy old chests brought from Charleston were drawn from their hiding places and the rich con-

tents exposed to the greedy gaze of the plunderers. Haversacks and pockets were filled, and when no dent of pressing could put more into them, snowy cases were drawn from pillows and converted into sacks into which they stored their booty. I watched them quietly until I saw the wretch styling himself "Colonel" take up a ring, which, more on account of associations than for any intrinsic value, I highly prized.

"You will not take that," I said, stepping forward and extending my hand. "That ring was the gift of one now dead, and I cannot afford to lose it."

"Some d——d lover I suppose, whose bones I trust are now bleaching on the battlefield! Well, give me a kiss and you shall have it."

I recoiled with the disgust I felt depicted in my face.

"You won't? Well, then, I'll keep it and give it to my mother or sister when I get home to Boston," and the ruffian pocketed the only souvenir I posessed of "the tender grace of a day that could never come back to me."

With wildly beating hearts, but betraying no outward signs of fear, we awaited the march of events. They returned to the lower portion of the house, filling the rooms with their dreadful oaths and calling on the negroes to give what information they could relative to the treasure. "Come here you black imp and tell us where these white people have hidden Jeff Davis's gold. Out with the truth and you shall have this." He drew out of his knapsack a white crepe shawl of exquisite texture and threw it around the sable form. "What I want with Missie's shawl?" the woman answered, taking it off and carefully folding it; "and all I can tell you is dere ain't no gold here." "You are lying like the rest," he replied, using a fearful oath, "but you will all lower your tones before I am done with you."

The ruffians drank and swore, and some uttered the most horrible blasphemies. Others, with a canteen of whiskey in one hand, and the other brandishing a gun, filed in and out of the house, filling our ears with threats of what they intended doing if the gold was not soon found.

It was about three o'clock in the afternoon, when the colonel, followed by some of the most desperate looking of his ruffians, rushed up to Earle, and shaking his gun at him exclaimed in a voice quivering with passion:

"Curse you! We won't wait another moment on you to deliver up the gold. Tell us where it is, or by G——I'll shoot you down."

I saw Earle's eyes flash fire, but for our sakes he kept quiet.

"Do you hear?" the villain continued, and

Searching for booty, Federal troops ransack a Southern bedroom.

raising his gun struck him sharply on the head.

"Wretch!" cried Earle, striving to break from the guards who now surrounded him. "I'll teach you to deal such cowardly blows!"

A second blow was dealt but fell on Iris, who had thrown herself between her husband and his persecutors.

In a shorter time than I can relate it, the inhuman wretches dragged my helpless brother beneath a large maple tree, and placing a strong rope around his neck, prepared to execute their threat.

The rope was tightening, when one of the men exclaimed: "Where's his wife? She must see him swing!" and, as if in answer to his call, Iris sprang forward and tightly grasped the rope.

"You dare not! You shall not kill him!" she cried, her face blanched to the dreadful whiteness of death.

"Who will stop us, you cursed Rebel," asked the colonel, who of all these brutal creatures seemed to me the most inhuman. "Here men, pull her off; and if she won't keep her distance, make her!"

Rudely they tore her hands from the rope and held them firmly despite her efforts to free herself. Then I saw the rope tighten once more and my poor brother swing into mid-air. They twice drew

Earle up and cut him down, each time calling upon him to confess where he had hidden the gold. Faint, almost dead as he was, they were preparing to hang him the third and what must have been the last time, when several armed newcomers, who seemed to be officers high in command, arrived and ordered them to release Earle.

The men fell back astonished and obedient while the leader exclaimed: "We have orders for you to mount and join the brigade immediately. But what the devil have you done! That fellow is almost dead; quick, bring some water!" And jumping from his horse he approached Earle, who was lying insensible on the ground with Iris bending over him.

"Save your tears, madam," turning from the unconscious form and addressing the poor girl. "I have seen a good deal of this kind of thing and I can assure you that your husband will get over this, though he has been rather badly served. Now, boys, mount and be off!"

In a short time we were relieved of their presence. Five miles distant they rejoined Stoneman's brigade from which they had been dispatched. They had gone, but traces of the ruin and desolation they had wrought looked upon us from all directions. . . .

"HAIN'T YE GOIN' TO WAIT FER YER DODGERS?"

Federal raids did not always yield the desired plunder. Sometimes the raiders were driven away by intervening Confederate troops; others were outwitted by quick-thinking civilians. For example, one detachment of Yankees, intent on seizing a supply of salt in eastern Kentucky, was forced to retreat by the clever action of a resourceful Bluegrass girl.

A record of the humiliating repulse was preserved by a Federal survivor.

I was in Col. Marshall's command, and we were camping in the eastern part of Kentucky. One day the officer in command was informed that the salt had given out. Col. Marshall sent for me, and said: "Lieutenant N——, the salt is out and we must have more right away."

"Yes sir," I replied, "Is there anything else?"

"That's all," said the Colonel. "Take some men and go after the salt, and don't come back without it. Get it honestly if you can—but get salt," he said.

Well, I selected twenty of my men, and we

started out on the forage. It was late in the spring and as we went on, we grew both tired and hungry, and at noon had not yet found any salt. We knew that the Rebels were not far away, and I didn't want to lead my men into any possible ambush; but when the pangs of hunger began to assert themselves, and we saw a large white house in the distance, we forgot Rebels and everything else but the inner man. On reaching the house, I called a halt and, entering the yard, knocked at the door. A black woman opened it.

"Good day, auntie," said I. "Can you get dinner for us, and get it right away?"

She looked at me, then out at the men with a glance of fine scorn. "Law, honey! I hain't got nuthin' to cook 'at you fine gemmen 'ud eat."

"Oh, I think you have," I said, encouragingly. "Anything will do; but where are the folks?" for I saw a bright little child come . . . down the stairs.

A frightened look crept over the woman's face as she perceived the child, and her voice wavered, though I was satisfied at the time that she lied as she said:

"Bless yer heart, honey, they ain't no folks 'ere, but jist me an' little Miss Lizzie. The menfolks is all in the war. I don't reckon ye'd want t' meet 'em, fer they'd kick th' life outen ye."

"All right, auntie, I'll try not to meet the menfolks, if you will just give us a little dinner," I said pleasantly.

"Will bacon an' corn-dodgers do?" she asked.

"Yes, give us that, if you have nothing better," I said. Taking the child by the hand, she went to the kitchen.

Just then one of my men came up to me and said: "Lieutenant N——, there are twenty-five or thirty hives of bees in the yard, all full of honey. We might get some for dinner and take the rest back to camp."

"Good!" I exclaimed, for I liked honey. I went at once to investigate the beehives, and all the men followed. Of course, every mother's son of them knew how to take honey from the hives. While the men argued, four or five of them began to make preparation.

Yankee foragers retreat before an angry swarm of Southern bees.

Just then, as we bent over in our eagerness, something strange occurred. Every hive began to move as if going to fall of its own accord, and before we could realize the calamity about to happen, the hives fell over with a crash, and the air was simply alive with angry, indignant honey bees.

They settled all over us—stung us in the eyes, the ears, all over our heads; everywhere that mortal man can be stung.

There was a small stream at the end of the garden, and while the men were rolling in agony on the grass, trying to kill their persecutors, I ran, plunged into the stream, and put my head entirely under water. Gad! I never had anything hurt so in my life.

When I rose up from the stream I heard a peal of merry laughter, and glancing in the direction of the sound, I saw the prettiest girl I think I have ever seen. She was leaning out of the upstairs window, dangling in her hand the rope that had been connected to those infernal beehives, and that had done all the mischief.

I bawled the command to mount, and as we were flinging ourselves into the saddle, that black devil put her head out of the door and called: "Honey, hain't ye goin' to wait fer yer dodgers?"

We galloped on to camp, half dead, and our heads were the size of water-buckets the next day. I felt ashamed that the cleverness of one Rebel girl and a swarm of bees could completely whip a company of Union soldiers.

"OH! MISS LUCY, DE TOWN'S BURNIN' UP!"

On April 2, 1865, the battered, overextended Confederate defensive line at Petersburg collapsed, putting Robert E. Lee's worn and depleted army on the road to Appomattox. Richmond no longer could be defended, and after four years of stubborn defiance, the Confederate capital finally fell.

When Federal forces entered the defeated city the next day, a wild, destructive fire was already blazing through Richmond; the Confederacy was dying. A witness to Richmond's final ordeal was young Virginia Dade, who lived in a Richmond boarding house with her infirm sister.

On the memorable Sunday, 2d April, 1865, having been kept from our church by the illness of my sister, about the time that I supposed the congregations would be dispersing from their various places of worship, I stepped to the door to inquire from any passing acquaintance the news from "the front."

The first person I saw at the door was a fellow-lodger, Miss Bowers, who came tottering up the steps, pale and agitated, exclaiming: "Oh! have you heard the dreadful news? General Lee's right flank has given away; he has been compelled to retreat, and Richmond is to be evacuated immediately! While Dr. Hoge was in the midst of his sermon a messenger came hurriedly into the church, walked up the aisle, handed him a note, and quickly left. Dr. Hoge glanced anxiously over the mysterious paper, bowed his head for a moment in silence on his desk, then rising, said: 'Brethren, trying scenes are before us. General Lee has been defeated; but remember that God is with us in the storm as well as the calm. Go quietly to your homes, and whatever may be in store for us, let us not forget that we are Christian men and women, and may the protection and blessing of the Father, Son and Holy Ghost be with you all.' "

Next came Mrs. Porter from St. Paul's Church crying "Oh! Miss Lucy, have you heard that the city is to be evacuated immediately and the Yankees will be here before morning? While we were in church a horseman dashed up to the door, dismounted, went up the aisle, and handed a paper to the President; then spoke in a whisper to some members of the Cabinet who were there and they all arose and went out. What can it all mean? And what is to become of us poor defenceless women, God only knows!"

All through the day the various gentlemen belonging to the house had been running in to get their haversacks, canteens, blankets, etc., with a view to following the retreating army.

Left to ourselves, our first thought was that it would be well to sit up all night and to be ready to meet the first warning of approaching danger, but we finally decided that the best preparation for the morrow would be to gain all the strength and refreshment we could by a night's sleep, if sleep were possible.

It seemed as if but a few moments had passed when we were awakened by the most awful and terrific sound that has ever sent the lifeblood curdling to my heart. From that time, 4 o'clock A.M., there was no more sleep for us, for explosion followed explosion in quick succession all through the day. It seems that the retreating soldiers had put slow-matches to all the government store-houses, arsenals, etc., and the fire was now reaching them, one after the other. One shock was so violent that we thought the house had been struck, for the window shades were knocked from their fastenings and fell to the floor with a terrible crash.

We were just making a feint to eat our ill-cooked breakfast, when, about a quarter past seven, Eddie Mills, a boy about twelve years old, came running into the room exclaiming: "The Yankees are coming!" I went to the front door to ascertain if this was really so. It was true indeed; for there, riding quietly up the street and looking cautiously and inquiringly about them, were two calvary officers, the first "blue coats" I had seen.

Very soon we were told that there was a soldier standing by our front steps who, on inquiry, proved to be on guard stationed there by the Union authorities; for to their credit the first act of the Federal commander on entering the city was to place a guard at every street corner for the protection of person and property.

About 9 o'clock, the terror-stricken face of the house cook appeared at the door, she crying in dismay, "Oh! Miss Lucy, de town's burnin' up!" And so indeed it was. The first sight that met my eyes on reaching the front door was Dr. Reed's Presbyterian Church, corner of 8th and Franklin Streets, enveloped in flames. In a few minutes the fiery tongues had lapped up and around the steeple, which they encircled in a serpent-like coil, fascinating my gaze with its fatal beauty, till it swayed, tottered a moment, and then fell with a

Burned-out Richmond residents seek safety on the grounds of the State Capitol as Richmond falls.

terrible crash from where it had stood for half a century.

To the south and southeast I beheld the most sublimely awful spectacle that it has ever been my fortune to witness—the whole city in that direction seemed one sheet of fire, while dark clouds of smoke hung like a pall over the scene, and rolled in vast volumes to the north and west. One frightful feature in the scene, investing it with an almost unearthly horror, was the death-like silence that prevailed. No cries of fire, no ringing of fire bells, no rattling by of engines, not even the shrieks of women and children, for all seemed dumb with terror, and shrank pale and mute into their dwellings. . . .

Immediately on the occupation of the city,

rations were issued by the Federal commander to such as needed them, and few there were who did not. In this state of things it is not surprising that even ladies reared in ease and luxury now crowded to the ration office to get their allotted portion of codfish, fat pork and yellow meal, for this was all there was between them and starvation. I made my way through the hungry throng with mingled feelings of gratitude and humiliation to receive our share. Though we knew our army had been defeated and was retreating we knew not whither, yet hope still flickered in our hearts. This continued till the night of Sunday, April 9. We were sitting in our dimly lighted chamber, when the stillness of night was broken by the boom of a cannon, followed in quick succession by a number of other reports.

The door burst open and in rushed Mrs. Brown, who, though a native of Ohio, had always professed to be a Southerner in sympathy, and as such had obtained and held a lucrative clerkship under the Confederate Government. But now, throwing off the mask which policy had drawn over her face, she rushed triumphantly in, clapping her hands and shouting: "General Lee has surrendered!" And such indeed, as it proved, was the cause of the firing we heard. . . .

A few days after the news of General Lee's surrender had extinguished the last spark in the smoldering ashes of hope, the sound of gay music caused me to look out upon the most imposing pageant that it has ever been my fortune to behold—the entrance into the city of a portion of General Grant's army. As far as eye could reach was one unbroken column of troops, with their fine horses and wagons, and equipped in elegant uniforms and accoutrements, which to my eyes—accustomed to looking only at our poor, ragged and oftentimes barefooted boys—appearing as if newly donned for some gala day. I could see them winding over Church Hill in the far distance and then down into the valley and up over Shockoe Hill; their bayonets brightly gleaming in the morning sun, the Stars and Stripes in countless numbers waving in the breeze.

4

The Flame of Battle

The War Between the States produced 10,455 military actions, ranging from the great contests like Gettysburg and Chickamauga to obscure skirmishes along backwoods roads. All were potentially deadly, and yet that was why Johnny Reb, like his Yankee counterpart, had gone to war—to fight. "War means fightin' and fightin' means killin'," said Confederate Gen. Nathan Bedford Forrest. And Johnny Reb knew how to fight.

His reputation in battle became a Southern legacy. Yet all the heralded feats of the Confederate armies, when reduced to basics, were composed of personal acts by individual soldiers caught in the flame of battle.

Confederate troops do battle beneath the Starry Cross.

"THE BALL WAS OPENED"

After all the drilling and all the time in camp, after all the speeches and good-byes, after all the boasting that one Confederate could whip a dozen Yankees—after all that, Johnny Reb finally fought his first battle. Initial exposure to the danger, destruction, and death of combat could produce a range of emotions: anxiety, excitement, anger, fear, shock, relief, depression, and, for some, even pity for the enemy.

For many, shot dead on the field, the first battle was also the last. Survivors, however, had "seen the elephant," as initiation to combat was called in soldier slang. "The ball had opened," they would say in camp, and they had lived through it. Those who survived their first battle knew they had passed through a momentous, unforgettable event. Confederate John H. Hines, a young cavalryman from Kentucky, first came under hostile fire at the Battle of Shiloh, and documented the experience in this letter home:

Near Corinth April 22nd 1862
Dear Ma and G. Pa

. . . I was in the battle of Shiloh from beginning to end. It is said to have been the hardest fought battle ever fought on this continent. Persons who were in the battles of Manassas and Ft. Donelson say they were skirmishes in comparison. . . .

Our squadron was ordered close to the federal lines on Saturday evening. We stopped close enough to hear their drums beating. We were very tired and hungry. Some of the men not having et for 36 hours. I gave a teamster 50 cents for a biscuit. Tied my horse close to me and laid down without taking off boots or pistols and slept soundly until just at dawn the loud peal of some half dozen cannons aroused us. In a few moments we were in our saddles, overcoats and extra equipment lashed to our saddles. In our shirt sleeves, we sat on our horses examining our arms, ready for the coming fray, for we knew we would give the enemy battle if they would stand.

The increased roaring of artillery and an occasional ambulance bearing off wounded soldiers told that, as we say in camp, the ball was open. Before the sun was up we were marching to the scene of action, which was perhaps a mile off. We had not marched very far before we came upon our line of infantry. For three miles in one unbroken line stood our troops, their fixed bayonets glistening in the new sunbeams, for the sun was just coming over the top of a small elevation.

Almost every hill now on both sides looked like a volcano, for the deep mouthed cannon were roaring on every side. Soon the rattle of musketry announced that our vanguard had found the foe. The dark line of men now moved quickly in. After minutes more the volleys of musketry announced that they too had entered the bloody arena. It was really a grand scene now: you could not distinguish a musket shot now, it was one continual roar like the rushing of a storm. The thundering of the artillery at regular intervals alone disturbed the continual sounds. A shell or cannonball would tear some of your comrades to pieces and a person could not tell whose turn it might be next.

Being mounted and ordered to different places during the day, I had an opportunity to see everything that happened almost and I can assure you that a battlefield is far from being a pleasant place, laying aside the dangers of being hurt, because you can't get out of hearing the groans of the dying or out of sight of the dead. It seemed to me like my acquaintances were always lying in the most auspicious places. Turn what way we might I could find some ghastly looking face that perhaps an hour ago I had seen rushing to the contest with a smile on his face. I could not enumerate a hundredth part of the incidents of note that occurred during both days. . . .

We have again returned to camp which is not outside of the former federal lines and are resting quietly. I've a good slice of cheese and a can of oysters which I took out of a federal tent before setting fire to it. I have nothing to do but think over what has happened in the last few days. . . .

I was glad to hear the opening of the battle because I wished to satisfy my curiosity for seeing a battle and I thought it would do one some good to see dead federals. But I had not seen many until the sight became sickening. I gave my canteen of water to a federal soldier who was badly wounded and felt glad I was able to relieve him. The same sight I thought an hour before I could glory in and even ride them down sick or well wherever I found them. . . .

Don't look for me unless I can come with the army which I hope to do soon.

Your affectionate son,
J. H. Hines

"THE BATTLE ROARED IN FRONT"

Face to face with the enemy, war became a reality. So it was for William W. Blackford, a young Virginia officer attached to Col. J. E. B. Stuart's Black Horse Cavalry at the Battle of First Manassas.

Astride his favorite mount, Comet, Blackford went into battle alongside Stuart, who would become the South's most famous cavalry leader. Like thousands of others entering battle for the first time, Blackford momentarily struggled with his emotions. However, he quickly learned that combat left little time for reflection.

The battle roared in front—a sound calculated to arouse the sublimest emotions in the breast of the soldier, but the prayers, the curses, the screams, the blood, the flies, the sickening stench of this horrible little valley were too much for the stomachs of the men, and all along the column, leaning over the pommels of their saddles, they could be seen in ecstasies of protest.

Upon reaching the edge of the wood a view of the battle burst upon us, and Stuart halted to take a look. Smoke in dense white clouds lit up by lurid flashes from the cannon wrapped the position of the artillery; while lines of thin, blue, misty vapor floated over infantry, pouring out their deadly hail. At one moment all beneath would be invisible—at another the curtain, lifted by a passing breeze, revealed the thousands of busy reapers in the harvest of death. Colonel Stuart and myself were riding at the head of the column as the grand panorama opened before us, and there right in front, about seventy yards distant, and in strong relief against the smoke beyond, stretched a brilliant line of scarlet—a regiment of New York Zouaves in column of fours, marching out of the

The Black Horse Cavalry scatters New York Zouaves at First Manassas.

Sudley road to attack the flank of our line of battle. Dressed in scarlet caps and trousers, blue jackets with quantities of gilt buttons, and white gaiters, with a fringe of bayonets swaying above them as they moved, their appearance was indeed magnificent. The Sudley road was here in a deep depression and the rear of the column was still hid from view—there were about five hundred men in sight—they were all looking toward the battlefield and did not see us. Waving his saber, Stuart ordered a charge, but instantly pulled up and called a halt and turning to me said, "Blackford, are those our men or the enemy?" I said I could not tell, but I had heard that Beauregard had a regiment of Zouaves from New Orleans, dressed, I had been told, like these men. Just then all doubt

was removed by the appearance of their colors, emerging from the road—the Stars and Stripes. I shall never forget the feelings with which I regarded this emblem of our country so long beloved, and now seen for the first time in the hands of a mortal foe. But there was no time for sentiment then. The instant the flag appeared, Stuart ordered the charge, and then we went like an arrow from a bow.

As we were in column of fours it was necessary to deploy, and our gallant Colonel waved his sabre for the rear to oblique to the left, "on right into line," so as to strike the enemy in "echelon" and this they did. While a Lieutenant in my company, I had carried a Sharp's carbine slung to my shoulder and this I still wore; I also had my sabre and a large sized five-shooter. In the occupation of the moment I had not thought which of my weapons to draw until I had started, and as it does not take long for a horse at full speed to pass over seventy yards, I had little time to make the selection. I found in fact that it would be impossible to get either my sabre or pistol in time, and as the carbine hung conveniently under my right hand I seized and cocked that, holding it in my right hand with my thumb on the hammer and finger on the trigger. I thought I would fire it and then use it for a crushing blow, in which it would be almost as effective against a man standing on the ground as a sabre.

Half the distance was passed before they saw the avalanche coming upon them, but then they came to a "front face"—a long line of bright muskets was leveled—a sheet of red flame gleamed, and we could see no more. Capt. Welby Carter's horse sprang forward and rolled over dead, almost in front of Comet, so that a less active animal would have been thrown down, but Comet recovered himself and cleared the struggling horse and its rider. The smoke which wrapped them from our sight also hid us from them, and thinking perhaps we had been swept away by the volley, they, instead of coming to a "charge bayonet," lowered their pieces to load, and in this position we struck them.

The tremendous impetus of horses at full speed broke through and scattered their line like chaff before the wind. As the scarlet line appeared through the smoke, when within a couple of horse's lengths of them, I leaned down, with my carbine cocked, thumb on hammer and forefinger on trigger, and fixed my eye on a tall fellow I saw would be the one my course would place in the right position for the carbine, while the man next to him, in front of the horse, I would leave to Comet. I then plunged my spurs into Comet's flanks and he evidently thought I wanted him to jump over this strange looking wall I was riding him at, for he rose to make the leap; but he was too close and going too fast to rise higher than the breast of a man, and he struck him full in the chest, rolling him over and over under his hoofs and knocking him about ten feet backwards, depriving him of all further interest in the subsequent proceedings, and knocking the rear rank man to one side. As Comet rose to make the leap, I leaned down from the saddle, rammed the muzzle of the carbine into the stomach of my man and pulled the trigger. I could not help feeling a little sorry for the fellow as he lifted his handsome face to mine while he tried to get his bayonet up to meet me; but he was too slow, for the carbine blew a hole as big as my arm clear through him.

Just beyond their line was a fence, and Comet, exasperated to frenzy by the unusual application of the spur, was almost beyond my control, and entirely beyond the control of one hand; so I had to drop the carbine in its sling, and use both hands to swing away from the fence which he seemed bent on clearing: the field beyond was filled with their troops and if he had gone over, there would have been small chance for return. With both hands I managed to turn the horse enough to bring him up to the fence so obliquely that even he did not like to attempt it, and he came round.

We now charged back, taking their line in the rear at another place, but they had begun to break and scatter clear down to the Sudley road before we reached them; all order was gone and it became a general melee or rather a chase. I might have put in some effective work with my revolver but it got hung in the case at my belt, and as I wanted to try the effect of a downward blow with the barrel of the carbine when swung high in air, I caught it up again; but the fellows dodged or parried every blow I got close enough to attempt, and I accomplished no more than chasing some of them back into the road where the rear of the regiment stood, and where I had no disposition to follow. This regiment—they say it was the Fire Zouaves—was completely paralyzed by this charge, and though their actual loss in killed and wounded was not very great, their demoralization was complete. The arrest of their dangerous move upon the exposed flank of our main line of battle was a result of the utmost importance and, I shall always think, saved the day.

"BATTLE IS TERRIBLE AND FEARFUL"

Amid the gore of combat, the imagined glory of war disappeared quickly, its heroic images abruptly replaced by an authentic, brutal vision. Exposure to combat was sobering, and even the youngest recruit could quickly acquire a battlefield maturity, as expressed by Capt. D. U. Barziza, a youthful officer in the 4th Texas Infantry.

No tongue can convey an adequate idea of the roar of cannon and the rattle of musketry—the cheering shout and hurried command—the tramp of horse and ominous rumble of artillery—the death-groan and parting shriek. No painting can portray the scenes of War—desolate homes and abandoned fields—homeless women and affrighted children; the battlefield—the long lines of troops—the glittering arms—the eager, restless countenance—the steady march—the desperate onset—the flashes of fire—the dead soldier—the smoke-thick air—the trampled ground—the dismantled trees—the mangled limbs—the broken musket—the strong horse writhing in the throes of death—the streaming of blood and matted hair—the death dew upon the brow of the dying soldier—the intensely, indescribably wild and thrilling aspect of strong men in the storm of Battle.

Abstractly, how positively foolish and senseless it seems for thousands of men to be engaged in deadly conflict with others, entire strangers to themselves, and, as the soldiers say, "nobody mad." In the morning, they will be in eager haste to take each other's lives; in the evening, the one kindly supporting and ministering to his wounded foe. A soldier's life tends to engender a feeling of indifference to future danger and an almost recklessness to the present. On his march, he is full of fun and humor, and sings his songs cheerily around his smoky camp fire—goes into ecstacies over a letter—shouts till his throat is sore at the waving of a white handkerchief, and jests with his comrades a minute before his own death.

A Battle is a terrible and fearful, but grand and magnificent display. How quiet and calm just before action! As though nature held its breath, and the very elements wait expectant upon the impending conflict. Men and cannon are moved into position quietly, deliberately and cautiously. Groups of generals are collected upon some commanding eminence. At a given signal the artillery begins to belch forth its horrid missiles. The air is filled with the bursting, screaming, hissing death-messengers. The roar is incessant. The very elements now appear to be at war, and all the thunderbolts of Heaven seem to be turned loose from the hands of an angry and destroying God. The tough trees, survivors of a thousand storms, are broken and dismantled; huge strong horses are felled in death like so many toys and playthings; whole ranks of living, moving men are mown down by the merciless shot and shell. Meantime, the supporting columns are ranged ready to advance, the men crouching down on the earth as they "lie under the shelling."

Half an hour upon an occasion like this seems an age; and the mind is so keenly tortured and oppressed by anxiety, that one feels as physically wearied, as if he had been on a long and tiresome march. The feelings that take possession of a

The reality of war: Confederate dead at Sharpsburg.

ing, cursing, raving—horses plunging and neighing wildly; then comes the deadly onset—the rush, the repulse, the victory!

The continued ring of musketry mingled with the louder reports of cannon, the long lines of burning flame, the dust, smoke, confusion and uproar, the sudden intervals of firing, only to recommence with redoubled fury, utterly defy conception, and seem as though ten thousand fiends were holding their infernal orgies.

Cold, heat, rain, fatigue and danger are alike disregarded, and even God himself is, for the time, forgotten. Borne along in this human current, the soldier steps over the body of his dead brother, and rushes on unheeding the imploring cries of his best friend. Men seem like devils who have wrested the instruments of wrath and destruction from the hands of the Almighty, and wield them for their mutual destruction.

And when the Battle is over, what a sight! Excitement allayed and passion subsided, the strong man becomes a child, obedient, full of sympathy, kind, tender and obliging.

For miles the ground is strewn with the dead and dying—the wrecks of battle—the warm blood yet pouring from them; every ditch and ravine is filled with the poor mangled wretches, who have dragged themselves thither for shelter—friend and enemy bathing in the same water. And this is War!

soldier on the eve of advancing into a fight, can be known only to those who have experienced them. The heart is heavy; the blood feels as if it was congealed; the breath comes short and quick, and it is a relief to move on. As the Battle progresses, the sharp, desultory fire of the skirmishers startles every one into energy. The line presses forward and the engagement becomes general. Shells are bursting, shrapnel screaming, grapeshot whistling, and bullets fly thick as rain-drops. Men are cheer-

"DESPERATION SEEMED TO SEIZE ME"

Combat could be a confusing, unpredictable experience, as Pvt. J. A. McKinstry learned at the Battle of Corinth in 1862. An eighteen-year-old soldier in the 42nd Alabama Infantry, McKinstry was among the troops who stormed a strong Federal position called Battery Robinett. Led by Col. William P. Rogers, who would not survive the fighting, the costly assault carried the enemy's works—for a few moments. Then, when four regiments of Federal reinforcements counterattacked, McKinstry saw how, in the confusion of battle, an apparent victory could become a deadly defeat.

We lay on our guns during the night, and just before daylight we took position in a skirt of

woods, directly in front of Robinette [sic] and some four or five hundred yards from it. We were discovered at dawn, and Fort Williams, Robinette, and College Hill opened a terrific enfilade fire of shot and shell upon us. We lay flat upon our faces, and the shells passed a few feet over us (we thought these feet were only inches), doing but slight damage. We remained in this position, hugging the ground, for four mortal hours before the signal gun was fired and the order to charge was given. The forts caught the sound of the signal gun and ceased firing. We raised the rebel yell and made a rush for the opening, some fifty yards in our front. There we were met by a deadly volley of shrapnel shells from the three forts and our men fell dead and wounded all along the line.

In front of us was the most obstructive abatis that it was my misfortune to encounter, or to see, during the war. Beyond this in our front, to our right and to our left, were the forts belching destruction into our ranks; yet our men did not waver or halt, but over the tops, under the limbs, around the stumps, along the fallen trunks of the

trees, like squirrels, they scrambled in their effort to reach the fort in front. Forts Williams and College Hill were soon devoting their attention to the columns in their respective fronts; and when about half through the abatis, Robinette changed shells for grape and canister on us.

Our yells grew fainter and our men fell faster; but at last we reached the unobstructed ground in front of the fort, which was still a hundred yards away. Minies had been added to the missiles of death by the battery's infantry support; still we moved onward as our badly scattered forces rallied on the flag. Twenty steps further and our colors were down again; Going had fallen with a bullet in his leg. Comrade Crawford of Company A dropped his gun and almost before the flag had touched the dust, hoisted it again and shouted: "On to the fort, boys!"

A few steps farther, and the guns of the fort again changed their charges; now whole bags of buckshot were being belched from the cannons'

Fallen Confederates lie in a gruesome heap near Battery Robinett.

mouths into our now nearly annihilated ranks and our flag went down the ill-fated third time to rise no more on that battlefield. Poor Crawford had caught nine buckshot—seven in his breast and two in his arm; but we, only a remnant now of those who started, pressed on and reached the outside of the fort and for a moment had protection; but before we could scarcely catch a breath, hand-grenades came flying thick and fast over the walls of the fort and, falling in the dust, which was ankle deep, began to explode under our feet, filling the air with dust and smoke and wounding our men. It took but a moment, however, to put a stop to this; for having been educated in the tactics of fort defense, we quickly answered the command of a comrade: "Pick them up, boys, and pitch them back into the fort"; and immediately these infernal machines were bursting upon the inside among those who first threw them.

Someone at this juncture shouted, "Over the walls, and drive them out"; and up the steep embankment we clambered. Comrade Luke was on my right and Comrade Franks was on my left. As we scaled the top of the parapet, a volley of musketry met us. Luke went on over, Franks was killed with a bullet in the forehead, and, as he fell backward, he clinched me around the neck and carried me tumbling back with him to the bottom of the ditch on the outside. I was considerably rattled by the fall; but I heard Luke shout from the inside of the fort, "Come on, boys; here they are"; and I picked up my gun to go back to him, when I saw a "blue coat" jump from behind a stump, on the right of the fort, and run back in the direction of Corinth. He was only a few steps from me and I held my gun on him and tried to fire, but could not. He soon got behind the fort so that I could not see him and I took my gun down to see what was the matter, and found that in my excitement I had only half-cocked it.

Firing had almost ceased and I heard the shout of "Victory! Victory!" and I thought we had won the day. I ran to the left of the fort whence the shout of victory came and joined a small squad of our men that were standing a few paces from the fort. Col. Rogers and Capt. Foster were in this squad. On seeing a line of Federals approaching, and before giving the situation a thought, I immediately raised my gun and fired full into the breast of a Federal sergeant, who was in front of the column, and only a short distance from us. 'Twas then that Capt. Foster shouted, "Cease firing, men! Cease firing!" and waved his handkerchief; and I realized the true situation. 'Twas too late! A fatal volley was turned on our little band from the muzzles of fifteen hundred muskets.

I was still standing just as I was when I fired my last shot, and within a few feet of Col. Rogers, when a minie ball went crashing through my left hip and turned me half round; another went tearing through my right shoulder, which changed my position to front; and another ball crushed through my left shoulder, causing me to drop my gun and my left arm to fall limp by my side. I looked and lo! every one of the fifteen men who were standing with me had fallen in a heap. I looked again and not a Confederate was in sight. The battle was lost and our men had fallen back to the cover of the woods. Desperation seemed to seize me; and though the blood was spurting from six gaping wounds and I was already staggering from weakness, I took my dangling left arm up in my right, and in the face of that deadly fire, I turned and ran for a quarter mile (in full view of that column of Federals, who were popping away at me every step that I took) and on for half a mile before I fell. He who seems to take special care of boys was certainly with me in my desperate flight; for, though hundreds of minies passed uncomfortably near my ears, I was not hit in the back nor was I captured.

I have only to add that Crawford, after being shot down, saved our flag by tearing it from the staff, putting it in his bosom, and crawling out with it. Poor Luke was killed inside the fort. Of the thirty-three men belonging to our company who went into the charge that morning only eleven answered to roll call next day.

"THE ORDER WAS GIVEN TO CHARGE"

The charge: great ranks of uniformed men, emitting excited cheers, rush shoulder-to-shoulder toward the enemy line in a glorious, irrepressible dash through fire. Such was the romanticized nineteenth-century perception of warfare. Johnny Reb did in fact make many such assaults throughout the war, but such tactics—masses of men racing wave after wave across an open field toward an entrenched, well-fortified enemy—did not suit the improved weaponry of the day.

The smoothbore musket of earlier American wars had been replaced by much more accurate rifled shoulder arms, including the breech-loading rifle with its rapid rate of fire, and a comparable modernization had also made artillery much more lethal. A well-entrenched enemy armed with such accurate, destructive weapons could—and did—transform the proverbial glorious charge into a murderous exercise in carnage.

So observed a Confederate private who endured a bloody frontal assault during the Battle of Atlanta in 1864.

About this time our regiment had reformed, and had got their breath, and the order was given to charge, and take their guns even at the point of the bayonet. We rushed forward up the steep hillsides, the seething fire from ten thousand muskets and small arms, and forty pieces of cannon hurled right into our very faces, scorching and burning our clothes and hands and faces from their rapid discharges, and piling the ground with our dead and wounded almost in heaps. It seemed that the hot flames of hell were turned loose in all their fury, while the demons of damnation were laughing in the flames like seething serpents hissing out their rage. We gave one long, loud cheer, and commenced the charge.

As we approached their lines, like a mighty inundation of the river Acheron in the infernal region, Confederate and Federal met. Officers with drawn swords met officers with drawn swords, and man to man met man to man with bayonets and loaded guns. The continued roar of battle sounded like unbottled thunder. Blood covered the ground, and the dense smoke filled our eyes, and ears, and faces. The groans of the wounded and dying rose above the thunder of battle. But the Federal lines waver, and break and fly, leaving us in possession of their breastworks and the battlefield, and I do not know how many pieces of artillery, prisoners and small arms.

Here is where Major Allen, Lieutenant Joe Carney, Captain Joe Carthell and many other good and brave spirits gave their lives for the cause of their country . . . weltering in their own life's blood. It was one of the bloody battles that characterize that stormy epoch, and it was the 22nd of July, and one of the hottest days I ever felt.

The victory was complete. Large quantities of provisions and army stores were captured. The Federals had abandoned their entire line of breastworks, and had changed their base. They were fortifying upon our left, about five miles off from their dead and wounded soldiers. I have never seen so many battleflags left indiscriminately upon any battlefield. I ran over twenty in the charge, and could have picked them up everywhere; did pick up one, and was promoted to fourth corporal for gallantry in picking up a flag on the battlefield.

Southern troops charge a Federal position.

On the final charge that was made, I was shot in the ankle and on the heel of my foot. I crawled into their abandoned ditch, which then seemed full and running over with our wounded soldiers. I dodged behind the embankment to get out of the raking fire that was ripping through the bushes, and tearing up the ground. Here I felt safe. The firing raged in front; we could hear the shout of the charge and the clash of the battle. While I was sitting here, a cannon ball came tearing down the works, cutting a soldier's head off, splattering his brains all over my face and bosom, and mangling and tearing four to five others to shreds. As a wounded horse was being led off, a cannon ball struck him, and he was literally ripped open, falling in the very place I had just moved from. . . . The casualties on our side were frightful. Generals, colonels, captains, lieutenants, sergeants, corporals and privates were piled indiscriminately everywhere. Cannon, caissons, and dead horses were piled pell-mell. It was the picture of a real battlefield. Blood had gathered in pools, and in some instances had made streams of blood. 'Twas a picture of carnage and death.

"STEADY MEN! STEADY! THEY ARE COMING"

Johnny Reb was often outnumbered. For every Confederate soldier in the war, there existed about three Federals, who were generally better fed, better supplied, and better equipped. Southern soldiers seldom went into battle with numerical superiority. It was a handicap Johnny Reb had to face throughout the war—often with deadly results. Such was the case for the depleted 17th Virginia Infantry at the Battle of Sharpsburg. Led by Col. Montgomery D. Corse, the few survivors of the battle-torn regiment tried to hold a hilltop position against several hundred advancing Yankees. One of the handful of Johnny Rebs left standing after the assault later recalled what it was like on that hill near Antietam Creek.

The shells begin to sail over us as we lay close behind the fence, shrieking their wild song, a canzonet of carnage and death. These missiles howled like demons, and made us cower in the smallest possible space. . . . But what is that infernal noise that makes the bravest duck their heads? That is a Hotchkiss shell. Thank goodness, it burst far in the rear. It is no more destructive than some other projectile, but there is a great deal in mere sound to work on men's fears, and the moral effect of the Hotchkiss is powerful.

It was now getting late in the afternoon, and the men were becoming cramped from lying in their constrained position; some were moving up and down, some stretching themselves, for there was a cessation of firing in our front—an interval of quiet. It was but a short time, for the guarded, stern, nervous voice of our officer, calling, "Quick men, back to your post!" sent every soldier into line. And then, as we waited, each man looked along the line—the slight, thin, frail line—stretched out behind that crest to withstand the onset of solid ranks of blue, and felt his heart sink within him. . . .

Our brigade was a mere outline of its former strength, not a sixth remaining. Our regiment, the Seventeenth, that once carried into battle eight hundred muskets, now stood on the crest, ready to die in a forlorn hope, with but forty-six muskets.

My company, which often used to march in a grand review in two platoons of fifty men each, carried into Sharpsburg but two muskets (the writer and one other), commanded by Lieutenant Perry. Is it a wonder that we deliberately made up our minds to die on that hill, knowing what a force must be sent against us?

All at once, an eight gun battery, detecting our position, tried to shell us out, preparatory to their infantry advance, and the air around was filled by the bursting iron. Our battery of four guns took its place about twenty steps on our right, for our right flank was entirely undefended. They replied to the enemy. During the fire a shell burst not ten feet above where the Seventeenth lay, prone on their faces, and literally tore poor Appich, of Company E, to pieces, shattering his body terribly and causing the blood to splatter over many who lay around him. A quiver in the form, and then it remained still. Another Hotchkiss came screeching where we lay, and exploded, two more men were borne to the rear; still the line never moved or uttered a sound. The shells split all around, and knocked up the dust until it sprinkled us so, that if it intended to keep the thing up, it threatened to bury the command alive.

Oh, those long minutes that we lay with closed eyes, expecting mutilation, and a shock of the plunging iron, with every breath we drew—would it never end? But it kept up for fully fifteen minutes, and the men clenched their jaws tight and never moved; a line of corpses could not have been more stirless.

At last! At last! The firing totally ceases, then the battery with us limbered up and moved away, because, as they said, their ammunition was exhausted; but murmurs and curses loud and deep were heard from the brigade, who openly charged the battery with deserting them in the coming ordeal. It was in truth a desertion, for instead of throwing their shells at the enemy's eight gun battery, thereby drawing their dreadful fire upon us, they should have laid low and waited until the infantry attack was made, then every shot would have told, every shell or solid shot a help—but they moved away and left us. An ominous silence followed the deluge. The Seventeenth lay with the rest of the brigade, recumbent on the earth, behind the fence, with their rifles resting on the lower rails. The men's faces are pale, their features set, their hearts throbbing, their muscles strung like steel.

The officers cry in low tones, "Steady men! Steady! They are coming. Ready!"

The warning click of the hammers raised as the guns are cocked runs down the lines, a momentary solemn sound—for when you hear that, you

A lone Confederate horse soldier: Johnny Reb was often outnumbered.

know that the supreme moment has come.

The hill in the front shut out all view, but the advancing enemy were close on us, they were coming up the hill, the loud tones of their officers, the clanging of their equipments, and the steady tramp of the approaching host was easily distinguishable.

Then our Colonel said in a quiet calm tone, that was heard by all, "Steady lads, steady! Seventeenth, don't fire until they get above the hill."

Each man sighted his rifle about two feet above the crest, and then, with his finger on the trigger, waited until an advancing form came between the bead and the clear sky behind.

The first thing we saw appear was the gilt eagle that surmounted the pole, then the top of the flag, next the flutter of the Stars and Stripes itself slowly mounting—up it rose; then their hats came in sight; still rising, the faces emerged; next a range of curious eyes appeared, then such a hurrah as only the Yankee troops could give broke the stillness, and they surged toward us.

"Keep cool, men—don't fire yet," shouted Colonel Corse; and such was their perfect discipline that not a gun replied. But when the bayonets flashed above the hill-top the forty-six muskets exploded at once, and sent a leaden shower full in the breast of the attacking force, not over sixty yards distant. It staggered them—it was a murderous fire—and many fell; some of them struck for the rear, but the majority sent a stunning volley at us, and but for that fence there would have been hardly a man left alive. The rails, the post, were shattered by the balls; but still it was a deadly one—fully one-half of the Seventeenth lay in their tracks; the balance that is left load and fire again and again, and for about ten minutes the unequal struggle is kept up. The attacking force, I learned, was a full brigade, three thousand strong, and against our little remnant is a full regiment. What hope is there? None. And yet for the space of a few rounds the combat is kept up, the combatants not over thirty feet apart. We stood up against this force more from a blind dogged obstinacy than anything else, and gave back fire for fire, shot for shot, and death for death. But it was a pin's point against Pelides' spear. Our Colonel falls wounded; every officer except five of the Seventeenth is shot down; of the forty-six muskets thirty-five are dead, dying or struck down; three, myself among them, are run over by the line in blue, and throw up our hands in token of surrender. . . .

"I SAW THAT HE WAS BREATHING HIS LAST"

The volunteer regiments of the South, like their Northern counterparts, were initially composed of companies recruited intact from local areas. So Johnny Reb went off to war with people he already knew—often with members of his own family. Childhood friends, rural acquaintances, fellow church members, next-door neighbors, former classmates—all entered service together. It was not uncommon for sons to go into battle alongside fathers or brothers alongside brothers.

Such an arrangement produced a sense of community and familiarity in the ranks, but it could also make battlefield casualties especially personal for the common soldier. In combat together at the 1862 Battle of Prairie Grove, for example, were Corp. Columbus H. Gray and Sgt. J. A. ("Ad") Gray—brothers in Company D of the 29th Arkansas Infantry. One survived the battle; the other died. In this anguished letter to the folks at home, Corp. Gray reported the loss.

Confederate dead on the field.

December 12, 1862

Dear Father,

I take my present opportunity of informing you all of the death of my dear beloved Brother. He was killed the seventh last. He was at the head of the company when he was shot dead. We were all laying down and the Federals came up in 50 steps of us when our colonel ordered us to rise and fire. We did so and loaded again and then he ordered us to charge. I was between Ad and W. T. Bradley all the time and we were ordered to charge. We all broke and Ad got ahead. He run up in 10 steps of the enemy before they hit him.

I stopped, squatted down by him, and laid my hand on his head and I said, Oh, my brother whare are you hurt but he could not answer me. I saw that he was breathing his last. Ad was hit in the left side rite under the rib. It almost run me distracted. I did not know what to do. I knew I could not do him any good by staying there with

him so I jumped up and run on with the company. W. T. Bradley was wounded in the thigh and three others was killed in the same charge, none that you know.

The fight commenced on Sunday evening the 7th about half past one and lasted until night. We made three desperate charges during the time with our little regiment and repulsed the Enemy every time with a great loss on both sides. Colonel Pleasants was wounded in the first charge, his leg was broke he sat on his horse and give commands until his horse was shot from under him. Colonel Gohagan's horse was shot from under him but he was not touched. Our regiment went into the fight with 304 men and we lost killed and wounded 142 men. Our company went in with 26 men and lost 14 killed and wounded. I will give you a list of the killed and wounded in our company. J. A. Gray killed, Croswell killed, John Goff killed, Bruce Goff killed, Yarbrough killed. I believe that is all that is killed on the battlefield that I know of for certain. I think Luke Hunt was killed. The wounded were Pete Sanders through the breast. J. H. Williams on the arm. W. T. Bradley in the thigh. W. Graves in the leg. McGoogan in the side, James Harrison in the thigh, J. Craig wounded, I believe that is all. Martin Garner came out safe so did J. T. Brown. I had my blanket on my shoulder and there was two ball holes shot through it.

Now I expect you want to know wat I did with my Brothers boddy. I am sorry to say that I had to leave him on the field. Just at night I went to him. Oh my God he looked so pale and bad and there was a tear in one of his eyes. I threwed my arms around him and hollowed to some of the boys to come help me carry him off the field and they

would not come. John Rich told me to come away from him that we could not take him off the field. So I laid him on his back and stritened him out and had to leave him. We left the field that knight and so did the Federals. They say that their killed and wounded was eight to our one. I can tell you we showed them shame.

I will wright again soon. We just got into our old camp this evening and we are all most tired down. You must all write me often for I do feel mity sad and lonesome. May God have mercy on us all is my prayer, so good by.

C. H. Gray

Judy, you must take it easy as possible for it cant be helped.

"THE EARTH IS RED WITH BLOOD"

"I heard a thud on my right as if one had been struck with a heavy fist," recalled a veteran Confederate. *"Looking around I saw a man at my side standing erect, with his head off, a stream of blood spurting a foot or more from his neck."*

Most of the young men who rushed to don the gray at the war's beginning had never been exposed to battle, and their patriotic, romantic notions of war had not prepared them for such horrors. Even the battle-tested veterans still in line near war's end continued to be stunned by the unprecedented bloodshed of this war—as described by a Confederate private who survived the Battle of Franklin.

Our regiment was resting in the gap of a range of hills in plain view of the city of Franklin. We could see the battleflags of the enemy waving in the breeze. Our army had been depleted of its strength by a forced march from Spring Hill, and stragglers lined the road. Our artillery had not yet come up, and could not be brought into action. Our cavalry was across Harpeth river, and our army was but in poor condition to make an assault. While resting on the hill-side, I saw a courier dash up to our commanding general, B. F. Cheatham, and the word, "Attention!" was given. I knew then that we would soon be in action. Forward, march. We

passed over the hill and through a little skirt of woods.

The enemy were fortified right across the Franklin pike, in the suburbs of the town. Right here in these woods a detail of skirmishers was called for. Our regiment was detailed. We deployed as skirmishers, firing as we advanced on the left of the turnpike road. . . .

As [our troops] marched on down through an open field toward the rampart of blood and death, the Federal batteries began to open and mow down and gather into the garner of death as brave, and good, and pure spirits as the world

*Lt. Robert B. Hurt, Jr., of the 55th Tennessee Infantry—
one of the Confederate dead at Franklin.*

ments of heaven and earth were in one mighty uproar.

Forward, men! And the blood spurts in a perfect jet from the dead and wounded. The earth is red with blood. It runs in streams, making little rivulets as it flows. Occasionally there was a little lull in the storm of battle, as the men were loading their guns, and for a few moments it seemed as if night tried to cover the scene with her mantle. The death-angel shrieks and laughs and old Father Time is busy with his sickle, as he gathers in the last harvest of death, crying, More, more, more! while his rapacious maw is glutted with the slain.

But the skirmish line is being deployed out, extending a little wider than the battle did— passing through a thicket of small locusts, where Brown, orderly sergeant of Company B, was killed—we advanced on toward the breastworks, on and on. I had made up my mind to die—felt glorious. We pressed forward until I heard the terrific roar of battle open on our right. Cleburne's division was charging their works. I passed on until I got to their works, and got over on their (the Yankees') side. But in fifty yards of where I was the scene was lit up by fires that seemed like hell itself. It appeared to be but one line of streaming fire. Our troops were upon one side of the breastworks, and the Federals on the other.

I ran up on the line of works where our men were engaged. Dead soldiers filled the entrenchments. The firing was kept up until after midnight, and gradually died out. We passed the night where we were. But when the morrow's sun began to light up the eastern sky with its rosy hues, and we looked over the battlefield, O, my God! What did we see! It was a grand holocaust of death. Death had held high carnival there that night. The dead were piled the one on the other all over the ground. I never was so horrified and appalled in my life. . . .

ever saw. The twilight of evening had begun to gather as a precursor of the coming blackness of midnight darkness that was to envelop a scene so sickening and horrible that it is impossible for me to describe it.

"Forward, men," is repeated all along the line. A sheet of fire was poured into our very faces, and for a moment we halted as if in despair, as the terrible avalanche of shot and shell laid low those brave and gallant heroes, whose bleeding wounds attested that the struggle would be desperate. Forward, men! The air loaded with death-dealing missiles. Never on this earth did men fight against such terrible odds. It seemed that the very ele-

"I WISH WE COULD ALL GO HOME IN PEACE"

It didn't take long for the typical soldier to tire of war. Repeated exposure to death, destruction, and suffering could make even the most zealous Southern patriot eager for a quick victory. After barely a year in uniform, Virginia artilleryman George M. Neese, a gunner in Chew's Battery, yearned for a merciful end to the slaughter. Excerpts from his diary at the Battle of Cedar Mountain reflect the melancholy mood Southern soldiers sometimes experienced.

August 8 [1862]—Today we moved to Orange Court House. We are camped in a field east of town. There are a great many infantry camped around here, and from all appearances the butcher business will be flourishing in a few days, and the war that is budding for bloom will soon break out in a fresh place.

This is a beautiful night. The moon hangs like a great refulgent shield in a clear sky and bathes the dewey hills with a flood of silvery light.

At midnight a brass band which I think came on an incoming train played some five or six pieces, the last of which was "Home Sweet Home." As the familiar strains of the grand old piece stole through the midnight air they seemed to me like sweet echoes from the bending skies which wake a thousand thoughts of other days, of home and friends far away, that perhaps I will never see again; of happy scenes in the peaceful days of childhood that now return no more; all rushed in solemn troops through my memory as sadly as a weird night wind that sighs and moans through the strings of a broken harp. I know that there are hundreds of men lying on the silent hills around me who will never see home again nor hear the friendly voices of loved ones that are dreaming far away.

I tried to banish the reverie, but it sticks to me even after the music has died away, and I wish for the power and might to rise and shell off my blanket and smash to atoms every implement of war in all creation, so that we could all go home satisfied and gratified and dwell in peace forevermore with all mankind.

August 9—This morning we were ordered to the front, which lies in the direction of Culpepper Court House. We started early, and even then the road was already crowded with baggage and ordnance wagons all headed toward Culpepper.

About three o'clock this afternoon we sighted the enemy nine miles from Culpepper Court House. Jackson's batteries were ordered to the immediate front, took position and opened fire on the enemy right away. The enemy was prompt in replying to Jackson's batteries, and the cannonading soon after became general along the front, and opened the battle. . . .

Jackson's batteries on the mountain side were still thundering away and doing good work, while on our right a continued blaze of fire flashed along the opposing lines of infantry and the musketry raged with terrifying fury. The surrounding air was full of flying messengers that gathered in with a dull thud many inhabitants for the silent city of the dead.

The battle lasted till about sunset, when the musketry ceased; but there was some artillery firing till nearly midnight. Our forces drove the enemy about four miles, and we held the battlefield.

The Federal dead lay all around our bivouac, and I heard the pitiful groans of the wounded and

Confederate infantry pour fire into the enemy ranks.

the low weakly murmur of the dying. When I lay down on blood-stained sod to snatch a few hours of sleep it was then two hours past midnight, and the desultory artillery fire that was kept up in the fore part of the night had fully died away and the dogs of war were silent once more.

The sudden and abrupt vicissitudes of sanguinary war rush a man rough-shod from one end of the scale of human experience to the other. Last night I was lulled to sleep, as it were, by the enlivening and inspiring strains of a band playing "Home Sweet Home"; today I heard the hideous roar of battle, and tonight I am kept awake by the constant and pitiful murmur of the wounded and the groans of the dying without any "Sweet Home" in it.

If this cruel war lasts seventy-five years, and the Yanks don't kill me before it ends, I hope I will never be compelled to bivouac on another fresh battlefield.

The same silvery moon that flooded the hills of Orange last night hangs again in an unclouded sky and bathes the plains of Culpepper with a sea of mellow light, and the battlefield lies in a weird silvery glow nearly as light as day. The moonbeams that played last night with velvety fingers, penciling with silvery sheen the silent hieroglyphics of hope that flashed over the cheeks of sleeping soldiers as they dreamed of home and loved ones far away, tonight silently fall and linger on many upturned faces that are cold as marble and wearing the pallid and ghastly hue that can alone be painted by the Angel of Death.

I wonder where that band is that played "Home Sweet Home" last night. I wish it would come right here and play "Come Ye Disconsolate," so as to drown this constant wailing of the wounded.

"I WAS SHOT JUST AS WE REACHED THE TOP"

When he went into battle, Johnny Reb knew he might be a casualty. More than 22,000 Confederates were killed or wounded at Gettysburg; almost 17,000 fell at Chickamauga; more than 11,000 were killed or wounded at Sharpsburg. Almost half of the estimated 750,000 Confederates in uniform became casualties during the war. One of them was Pvt. Lamar Fontaine, who was seriously wounded at First Manassas, yet lived to record what it was like to be shot down on the field of battle.

"Forward, double-quick, march."

We trotted in the direction of the roll of musketry and the quick, heavy crack of the rifled Parrott guns. After about a mile and a half of double-quicking, with here and there the hiss of a deadly minie, the shriek of a shell, or the hum of a solid shot above our heads, we halted. We could hear the yells of the Confederates and the huzzahs of the Yanks; louder and nearer they came. The excitement was intense, and we wondered why they would not let us go on. Several of our officers and a few men went forward to the top of a hill that was in front of us, and were gone some time. In the meantime the roll of musketry was increasing, and we were standing stock-still in an open field, but near the skirts of a small belt of timber.

For a while the incessant roar of the musketry increased, and the huzzahs of the Yankees seemed to grow fainter, and we saw our officers returning. Again a courier galloped up and gave our general another dispatch. We were about-faced and in a double-quick hurried back past our starting point, and on down in the direction of Union Mills, far on our extreme right, some five miles from the fight at the Henry house. We crossed Bull Run, stopped under a hill, and were ordered to rest in line. Many of the men looked pale and exhausted, and fell down from the long run of five miles. I leaned on my musket and retained my position in the ranks.

Presently an old gentleman of General D. R. Jones' staff, Colonel J. J. B. White, came dashing up from our rear and rode to the front. Orders were given to "fall in," and the lines were instantly formed. Shells began to burst around us in close proximity. I saw one cover Colonel White and his horse with smoke and dust, but it did not injure him.

A wounded Reb bids farewell to his messmates.

We were moved forward in the direction of the cannonading, and crossed over a hill into a small valley, through which flowed a small branch. In a crooked road, with our left in the front, we marched alongside of this branch. Its banks were about eight feet high above the water and almost perpendicular, with blackberry vines between us and the branch.

While in this narrow valley we came in sight of the Yankees posted on a hill, directly in our front, and with a line of skirmishers to the right and left of us on high hills. I could look right into the mouth of a ten-gun battery, and could see a brigade of regulars of the old United States Army on the brow of the hill below it. We heard a voice sing out in a clear, sharp tone:

"Are you friends?"

Not a sound was uttered by us, but our hands were raised for silence, and the signal passed down the line. Our colors were rolled up in an oilcloth cover, and never unfurled during the day that I am aware of. We marched straight ahead and kept our eyes on the Yankees in our front. Again came the voice from the Yanks, but we paid not the slightest attention to it, and marched on toward them. They ordered us to halt, but we did not obey. Then came the command, "Ready," and involuntarily each of us cocked his gun, but did not halt. We heard the command given by the Yanks, "Aim," and saw every one of their guns come into position, like clockwork. Before the word "Fire" rang out, every man of us, with the exception of a dozen or more, jumped through the blackberry thicket into the bottom of the branch, and the two volleys of the Yanks were poured into vacant space, and we felt the wind of the bullets as they passed over our heads.

Some of the guns of the boys were discharged as they reached the bottom of the branch. Cass Oltenberg's gun jarred me as it went off not more than a foot from my head. Just after the Yankees gave us their volleys from the front, rear and side, someone gave the order for us to charge. Up we rose out of the branch and with a loud yell rushed straight at the nearest body of Yanks. As we mounted the top of the steep bank and went toward the hill on which the Yanks were, we came to the top of a steep bluff that we could not get down. There they poured a galling fire into us which we returned, but it was foolish for us to stand exposed to the fire of a whole brigade of infantry and ten rifled Parrott guns. [We were led] by the right flank into the rear of their line.

I was shot just as we reached the top of the bluff and lay there until ten o'clock that night. I heard the first volley our boys poured into the brigade from their rear, and heard the awful roar of the retreating Yanks as the volley, delivered in their rear, surprised them. They thought that they were surrounded and cut off from their line of retreat.

I can never forget those long hours I lay, on that July Sunday, in the blazing sun after I fell on the top of the bluff. The roar of the cannon was around me and the incessant hiss of the deadly minies, as they threw the dust into my eyes and ears, was fearful. I could not move hand or foot. We sometimes live a whole lifetime in a few short minutes, but here I had hours, and they were fearfully long ones at that. I was not in any very great pain, as I was completely paralyzed. My neck was twisted and my chin rested against my backbone; I was doubled up into a short space and wedged in a small gully.

Toward night everything grew dim and confused and the silence of death fell on the field. Close by me a little drummer boy was lying, cut nearly in two by a cannon ball. His blood and entrails had been scattered over me until I, too, looked as if torn to pieces. Near my feet lay Captain McWillie, a son of Governor McWillie of Mississippi.

It was not long before my eyes began to grow dim; everything had put on a lurid glare, then it faded to a yellow tinge, then to a dark blue, and finally to a black. I tried to speak, but my tongue and throat, like the rest of my body, were numb, and would give no response to my efforts. My brain and thoughts alone were active. I felt no pain, only a tingling sensation, just as you feel when any of your limbs are asleep.

Sometime in the night I heard the approach of voices and the tramp of men. Soon I heard the sounds of picks and spades and caught the gleam of lanterns, and knew a burial party was on the field, and that surgeons, with their attendants, had come to pick up and care for the wounded. Again and again I tried to speak, but no sound came. Presently I felt the jar of the picks and spades as they dug a grave by my side, and then I felt a strong hand grasp my head and another my feet, and lift me clear of the ground. There was a sharp click, and then a loud buzzing sound in my ears,

and my whole body was in an agony of pain. A fearful thirst tortured me. I spoke, and my friends let me drop suddenly to the ground. The jar awoke every faculty to life. I asked for water, and at once a strong light was flashed in my face, a rubber canteen applied to my lips, and I felt a life-giving stream of cold, refreshing water flow down my swollen throat, and seemingly into every part of my frame. I was carefully lifted from the ground and placed upon a caisson box of a captured cannon. I saw them lay the mangled form of the drummer boy in the grave which they were preparing for me. . . .

"HE FELL ALMOST AS SOON AS THEY STARTED"

"Dying on the field of battle," a Confederate private observed, "is about the easiest duty a soldier has to undergo." In the flame of battle death was quick and common. Countless Confederates sacrificed themselves in courageous, unselfish acts or in loyal obedience to orders, but more often than not death on the battlefield held no glory. Men died in awesome, impersonal numbers and were buried anonymously in great mass graves gouged in the earth. Many soldiers were killed in actions that accomplished little or nothing. Others were killed through foolish orders or the blundering of incompetent commanders.

Some, like Capt. Charles Seton Fleming, were killed executing orders they personally opposed. A twenty-six-year-old officer in the 2nd Florida Infantry, Fleming was killed on June 3, 1864, at the Battle of Cold Harbor. Reproduced here are his final letter to his mother and a letter from a friend to Fleming's brother, reporting the young captain's death on the field of battle.

"Perry's Brigade"
Near Hanover Junction, Va.
May 23, 1864

My Dear Mother:

I only write you a line or two now, to let you know that I am still safe and well. I wrote you several days ago, giving you a brief account of the battles of the Wilderness and Spotsylvania Court-House, in the former of which, Perry's Brigade was engaged and lost heavily. I received two very slight wounds from glance shots, having been knocked down twice during the battle, both times

from minie balls; but only being bruised, I have entirely recovered. We were not actually engaged in the latter fight.

In both battles the Yankees were the attacking party. We succeeded in repulsing their repeated and desperate attempts to drive us from our breastworks, slaughtering them as they came up, by thousands.

Day before yesterday, Grant withdrew from before us and we arrived here this morning so as to keep up with him. He seems to be trying to go around our army and get to Richmond that way,

Captain Charles S. Fleming—killed at Cold Harbor.

Our troops are in the best of spirits, and are actually anxious for Grant to continue to attack us. The news from the West is also glorious. God seems to be on our side; may He continue to be so!

Good-by for the present. Hope to write you in a few days, giving you an account of another victory for our army.

Much love to all, and remember me to Mr. Brantly and family, Mr. Bell and Mr. Causey. Accept much love from me.

"Your affectionate son,
C. Seton Fleming."

Field Hospital
Gaines' Farm, June 9, 1864
My Dear Friend:

I enclosed you a note a few days [ago], in which it was my sad and painful duty to convey to you, and through you to his mother and other relatives, the death of Captain Seton Fleming. Since writing that note, the slight room for doubt permitted by the non-recovery of his body, has been removed. On night before last, an armistice of two hours was agreed upon between the commanding Generals for the purpose of burying the dead and removing the wounded. Our command was in reserve and unfortunately, did not know of the opportunity until half an hour before it expired; and then by the arrival of a courier from Wilcox's Brigade, which occupied the front, which we had held, to say that Captain Fleming's remains had been found and were being guarded. Colonel Lang promptly sent out a detail (or rather gave permission for the men to go—they needed no ordering) to bring them in. A man came up to the hospital and told me and I went down and waited until near midnight. Our party missed their way, unfortunately, and the Alabamians finally brought the body to a spot within our lines and interred it without any of us being able to see it. I would have had it taken up again but from the length of time since his death (from the evening of the 3d to that of the 7th inst.), the warm weather, and represen-

as he has found it a hard job to whip us. But, thus far, God has led us through and given us the victory, and I do not fear His deserting us as long as we trust in Him.

I wrote you that Jenckes Reed had been mortally wounded in the battle and died the next day. Poor fellow! He was a good soldier. May God comfort his afflicted mother. I hope that God will continue to protect me as He has heretofore done; but if it is His will that I be killed, we must bow to it. He does everything for the best.

Since I last wrote, there has been some little fighting with us, but not much. We may fight another great battle here any day. The Yankees have fought more desperately during the last battles in this state than I have ever known them to do before. They appear to think that this is the last struggle of the war, and that if they are defeated now, all will be lost with them.

tations of the party who buried it, we concluded it would not be advisable.

A package of papers and a ring were removed and given me. The sword-belt and scabbard they did not attempt to take off. The sword was gone, probably drawn when he fell and afterwards picked up by someone. His remains are lying in rather a pretty place, among fine trees.

I have had a head-board prepared and placed there and will have the spot enclosed with some rails. If you or his mother think proper, I will have a plain marble slab placed there until the times are such as will allow his removal.

Seton fell nobly, in what all our old officers, and he among the rest, considered a rash and desperate move. . . .

On the evening of the 3d inst., a portion of the enemy's picket line had been allowed to establish themselves strongly and near our front; and our line making a salient, their sharp-shooters almost enfiladed it.

This line of skirmishers, as I understand it, had remained until they became very near supported by a line of battle before any attempt at their dislodgement. General Finegan issued the order that at dusk, after preparatory shelling, the old regiments, some two hundred and fifty odd men, (the Second reports forty-five muskets for duty now) should deploy, advance and drive the sharp-shooters of the enemy out.

Seton was in command of the Second. His men appreciated what they were called upon to attempt to do so well, that they spoke of it, and Seton passed a note down the line from hand to hand, as it was worth a man's life to pass out of the traverses any distance, to Lieutenant-Colonel Baya, of our regiment, asking how his men felt about going out. The latter replied that they considered it desperate, and fraught with no good result, but thought the Eighth would go if called upon.

Seton then made a little speech to his men—told them he was ordered to go—was going—and called upon them to support him and follow him; and that in all probability it was the last time he would give them an order. About this time he was exposing himself very unnecessarily upon the works. Someone remonstrated. He remarked that it did not matter; 'twas only the difference of a few moments.

He fell almost as soon as they started, not more than thirty or forty yards in front of our works, as was discovered when his body was recovered.

He seemed to have, and expressed himself as having, a decided presentiment that he would be killed. He had appeared to me, for some considerable length of time, as one who was looking death calmly in the face and was ready to meet it. As an officer, he had not an equal in the Brigade, and all felt this, and felt that injustice had been done him in not receiving staff promotion. He was respected by all who knew him, alike for his kind and gentlemanly consideration to those with whom he was thrown, as for his conscientious and thorough performance of all duties that devolved upon him. I had learned to respect and love him very much, and I was prejudiced against him at the commencement of the war.

If it can be of any small consolation to those who have lost so much, to know that his worth was throughly appreciated, I can assure you that the officers and the men of the old Brigade did so.

I do not know his mother, and have consequently written to you, thinking you would communicate with her. If she desires in the least I should do so, I will write and answer any inquiries she may make. She has my warmest sympathy in her great bereavement.

Dr. Richard P. Daniel
Surgeon of the Eighth Florida

"ANOTHER HERO TAKES THE FALLING STANDARD"

Among the first to fall in battle was the regimental color-bearer. Carrying the colors into combat was a high-risk responsibility and produced an abnormally high casualty rate. The standard bearer was an obvious target, and both sides routinely tried to damage one another's morale by shooting down the colors.

Despite the danger, Southern soldiers competed for the honor of bearing the colors into action. Battle flags were sometimes shot to ribbons and often passed from color-bearer to color-bearer as, one by one, they were struck down. In a bloody charge at the Battle of Gaines Mill, June 27, 1862, the state flag of Gen. Maxcy Gregg's 1st South Carolina Infantry fell into the hands of five successive color-bearers, all teenagers: Sgt. James H. Taylor, Corp. Edmund Shubrick Hayne, Pvt. Alfred Gaillard Pinckney, Pvt. Gadsden Holmes, and Pvt. Dominick Spellman. Within minutes, according to this eyewitness account, four of the five boys were dead on the field.

Two of the four South Carolina color-bearers who fell at Gaines Mill: Sgt. James Hunt Taylor, age sixteen (left), and Corp. Edward Shubrick Hayne, age eighteen.

Maxcy Gregg orders his brigade to charge, and with a yell that awakes the slumbering echoes of meadow and stream, they press irresistibly along. The chivalrous Colonel A. M. Smith falls mortally wounded, and the blue flag of South Carolina— which he told his men to die by but never let trail—wavers, for James Taylor, the boy hero who bore it, had his breast fatally pierced by a bullet after being twice wounded.

It is [down] for but a moment, for the daring young Shubrick Hayne takes it from [Taylor's] dying grasp and again it floats on high. Alas! He too, falls to the earth to rise no more. It is now in the hands of the youthful but fearless Alfred Pinckney, but soon it drops from his nerveless grasp as he falls mortally wounded across the body of his friends.

Then the fourth, Gadsden Holmes, springs forward to rescue it, but falls pierced with seven balls before he reaches the flag. It does not touch the earth, for another hero rushes from the ranks of the color company and takes the falling standard, and again the Palmetto rustles in the breeze, held by the stalwart arms of the lion-hearted Dominick Spellman, who bore it through the fight. Many others perished beneath the withering flame, but the column moved victoriously on, and after a most stubborn and bloody resistance the enemy retreated, and the danger that menaced the capital of the Confederacy disappeared with the setting sun.

"AN ENTHUSIASM I WILL NEVER FORGET"

The war sometimes produced emotions that led to audacious acts of courage. In the summer of 1863, for example, five young Confederates stationed near Charleston, South Carolina, were seized by the zeal of war—and the result was a daring display of battlefield bravery. A survivor recounted the experience:

Battery Wagner was situated on Morris Island, about six miles from Charleston. Its guns commanded the channel approach to that city, and the possession of the island was considered the key to the city. The enemy had effected a landing on the southern end of the island, and moving up their forces, had erected heavy batteries about sixteen hundred yards in front of Wagner. This island was a long, low, sandy sea island, almost denuded of growth, save a few palmetto trees, a number of which grew along the banks of Vincent Creek. There was situated near the banks of this creek an abandoned two-story wooden house, much nearer the enemy's works than ours, of which a small body of the enemy took possession; in fact, it was the headquarters of their night outpost picket.

From the upper windows of this house a band of sharpshooters had been constantly harassing the garrison at Wagner by firing plunging shots in their elevated positions from their long-range rifles, and scarcely a day passed without some soldier in the open parade of the fort being killed or wounded.

At the time mentioned I was a captain of infantry, but detached from my regiment in Virginia, and was temporarily assigned to staff duty as inspector general with Gen. William B. Taliaferro, who commanded Fort Wagner. One morning in July of 1863, Lieut. J. J. Doughty of Augusta, Ga. received a box of eatables from home, and invited the writer, Lieut. W. H. Hitt, and Lieut. Thomas Tutt, also of Augusta, and Sergt. Hopps, from Missouri, to dine with him in his quarters in the fort. We were enjoying, as only ravenous soldiers could, the delicious viands

A battle-scarred beacon house overlooks the dunes on Morris Island.

which tender hands at home had stored away in this precious box, and had nearly finished our meal, when one of Tutt's men came in hurriedly and reported, with a voice quivering with emotion, that a well-known comrade of his command had just been shot dead in the open fort by one of the enemy's sharpshooters.

Tutt sprang from his seat, his dark eyes flashing fire, with a strange light gleaming from their depths, and, looking into our faces, said, with his own set hard with determination, and with fury written in every line: "Boys, let us get a rifle apiece and drive the d——d rascals from that house and burn it, or perish in the attempt." There were five of us present—Tutt, Doughty, Hitt, Hopps, and myself in that party. We were all quite young, and the strange magnetism of Tutt, who was our senior by several years, and his determined bearing immediately fired us all with an enthusiasm which I will never forget, and, without taking time to reflect upon the peril or the consequences of the enterprise, we agreed, and at once formed our plan of action.

We quickly made our plans, and, each procuring a rifle and ammunition, we secretly left the fort about 3 P.M. on the perilous expedition. Being a staff officer, I was enabled to pass the party out at

the sally port, and, crouching low and stealthily, in Indian file, Tutt being in the lead, we glided slowly up the creek, taking advantage of its banks, the palmetto trees, and occasional sand dunes to hide us from view (which we found it to be a very difficult matter to do). The house was about fifty yards from the creek, and when we had reached a point about one hundred yards from it, we halted, and lying down together behind some stunted shrubbery, held a council of war.

It was impossible to retreat then, because the sharpshooters had evidently seen some movement, and, with their rifles in hand, we could see them at the windows, looking intently in our direction. The space between us and the house was a perfectly open sand area, without the slightest shelter or protection. There was not a moment to lose, as the enemy was growing more and more suspicious. There were eight sharpshooters in the house, but at the time we did not know the number. There were only five of us. We at once concluded to make a dash for the house.

At a signal from Tutt, and on the full run, we rushed for the building, a scattering volley being fired at us, providentially without effect. Meeting together on the opposite side of the house, we ran pellmell into the building through the open door in the back of the same. The enemy seemed stunned by the suddenness of the attack, and we were fairly in the hall before they were enabled to start down the narrow stairway to meet us. A general fusillade followed. The vivid flashes of the rifles lighting up the hall, which was soon filled with dense smoke, caused them to retreat to their former position, and Tutt, raving like a demon, started upstairs alone, but we pulled him back. He then, in a loud voice, ordered the house set on fire, which we at once did, retiring to the open area in the rear after the fire had made considerable headway.

The building was old and dry, and burnt like tinder, and it was a case of the enemy being cremated or leaving the house. Some of them ran out of the doors, and others jumped from the windows. We stood around with our rifles cocked, firing at them as they appeared. They made a feeble resistance, shooting wildly, and the survivors took to their heels. Some of them were shot and the others made good their escape.

By this time the musketry and the burning building had aroused the respective garrisons of the two forts, which swarmed in masses on their parapets; we were at easy rifle range of the Yankee garrison, and if we attempted to retreat across the open area of sand, death to us would have been the inevitable result. The only way back, by the creek, was already swept by a hurricane of bullets, the enemy evidently supposing that there was a large body of us concealed in the shrubbery near the now consumed house. We realized too late that we were caught like rats in a trap.

In front of us, two hundred yards nearer the enemy's works, was a little hillock or sand dune on this open area of sand, and although it brought us much nearer the Federal works, we made a dash for it in order to shelter ourselves from the terrific fire which was now concentrated upon us by the thoroughly aroused Yankee garrison. With only a slight wound received by Hopps, though some of us had our clothing torn by bullets, we providentially gained the sand hill, which was only a few feet higher than the surrounding plane, and each of us sank down at full length behind it. For the time being [we] were comparatively safe from the enemy's leaden missiles, which sung around us, intermixed with that ominous sound of the bullet—s-t, s-t, s-t—familiar to all soldiers who saw service in that war.

After lying in the position described, under the pitiless rays of a scorching July sun for some little time, the enemy's fire greatly slackened. I stealthily peeped over the sand dune to take an observation, when, to my horror, I saw a full company of Yankee infantry, which had silently moved out of their works, rapidly approaching us, the sunlight flashing from their bright bayonets as they marched. Turning to my companions, I said: "Boys, look yonder, it's all up with us now." Certain death or capture indeed seemed inevitable, and we each realized it.

With elbow touching elbow, and our heads alone visible above the sand bank, we kept up a steady fire upon the line of blue rapidly nearing us. At the first volley they halted, returned the fire, and then with huzzas came for us on the full run. The situation was appalling, but we continued to pour our fire into them. What was it, then, that shook the island from center to circumference? Turning our heads in the direction of the sound, we witnessed a sight which sent the blood tingling in our veins.

The entire face of Wagner was enveloped in rolling clouds of smoke, lit up with crimson flame from bastion to bastion by the guns of the fort. The heaviest batteries of siege guns on this entire face of Wagner were suddenly opened upon the approaching Federal infantry. Charlie Olmstead, my old schoolmate, who was commanding in the absence of Gen. Taliaferro, had come to the rescue. The artillery fire was directed with wonderful precision, the shells passing over our heads and bursting beyond us uncomfortably close, in the very face of the enemy, scattering them like chaff before the wind. But something we had not counted on followed.

The Yankee fort immediately opened their batteries of heavy guns upon Wagner, and one of the most terrific artillery duels I ever witnessed during the war was thus precipitated between the respective forts, and all stirred up by our little band. The scene was grand and awe-inspiring, both sides shelling furiously over our heads at each other. Of course all the infantry on both sides were driven from the parapets by this terrific artillery fire. It was plain that this demonstration on the part of Col. Olmstead was made to safely cover our retreat, and we rapidly raced for our works. We arrived safely, completely winded and exhausted.

"THE TORPEDO STRUCK THE VESSEL AND EXPLODED"

Sometimes bravery was a carefully calculated act, as demonstrated by the commander and crew of the C.S.S. David. A fifty-foot semisubmersible torpedo boat equipped with a 100-pound spar torpedo, the David steamed quietly across darkened Charleston harbor on the night of October 5, 1863, heading for the offshore anchorage of the Federal blockading fleet. The David was commanded by Lt. William T. Glassell of the Confederate Navy, who was assisted on board by Engineer James H. Toombs, a ship's pilot named Cannon, and an unidentified fireman. Their mission was to torpedo and sink a powerful new Federal warship, the 230-foot armor-plated steam frigate New Ironsides. They completed their precarious voyage and managed to damage their target before the David itself was crippled.

Lieutenant Glassell's account of the bold attack:

The 5th of October, 1863, a little after dark, we left Charleston wharf and proceeded with the ebb-tide down the harbor.

A light north wind was blowing and the night was slightly hazy but star-lit, and the water was smooth. I desired to make the attack about the turn of the tide and this ought to have been just after nine o'clock, but the north wind made it run out a little longer.

We passed Fort Sumter and beyond the line of picket-boats without being discovered. Silently steaming along just inside the bar, I had a good opportunity to reconnoiter the whole fleet of the enemy at anchor between me and the camp-fires on Morris' Island.

Quietly maneuvering and observing the enemy, I was half an hour more waiting on time and tide. The music of drum and fife had just ceased and the nine o'clock gun had been fired from the admiral's ship, as a signal for all unnecessary lights to be extinguished and for the men not on watch to retire for sleep. I thought the proper time for attack had arrived.

The admiral's ship, *New Ironsides*, lay in the midst of the fleet, her starboard-side presented to my view. I determined to pay her the highest compliment. I had been informed, through pris-

oners lately captured from the fleet, that they were expecting an attack from torpedo boats and were prepared for it. I could, therefore, hardly expect to accomplish my object without encountering some danger from riflemen and perhaps a discharge of grape or canister from the howitzers. My guns were loaded with buck-shot. I knew that if the officer of the deck could be disabled to begin with, it would cause them some confusion and increase our chance for escape, so I determined that if the occasion offered, I would commence by firing the first shot. Accordingly, having on a full head of steam, I took charge of the helm, it being so arranged that I could sit on deck and work the wheel with my feet. Then directing the engineer and fireman to keep below and give me all the speed possible, I gave a double-barrel gun to the pilot, with instructions not to fire until I should do so, and steered directly for the [*New Ironsides*]. I intended to strike her just under the gang-way, but the tide still running out, carried us to a point nearer the quarter. Thus we rapidly approached the enemy.

When within about 300 yards of her a sentinel hailed us: "Boat ahoy! Boat ahoy!" repeating the hail several times very rapidly. We were coming towards them with all speed and I made no

David *torpedo boat grounded at Charleston.*

answer, but cocked both barrels of my gun. The officer of the deck next made his appearance and loudly demanded, "What boat is that?" Being now within forty yards of the ship and plenty of headway to carry us on, I thought it about time the fight should commence and fired my gun. The officer of the deck fell back mortally wounded (poor fellow), and I ordered the engine stopped. The next moment the torpedo struck the vessel and exploded. My little boat plunged violently, and a large body of water which had been thrown up descended upon her deck, and down the smoke-stack and hatchway.

I immediately gave orders to reverse the engine and back off. Mr. Toombs informed me then that the fires were put out, and something had become jammed in the machinery so that it would not move. What could be done in this situation? In the meantime, the enemy, recovering from the shock, beat to quarters, and general alarm spread through the fleet. I told my men I thought our only chance to escape was by swimming, and I think I told Mr. Toombs to cut the water-pipes and let the boat sink. Then, taking one of the cork floats, I got into the water and swam off as fast as I could.

The enemy, in no amiable mood, poured down upon the bubbling water a hail-storm of rifle and pistol shots from the deck of the *New Ironsides*, and from the nearest monitor. Sometimes they struck very close to my head, but swimming for life, I soon disappeared from their sight and found myself all alone in the water. I hoped that, with the assistance of flood-tide, I might be able to reach Fort Sumter, but a north wind was against me, and after I had been in the water more than an hour, I became numb with cold and was nearly exhausted. Just then the boat of a transport schooner picked me up and found, to their surprise, that they had captured a rebel.

The captain of this schooner made me as comfortable as possible that night with whiskey and blankets, for which I sincerely thanked him. I was handed over next morning to the mercy of Admiral Dahlgren. He ordered me to be transferred to the guard-ship *Ottawa*, lying outside of the rest of the fleet. I learned that my fireman had been found hanging on to the rudder chains of the *New Ironsides* and taken on board. I had every reason to believe that the other two, Mr. Toombs and Mr. Cannon, had been shot or drowned, until I heard of their safe arrival in Charleston. Pilot Cannon states that, not being able to swim, when the fires were extinguished he jumped overboard and clung to the unexposed side of the *David*. The boat gradually drifted away from the *New Ironsides*, without being materially injured, though a bull's-eye lantern afforded a mark to the Federal cannoneers. After drifting about a quarter of a mile, Pilot Cannon got aboard. Seeing something in the water he hailed, and heard to his surprise a reply from Engineer Toombs. Toombs got aboard, caught up the fires with the light from the lantern, got up steam and started for the city. They were fired at several times while passing the Federal monitors and picket-boats, but escaped them unhurt and reached Atlantic wharf at 12 o'clock.

I was retained as a prisoner in Fort LaFayette and Fort Warren for more than a year and learned while there that I had been promoted for what was called "gallant and meritorious service."

"I LUNGED MY BAYONET AT HIS SIDE"

In the War Between the States, combat could be personal and face-to-face— like that experienced by Southern soldiers at the Battle of the Crater. In the summer of 1864, Northern troops secretly tunneled under a portion of the Confederate line at Petersburg and at 4:45 A.M. on July 30, 1864, exploded 8,000 pounds of powder beneath two regiments of sleeping defenders. The explosion caused almost 300 Confederate casualties, breached the line, and created a giant crater. In an attempt to overwhelm the stunned Southerners, Federal forces—including eight black regiments—charged through the crater, but became trapped under heavy fire in the huge pit, where some of the bloodiest hand-to-hand combat of the war occurred.

George S. Bernard, a Confederate survivor of the engagement, later recalled what this face-to-face fighting was like.

I fired my gun into a mass of human beings, with what effect I do not know, nor do I care to know. As soon as I fired I sprang into one of the numerous traverses that ran through and about the lines of the breast-works and ditches that constituted the fortifications at this point. This traverse, by a somewhat winding route, led directly into the main ditch at this point. I followed it—meeting several unarmed, terrified negroes, some wounded and some not, all begging for mercy and trying to get to our rear—until it brought me to this main ditch. It seems that there was one Confederate soldier—a mere youth— ahead of me in this traverse and on his way to the main ditch.

As soon as I entered the main ditch, which was filled with the enemy, white and black, in perfect confusion, some running and some fighting, I saw this youth to my left leaning with his back against the breast-work, with a large negro soldier standing over him, with musket in hand, attempting to send his bayonet into his body. The youth having

Hand-to-hand combat at the Battle of the Crater.

hold of the bayonet and resisting with all his might the efforts of the negro to stick it into him. I immediately made for them, lunged my bayonet at his side, but, either from bad aim on my part or quick motion on his, the bayonet, instead of entering his body and putting an end to him, struck plumb upon his hip bone. He immediately turned loose his gun and seized mine before I could recover myself for another lunge at him, and endeavored to disarm me, and would perhaps have done so, but for the fact that I was possessed of considerable physical strength.

While this negro and I were scuffling over my gun a Federal lieutenant, a white man, with pistol drawn and pointed to my face, ordered me to surrender, which perhaps I would have done but for the fact that at that moment our boys were pouring over the embankments into the ditch where I was, and I saw it was safer to fight on than

to surrender. So I declined to surrender and went on with my efforts to get control of my gun. This lieutenant then pulled the trigger, but his pistol only snapped. As quick as thought he again cocked it, and putting it to my face, pulled the trigger. It fired, but it was so close to me that as it fired, it was knocked out of position by my arm and its charge missed me. Before he could get ready for another fire a member of the Richmond Grays—Jake Old, I believe it was—had pierced him with his bayonet and he fell to the ground.

Just at this juncture—it all happened in less than one-tenth of the time I have taken to tell about it—the youth whom I had rescued had picked up a large army pistol and with its butt end knocked my negro antagonist a blow on the forehead which felled him to the ground, a dead man I think, and left me master of my gun and unhurt.

"WOH—WHO—EY! WHO—EY! WHO—EY!"

"Then arose that do-or-die expression, that maniacal maelstrom of sound; that penetrating, rasping, shrieking, blood-curdling noise that could be heard for miles on earth and whose volumes reached the heavens. . . ."

It was the Rebel yell, described here by an aging Southern veteran who had heard it raised above the roar of combat on numerous fields of battle. It was an odd mixture: part hunting shout, part hog-call, part excitement, part fear, and part bravado. Those who heard it never forgot it, and those who emitted it said it could never be duplicated outside battle. It became an enduring symbol of Johnny Reb—an audible and ecstatic expression of the decidedly Southern, almost joyful, all-or-nothing attitude that carried the Starry Cross of the Confederacy to repeated victories over a normally stronger foe.

J. Harvie Dew, a horse soldier in the 9th Virginia Cavalry, offered this analysis of the Rebel yell as he heard it in 1863 at Brandy Station.

Southerners have always been recognized by those who have known them best as a people possessed of unbounded enthusiasm and ardor. They have been considered and often called a "hot-headed," a "hot-blooded," people.

These peculiarities of birth, character, and temperament, coupled with the fact that they were chiefly an agricultural people inhabiting a broad expanse of country but thinly settled, and confined in no large numbers to the narrow limits that city and town life impose, had much to do with the development of their soldierly qualities as well as of their capacity for yelling.

Life in the country—especially in our Southern country where people lived far apart and were employed oftentimes at a considerable distance from one another and from the houses or homes in which they ate and slept—tended, by exercise in communicating with one another, to strengthen and improve their voices for high and prolonged use.

Hollering, screaming, yelling for one person or another, to their dogs, or at some of the cattle on the plantation, with the accompanying reverberations from hilltops, over valleys and plains, were familiar sounds throughout the farming districts of the South in the days gone by.

Hunting, which was enjoyed and indulged in more or less by nearly every citizen of the South, was also conducive to this characteristic development.

The Federal or "Yankee" yell, compared with that of the Confederate, lacked in vocal breadth, pitch, and resonance. This was unquestionably attributable to the fact that the soldiery of the North was drawn and recruited chiefly from large cities and towns, from factory districts and from the more densely settled portions of the country.

It is safe to say that there are thousands upon thousands of men in the large cities and in other densely populated portions of the North, who have not elevated their vocal tones to within anything like their full capacity since the days of their boyhood and many not even then.

To afford some idea of the difference between these "yells," I will relate an incident which occurred in battle on the plains at Brandy Station, Virginia, in the fall of 1863. Our command was in full pursuit of a portion of Kilpatrick's cavalry. We soon approached their reserves (ours some distance behind), and found ourselves facing a battery of artillery with a regiment of cavalry drawn

Confederates in combat: the Rebel yell rose above the clamor of battle.

up on each side.

In a moment more one of the Federal regiments was ordered to charge, and down they came upon us in a body two or three times outnumbering ours. Then was heard their peculiar, characteristic yell—"Hoo-ray! Hoo-ray! Hoo-ray!" (This yell was called by the Federals a "cheer," and was intended for the word "hurrah," but that pronunciation I never heard in a charge. The sound was

as though the first syllable, if heard at all, was "hoo," uttered with an exceedingly short, low, and indistinct tone, and the second was "ray," yelled with a long and high tone slightly deflecting at its termination. In many instances the yell seemed to be the simple interjection "heigh," rendered with the same tone which was given to "ray.")

Our command was alone in the field, and it seemed impossible for us to withstand the coming shock; but our commander, as brave an officer as ever drew a saber, frequently repeated, as the charging column approached us, his precautionary orders to "Keep steady, boys! Keep steady!" and so we remained till the Federals were within a hundred yards of us. Then, waving his sword in air, he gave the final order loud enough to be heard the field over: "Now is your time, boys! Give them the saber! Charge them, men! Charge!"

In an instant every voice with one accord vigorously shouted that "Rebel yell," which was so often heard on the field of battle. "Woh—who—ey! Who—ey! Who—ey! Woh—who—ey! Who—ey!" (The best illustration of this "true yell" which can be given the reader is by spelling it as above, with directions to sound the first syllable "woh" short and low, and the second "who" with a very high and prolonged note deflecting upon the third syllable "ey.")

A moment or two later the Federal column wavered and broke. In pursuit we chased them to within twenty feet of their battery, which had already begun to retreat. The second regiment to the right and rear of the battery then charged upon us, and for a moment we were forced back; but by that time our reserves were up, and we swept the field.

"WE HAVE SURRENDERED"

"We persisted," recalled a Confederate veteran, "in vaguely hoping and trying to believe that success was still to be ours, and to that end we shut our eyes to the plainest facts, refusing to admit the truth that was everywhere evident, namely, that our efforts had failed, and that our cause was already in its death struggles."

Johnny Reb did not give up easily, yet by early 1865, many Confederates went into battle resigned to a belief that their sacrifices were all in vain. When Lee withdrew his troops from their lines at Petersburg and retreated toward Appomattox, much of the worn and depleted army dissolved en route. Yet many soldiers of the South were determined to keep fighting until death if necessary.

Confederate Carlton McCarthy, a private in the Army of Northern Virginia, remembered how the long and deadly contest finally staggered to an end at Appomattox.

Sunday morning, April 9th. After a short march, the column entered the village of Appomattox Court House by what seemed to be the main road. Several dead men, dressed in the uniform of United States regular artillery, were lying on the roadside, their faces turned up to the blaze of the sun. One had a ghastly wound in the breast, which must have been made by grape or canister.

On through the village without halting marched the column. Whitworth shots were hurtling through the air every few minutes, indicating very clearly that the enemy was ahead of the column and awaiting its arrival. On the outskirts of the village the line of battle was formed. Indeed, there seemed to be *two* lines, one slightly in advance of the other. Wagons passed along the line and dropped boxes of cartridges. The men were ordered to knock them open and supply themselves with forty rounds each. They filled their breeches pockets to the brim. The general officers galloped up and down the line, apparently hurrying everything as much as possible. The shots from a battery in advance were continually passing over the line, going in the direction of the village, but without harm to any one. The more experienced

men predicted a severe struggle. It was supposed that this was to be an attack with the whole army in mass, for the purpose of breaking through the enemy's line and making one more effort to move on.

Finally the order "Forward!" ran along the line, and as it advanced the chiefs of detachments, gunners, and commissioned officers marched in rear, keeping up a continual cry of "Close up, men; close up!" "Go ahead, now; don't lag!" "Keep up!" Thus marching, the line entered a body of woods, proceeded some distance, changed direction to the left and, emerging from the woods, halted in a large open field, beyond which was another body of woods which concealed further view in front.

After some delay, a detail for skirmish duty was ordered. Captain Jones detailed four men, Fry and Garber the same number. Lieutenant McRae was placed in command. The infantry detailed skirmishers for their front. All arrangements completed, the men deployed and entered the woods. They had advanced but a short distance when they encountered a strong line of picket posts. Firing and cheering, they rushed on the surprised men, who scampered away, leaving all their little conveniences behind them and retreating for about a mile. From this point large bodies of the enemy were visible, crowding the hill-tops like a blue or black cloud. It was not many minutes before a strong line of dismounted cavalry, followed by mounted men, deployed from this mass to cover the retreat of their fleeing brethren and restore the picket line. They came down the hills and across the fields, firing as they came. On looking around to see what were the chances for making a stand, Lieutenant McRae found that the infantry skirmishers had been withdrawn. The officer who had commanded them could be seen galloping away in the distance. The little squad, knowing they were alone, kept up a brisk fire on the advancing enemy, till he was close up in front and well to the rear of both flanks. On the left not more than two hundred yards a column of cavalry, marching by twos, had crossed the line and was still marching, as unconcernedly as possible, to the rear of McRae. Seeing this, McRae ordered his squad to retire, saying at the same time, "But don't let them see you running, boys!"

So they retired, slowly, stubbornly, and returning shot for shot with the enemy, who came on at a trot, cheering valiantly, as they pursued four men and a lieutenant. The men dragged the butts of their old muskets behind them, loading as they walked. All loaded, they turned, halted, fired, received a shower of balls in return and then again moved doggedly to the rear. A little lieutenant of infantry, who had been on the skirmish line, joined the squad. He was armed with a revolver and had his sword by his side. Stopping behind the corner of a corn-crib, he swore he would not go any further to the rear. The squad moved on and left him standing there, pistol in hand, waiting for the enemy, who were now jumping the fences and coming across the field, running at the top of their speed. What became of this singular man no one knows. He was, as he said, "determined to make a stand." A little further on the squad found a single piece of artillery, manned by a lieutenant and two or three men. They were selecting indi-

Grief at Appomattox.

viduals in the enemy's skirmish line, and *firing at them with solid shot!* Lieutenant McRae laughed at the ridiculous sight, remonstrated with the officer and offered his squad to serve the gun, if there was any canister in the limber chest. The offer was refused and again the squad moved on. Passing a cow-shed about this time, the squad halted to look with horror upon several dead and wounded Confederates who lay there upon the manure pile. They had suffered wounds and death upon this the last day of their country's struggle. Their wounds had received no attention, and those living were famished and burning with fever.

Lieutenant McRae, noticing a number of wagons and guns parked in a field near by, surprised at what he considered great carelessness in the immediate presence of the enemy, approached an officer on horseback and said in his usual impressive manner, "I say there, what does this mean?" The man took his hand and quietly said, "We have surrendered." "I don't believe it, sir!" replied McRae, strutting around as mad as a hornet. "You mustn't talk so, sir! You will demoralize my men!" He was soon convinced, however, by seeing Yankee cavalrymen walking their horses around as composed as though the Army of Northern Virginia had never existed.

"IN PROUD HUMILIATION STOOD THE EMBODIMENT OF MANHOOD"

The end of Johnny Reb's fighting days began on Palm Sunday, April 9, 1865, at Appomattox, when the Army of Northern Virginia was surrendered in the parlor of Virginia farmer Wilmer McLean. Generals Joseph Johnston, Richard Taylor, and Edmund Kirby Smith still had Confederate armies in the field, but they too would soon surrender. Johnny Reb finally laid down his arms at Appomattox, but his legacy as a fighter was already established. His reputation was noted with obvious respect by a former enemy, Gen. Joshua L. Chamberlain, who wrote this description of the final moment at Appomattox, when Johnny Reb folded his flags and stacked his arms for the last time.

Before us in proud humiliation stood the embodiment of manhood: men whom neither toils and sufferings, nor the fact of death, nor disaster, nor hopelessness could bend from their resolve; standing before us now, thin, worn, and famished, but erect, and with eyes looking level into ours, waking memories that bound us together as no other bond. Was not such manhood to be welcomed back into a Union so tested and assured?

Instructions had been given; and when the head of each division column comes opposite our group, our bugle sounds the signal and instantly our whole line from right to left, regiment by regiment in succession, gives the soldier's salutation, from the "order arms" to the old "carry"— the marching salute. [Confederate Gen. John B.] Gordon at the head of the column, riding with heavy spirit and downcast face, catches the sound of shifting arms, looks up, and, taking the meaning, wheels superbly, making with himself and his horse one uplifted figure, with profound salutation as he drops the point of his sword to the boot toe; then facing to his own command, gives word for his successive brigades to pass us with the same position of the manual—honor answering honor. On our part not a sound of trumpet more, nor roll of drum; not a cheer, nor word nor whisper of vain-glorying, nor motion of man standing again at the order, but an awed stillness rather, and breath-holding, as if it were the passing of the dead!

As each successive division masks our own, it halts, the men face inward towards us across the road, twelve feet away; then carefully "dress" their line, each captain taking pains for the good appearance of his company, worn and half starved as they were. The field and staff take their positions in the intervals of regiments; generals in rear of their commands. They fix bayonets, stack arms; then, hesitatingly, remove cartridge-boxes and lay them down. Lastly, reluctantly, with agony of expression, they tenderly fold their flags, battle-worn and torn, blood-stained, heart-holding colors, and lay them down; some frenziedly rushing from the ranks, kneeling over them, clinging to them, pressing them to their lips with burning tears. And only the Flag of the Union greets the sky!

What visions thronged as we looked into each other's eyes! Here pass the men of Antietam, the Bloody Lane, the Sunken Road, the Cornfield, the Burnside-Bridge; the men whom Stonewall Jackson on the second night at Fredericksburg begged Lee to let him take and crush the two corps of the Army of the Potomac huddled in the streets in darkness and confusion; the men who swept away the Eleventh Corps at Chancellorsville; who left six thousand of their companions around the bases of Culp's and Cemetery Hills at Gettysburg; these survivors of the terrible Wilderness, the Bloody-Angle at Spotsylvania, the slaughter pen of Cold Harbor, the whirlpool of Bethesda Church!

Here comes Cobb's Georgia Legion, which held the stone wall on Marye's Heights at Fredericksburg, close before which we piled our dead for breastworks so that the living might stay and live.

Here too come Gordon's Georgians and Hoke's North Carolinians, who stood before the terrific mine explosion at Petersburg, and advancing retook the smoking crater and the dismal heaps of dead—ours more than theirs—huddled in the ghastly chasm.

Here are the men of McGowan, Hunton, and Scales, who broke the Fifth Corps lines on the White Oak Road, and were so desperately driven back on that forlorn night of March 31st by my thrice-decimated brigade.

Now comes Anderson's Fourth Corps, only Bushrod Johnson's Division left, and this the remnant of those we fought so fiercely on the Quaker Road two weeks ago, with Wise's Legion,

Lee's depleted legions stack arms at Appomattox.

too fierce for its own good.

Here passes the proud remnant of Ransom's North Carolinians which we swept through Five Forks ten days ago—and all the little that was left of this division in the sharp passages at [Sayler's] Creek five days thereafter.

Now making its last front, A. P. Hill's old Corps, Heth now at the head, since Hill had gone too far forward ever to return: the men who poured destruction into our division at Shepardstown Ford, Antietam, in 1862, when Hill reported the Potomac running blue with our bodies; the men who opened the desperate first day's fight at Gettysburg, where withstanding them so stubbornly our Robinson's Brigades lost 1185 men, and the Iron Brigade alone 1153,—these men of Heth's Division, here too, losing 2850 men, companions of these now looking into our faces so differently.

What is this but the remnant of Mahone's Division, last seen by us at the North Anna? Its thinned ranks of worn, bright-eyed men recalling scenes of costly valor and ever-remembered history.

Now—Longstreet and his men! What shall we give them for a greeting that has not already been spoken in volleys of thunder and written in lines of fire on all the riverbanks of Virginia? Shall we go back to Gaines' Mill and Malvern Hill? Or to the Antietam of Maryland, or Gettysburg of Pennsylvania?—deepest graven of all. For here is what remains of Kershaw's Division, which left 40 per cent of its men at Antietam, and at Gettysburg with Barksdale's and Semmes' Brigades tore through the Peach Orchard, rolling up the right of our gallant Third Corps, sweeping over the proud batteries of Massachusetts—Bigelow and Philips—where under the smoke we saw the earth brown and blue with prostrate bodies of horses and men, and the tongues of overturned cannon and caissons pointing grim and stark in the air.

Then in the Wilderness, at Spotsylvania and thereafter, Kershaw's Division again, in deeds of awful glory, held their name and fame, until fate met them at [Sayler's] Creek, where Kershaw himself, and Ewell, and so many more, gave up their arms and hopes—all, indeed, but manhood's honor.

With what strange emotion I look into these faces before which in the mad assault on Rives' Salient, June 18, 1864, I was left for dead under their eyes! It is by miracles we have lived to see this day—any of us standing here.

Now comes the sinewy remnant of fierce Hood's Division, which at Gettysburg we saw pouring through the Devil's Den, and the Plum Run gorge; turning again by the left our stubborn Third Corps, then swarming up the rocky bastions of Round Top, to be met there by equal valor, which changed Lee's whole plan of battle and perhaps the story of Gettysburg.

Ah, is this Pickett's Division?—this little group left of those who on the lurid last day of Gettysburg breasted level cross-fire and thunderbolts of storm, to be strewn back drifting wrecks, whereafter that awful, futile, pititul charge we buried them in graves a furlong wide, with names unknown!

Met again in the terrible cyclone-sweep over the breastworks at Five Forks; met now, so thin, so pale, purged of the mortal—as if knowing pain or joy no more.

How could we help falling on our knees, all of us together, and praying God to pity and forgive us all!

5

In Yankee Prisons

A Northern prison camp was a deadly place for a Confederate soldier. The death rate for Southern prisoners of war in the North was only slightly less than that for Northern troops in Southern prisons—12 percent as compared to a 15 percent death rate in Confederate prisons—but the postwar reports of suffering in the Confederacy's infamous Andersonville overshadowed gruesome accounts from Federal prisons.

The North too had its hellholes: Camp Douglas, Elmira, Point Lookout, Fort Delaware, Johnson's Island, Camp Chase, Rock Island, Camp Morton, and others. A prison camp—on either side—was not a healthy place. Almost 26,000 of the nearly 215,000 Southern soldiers who entered Northern prisons died there. Those who did survive usually came home with bitterly painful memories of life in Yankee prisons.

In line and under guard, captured Johnny Rebs await transportation to prison.

"OUR GLOOMY JOURNEY"

Sometimes Johnny Reb fell into enemy hands by the thousands, sometimes one by one. When Fort Donelson was surrendered to Federal forces, as many as 12,000 Confederate troops became prisoners of war; at Gettysburg approximately 5,000 were captured; at Fort Fisher, some 2,000 became prisoners. Sometimes captured troops were exchanged quickly. When Vicksburg fell, for instance, its garrison of more than 20,000 was immediately exchanged for a like number of Federal prisoners held by the Confederacy.

For many Johnny Rebs, however, whether captured with their regiments or singly, being taken by the enemy usually meant internment in a Northern prisoner of war camp for the duration—if they survived the hazards of prison.

Confederate cavalryman John H. King, a veteran of more than a dozen battles, was shot in the face and captured during fighting in Eastern Tennessee in early 1864. As soon as he could travel, he was sent to Camp Chase, the Federal prisoner of war camp at Columbus, Ohio, where he spent the final year of the war. Afterward, he recorded this account of his "gloomy journey" to prison.

On the 27th of January near Sevierville, Tennessee, I received in battle a wound in my face and neck which at the time was thought to be mortal. The enemy's bullet entering at the [symphysis] of the chin, shattered my lower jaw bone and passing through the neck made its exit a little to the left of the vertebral column. At the time I received this wound I was on horseback but soon fell to the ground, bleeding profusely and partially paralyzed. I can recall but slightly the sensation at first experienced when reeling in the saddle I fell forward, clutching at the neck of my horse, to which I endeavored to cling, and from which I fell senseless to the ground. I have a distant recollection of trying to free my feet from the stirrups and of my apparent inability to move them.

When I regained consciousness I found Yankee soldiers standing around me, while their army was passing by, and discovered that I had been rifled by these remorseless thieves from head to foot, each straggler as he came up, turning my limp body over in search of some trophy that might have been left by the preceding thief. At last the "good Samaritan" came in the person of one who, while he wore the uniform of an enemy, had within him the impulses of an honest Christian heart. Approaching me, he gently asked if I wanted a drink of water. It was impossible for me to speak, but I answered the good man by nodding my head affirmatively, when he at once handed me his canteen. I managed with great difficulty to swallow a little, as my throat was constantly filling with blood and its muscles partially paralyzed. I grasped my throat below the fractured jaw and, pressing upward, forced the hemorrhage to cease.

Night was now fast coming to envelope me in the gloom of its sable mantle. Chilled to the bone, I began to realize the certainty of freezing to death if I remained where I was. With all the willpower I could command, holding my jaw in position as best I could, I exerted my utmost strength in an endeavor to reach a house I had seen during the retreat of the morning. By the light of a young moon I made out to slowly climb the ascent, and to reach the log cabin, utterly exhausted and in such pain that no pen can describe.

I found a woman to be the only occupant of the cabin, and a fire burning in uncertain glow, to which, with this good woman's aid, I crawled gratefully for warmth. This good woman with the characteristic sympathy of her sex brought a pillow for my head and aided me to stretch my benumbed limbs on the hearth. About nine o'clock, just as I was getting well thawed and beginning to find some release from the pain that had racked my nerves, a wagon drove up to the cabin, and [two Federal soldiers] entered. I was ordered at once to get up, and while making the effort was seized by these men and almost dragged to the wagon.

Without the slightest regard for my suffering, the wagon into which I had been almost thrown was driven with reckless speed over a very rough road to Sevierville and to the county courthouse, in which had been improvised a kind of field hospital for both Yankee and Confederate soldiers. The floor of the courtroom had been covered with wheatstraw, while on the hearth of two small fireplaces a few embers were still burning when I entered this revolting place. I was assisted by the guard to a pile of straw, but as I was very cold and sore from the long, rough ride, I preferred to get as close to one of these small fires, where in misery I spent the night. In the meantime nothing had been done towards dressing my wound or alleviating my sufferings.

Near midday [the next day] I was assisted downstairs and ushered into the presence of two physicians. Administering an opiate, my broken bone was set in position, the wound in my neck was dressed and I was taken again up-stairs to a pallet of straw.

Under the influence of the opiate administered by the physicians I had fallen asleep and resting quietly when a guard rudely shook me saying "Come, get up Reb, you have to get away from here." Without further ceremony I was led to an ambulance, which I found waiting in the village street, and almost lifted into it. . . .

Arriving at Knoxville, I was quite exhausted, so much so that a guard was deemed unnecessary to secure my person. Indeed I could not have made an escape had I been set at liberty to make the effort. From the ambulance I was carried into a hospital whose inmates I found to be a mixture of Confederate and Federal soldiers, wounded and sick, waiting, like myself, the issue of a problematic future.

During the month of March I was transferred to the Female Academy Building, which was then known as the "Rebel" Hospital. Here I found none but my unfortunate Confederate comrades who, like myself, had been wounded in battle following the glorious ensign of Dixie. . . .

Under escort of a guard, we were marched to the railway cars and were soon on the way to Loudon, Tennessee, on the Tennessee river, where we were transferred to a steamboat to be transported to Chattanooga.

Reaching Chattanooga the next day, we had a foretaste of what we were to experience hereafter by being confined in a filthy jail. From Chattanooga, we were carried to Louisville, Kentucky, via Nashville, at which place we were again confined for a night like convicted felons in the State Penitentiary. From Louisville we were carried by rail via Jeffersonville, Indiana, and Cincinnati, to our ultimate destination: Columbus and Camp Chase, Ohio.

While waiting in Cincinnati for the cars to take us on our gloomy journey, we were surrounded by a rabble of men, women, and children who with jeer and gibe would insult us in every possible way that their filthy language would permit.

"Look at the dirty, ragged Rebels," we could hear on all sides.

It was in the month of April 1864, weary with a long and uncomfortable travel, suffering from my unhealed wound, chilled by the bleak winds of a climate to which I was a stranger, that with other comrades, I reached the city of Columbus, Ohio, a prisoner of war. We had but a glimpse of this, the capital city of a great state, as we were hurried through its streets to the prison that for months to come was to be our cheerless, inhospitable and wretched abode. We had heard of these cheerless prisons, of the inhuman treatment of the helpless inmates, and had tried hard to prepare our minds for the realization of a life which had speedily ended in the death of hundreds who had preceded us.

"TWENTY-FIVE DEGREES BELOW ZERO"

The bitter Northern winters were among the worst hardships for Confederate prisoners, who were accustomed to mild Southern weather and were often clothed in little more than rags. For the rest of his life, New Orleans native H. Carpenter, a lieutenant in the 9th Louisiana, would remember suffering through winters on Johnson's Island, a prisoner of war facility located off Sandusky, Ohio, on a spit of land in Lake Erie.

His terse account is followed by the prison memoir of Pvt. John A. Wyeth, a young Alabama cavalryman who survived wintertime privation at Indiana's Camp Morton.

It was the severity of the winters that told so heavily on us. Many were from the extreme South, and some had never seen a fall of snow. Coming from New Orleans, and wearing such clothing as was adapted to its climate in the month of September, the first day of January, 1864, was a revelation. On that day the thermometer marked twenty-five degrees below zero. . . . So intense was the cold that the sentries were taken from the walls and the ice king kept watch and ward for Uncle Sam. The big gate could have been left open and few of the prisoners would have taken the chance of escape in view of the almost certain death. The entire winters were bitter cold, and from our exposed position I am satisfied that the cold was much more intense than on the mainland.

At the time I was at Johnson's Island there were about 2,500 officers in confinement, and the quarters were well crowded. The sleeping arrangements consisted of bunks in tiers of three, each furnished with the usual army bedtick stuffed with straw, and far superior to the earth and ditch which had been our beds for months previous to our capture. The crowded condition of the prison necessitated that two men should occupy each bunk, which had the redeeming feature in winter that the occupants were sheltered by two blankets instead of one.

It was an evil genius that selected my bunk, for it lay just under the roof, and sometimes the snow, finding its way in, would cover me with a wet blanket. With the thermometer well down the tube, scantiest of bedclothing, and no fire, it is not strange that pulmonary and rheumatic complaints should have prevailed to a great extent. . . .

To men the greater number of whom had never been in a cold climate the suffering was intense when with such surroundings, the mercury was near zero. A number were frozen to death, and

Confederate prisoners of war endure a Northern winter.

carried into the death house one morning after an intensely cold night.

During these very cold spells it was our habit to sleep in larger groups or "squads," so that by combining blankets and body heat the cold could be better combated. Another practice was, just at sundown, when we were forced to "go to bed," to dip the top blanket in water, wring it out fairly dry, so that, being thus made more impermeable, it would retain the warmth generated by the body. Lots were drawn for positions, and woe to the unfortunate end men, who, although captains of the squad for the night, paid dearly for their honors in having to shiver through the weary hours. And yet all this was not without a strong suggestion of the grotesque. The squad or file of men slept "spoon fashion." No one was allowed to rest flat on the back, for this took up too much room for the width of the blankets. The narrower the bulk to be covered, the thicker the blanket on top. At intervals through these intensely cold nights, above the shivering groans of the unhappy prisoners could be heard the order of the end men. "Boys, spoon!" and, as if on parade, they would flop over upon the other side, to the gratification of one end man and the disgust of the other, whose back by the change was once more turned on a cold world. Of course it was only in the winter months that we had such intense cold, but no one can imagine how long these days and nights seemed unless he has gone through this experience. . . .

many more perished from disease brought on by exposure, added to their condition of emaciation from lack of food. I counted eighteen bodies

"HUNGRY, HUNGRY, HUNGRY ALL THE TIME"

"All the rats which could be caught were eaten," recalled a former Confederate prisoner, "and woe to the dog that ventured on our territory."

Hunger was the overwhelming preoccupation of many imprisoned Johnny Rebs. In prisons throughout the North—Camp Douglas, Elmira, Rock Island, Fort Delaware, and others—Confederate POWs endured what many described as slow starvation. Through the first half of the war, rations in Northern prisons were generally adequate compared to the meager sustenance Confederates received in the field. However, as the slim rations issued to Federal prisoners in the stricken South became public knowledge in the North, rations for Confederate prisoners were reduced in retaliation. By 1864, captive Confederates were desperately hungry.

Col. George H. Moffett lived through imprisonment at Camp Chase and Fort Delaware to record the sustained pain of prison hunger:

It is a horribly excruciating form of suffering to be hungry, hungry, hungry all the time—with just enough food to sharpen the appetite, but never enough to satisfy that everlasting gnawing sensation at the stomach. When a person dies of starvation caused from a total lack of food, there is a shorter limit to the suffering. But here the starvation process was long and drawn out, all the more agonizing because of its protracted duration. . . .

As the vitality lowered from insufficiency of food and the consequent nerve exhaustion, the brain sympathized with the empty stomach until this hunger became a mania. It filled our thoughts by day and our dreams by night. Men would sit around in groups, indulging in reminiscences of bygone days when they had plenty of good eating. One remembered a Christmas dinner when the table groaned with good things; another recalled a certain wedding feast; still another would tell of the big peach cobblers and apple dumplings his mother made; and so the talk went the rounds, until the big-hearted Scotchman, McAlpin, would bring an end to these reminiscences with the remark: "What is the use of talking about all those things now, when I would be perfectly content to be my dog at home eating from the slop pail?" Then at night there would be dreams of roast turkey, plum puddings, of fruits clustering in the arbors, of strawberries growing wild; but just as the hand was reached forth to seize the tempting viands the dream vanished. The prisoner would turn over on his hard bunk to dream it all over again. And this in a land of plenty!

And, as if to intensify the tantalization of the situation, officers and guards would frequently come into the prison enclosure eating fruits, ap-

Hungry Rebs swap rations in a Yankee prison camp.

ples, and oranges, and then would scatter the peelings around to see the famished prisoners scuffle for them. A favorite form of this malicious tantalizing process was to come in with a large slice of watermelon and eat it in the presence of the hungry prisoners. All eyes were riveted upon the luscious melon, jaws would drop and mouths water, and all they could get were the scattered fragments of the rind thrown out to them like bones to dogs. . . .

Did we eat rats? I answer affirmatively, and will say that in our opinion the Chinese are right when they class rat meat as a delicacy. A "rat killing" was about the only real amusement we had. Fresh meat, regardless of the species, was too much of a rarity among these hungry men to be discarded on account of an old prejudice. When properly dressed and fried in pork grease, a rat has the exact flavor of a squirrel. The uninitiated would never know the difference.

Virginian George W. Nelson experienced the dire effects of the prison diet—and witnessed the extreme measures taken to fill empty stomachs while he was imprisoned at Fort Pulaski, formerly a Confederate bastion on the Georgia coast.

Crumbs and bones that would have made the eyes of the famished men in that prison glisten were daily thrown to the dogs or carried to the dunghill. The consequences of all this was that the prisoners died like sheep. Whatever the immediate cause of their death, that cause was induced by starvation, and over the dead bodies of nine-tenths of those brave, true men there can be given but one true verdict: Death by starvation . . .

Fortunately for some of us, there were a great many cats about the prison. As may be imagined, we were glad enough to eat them. I have been partner in the killing and eating of three, and friends have frequently given me a share of their cat. We cooked ours two ways. One we fried in his own fat for breakfast—another we baked with a stuffing and gravy made of some corn meal—the other we also fried. The last was a kitten—tender and nice. A compassionate Yankee soldier gave it to me. I was cooking at the stove by the grating which separated us from the guard. This soldier hailed me: "I say, are you one of them fellows that eats cats?" "Yes." "Well, here is one I'll shove thro' if you want it." "Shove it thro'," I answered. In a very few minutes the kitten was in frying order. Our guards were not allowed to relieve our sufferings, but they frequently expressed their sympathy.

Mississipian Milton A. Ryan survived internment at Camp Chase and Chicago's Camp Douglas. Although hardened by prison life, he was still unnerved by the desperate acts of hungry men.

The hospital was just outside the prison wall. There was a ditch four feet wide and three feet deep. It was planked up sides and bottom and from the hospital it passed through our prison, and in it all the fifth of the prison was deposited, including the scraps from the hospital, such as scraps of meat, baker's bread, onions and beef bones, etc. At the head of the ditch there was a large tank. It was pumped full of water every day by a detail of prisoners. We all knew when the floodgate would be raised and the water turned loose. It would come sweeping down, bringing the garbage and other filth deposited in it during the day. Our boys would be strung along the sides of the ditch and as it came floating by, they would grab it and eat it like hungry dogs. . . .

"MUCH SICKNESS PREVAILED"

Poor diet, exposure, and unsanitary conditions made Southern prisoners susceptible to disease, producing a high mortality rate in most prisons. At New York's Elmira Prison, almost one third of the 10,000 inmates died of illness. One who survived, Pvt. John R. King of the 25th Virginia Infantry, saw many of his companions succumb to disease.

There were nearly 10,000 prisoners at Elmira one time; sometimes less and sometimes more. During the winter those who came from the South felt the cold exceedingly and died from pneumonia. Our clothes were poor. The pants I had when arriving at Elmira were in such a bad condition that for a time I wore nothing but my underwear. However, when the cold weather appeared I was glad to welcome old pants again and after much patching they were a great comfort. In the late winter,

New York's Elmira Prison, where some 3,000 Southern soldiers died of illness.

out-of-date government coats were presented to us for overcoats: for some reason unknown to us the tails had been cut unevenly, one side being a foot long and the other extending only a few inches below the waist line. They helped us to keep warm, but should we have been out in the world in such costume, one might have mistaken us for scarecrows eloping from the neighboring cornfield. Oilcloth and two blankets was the covering in our bunks, with a big snow outside and the bitter wind raging around the plank building and whistling in at the cracks.

We didn't dream of comforts and many of us had very poor shoes. Mine were ready to be cast aside and I did not get a new pair until the last day of February. While in the house I wrapped my feet in old rags which kept them warm, but in the late winter we were compelled to stand in the snow every morning for roll call, consequently my feet and shins were badly frozen. In the spring they had the appearance of a gobbler's legs and it was

many years after I returned home before they were entirely cured. Many besides myself had frozen feet.

The man who looked after the fires made only two fires in 24 hours. Each ward had two stoves. The first fire was made at 8 o'clock in the morning, the other at 8 P.M. Near noon and midnight, we were comfortable, but during the twelve hours between fires when the temperature of the stoves lowered we often suffered with the cold. A dead line nailed to the floor three feet in circumference surrounded the stoves. Of course we could not cross the dead lines and often a petty officer who entered on a cold evening would find some of the ragged shivering men standing too near the fast-cooling stove, would become enraged and would run cursing, striking right and left through the crowd, little caring who received the blows or what he did.

Much sickness prevailed among the prisoners. In the latter part of the winter many came from near Mobile Bay and brought with them smallpox. There were more than forty cases in our ward, and many died. When seven years of age I was vaccinated, and although surrounded with it, I escaped.

There were also many cases of pneumonia and measles, and thousands of us were afflicted with the stubborn diarrhea. The poor fellows died rapidly, despondent, homesick, hungry and wretched. I have stood day after day watching the wagons carrying the dead outside to be buried, and each day for several weeks sixteen dead men were taken through the gate. While the prison was occupied by us, which was about one year, it was estimated that 3,000 men died. The physicians were very good, but it was impossible to save all.

At one time scurvy was among us. There were not many deaths, but it caused much suffering. I was among the victims. It frequently attacked the mouth and gums, which became so spongy and sore that portions could be removed with the fingers. Others became afflicted in their limbs, the flesh became spotted and the pain was almost unbearable. The remedy was raw vegetables and a medicine called "chalk mixture."

Our dead were buried outside with a detail of 16 or 17 prisoners. The name, company, and regiment of the dead were written on a piece of paper, put in a tightly corked bottle and buried with the corpse. All were buried in that way. Their caskets were made in the pen by prisoners detailed for that purpose.

During the early spring, the 40th, 41st, and 42nd wards were converted into hospitals. We all decided beds made of shavings would be a luxury, so every fellow that was able procured a sharp knife and a pine board and I doubt if the world ever saw such a universal whittling in so short a time. All tried to possess a comfortable bed, but in a few days the provost marshall inspected our quarters and ordered every shaving burned. He advocated that the shavings would breed vermin, but we had already been made very uncomfortable by their presence. Near the cookhouse there were vessels for heating water, but few of us could get soap, and consequently the few clothes we had never were washed.

After warm weather came we had many visitors, often ladies. Some of them spoke pleasantly and were well behaved, while others were impudent and insulting. I remember one day Colonel Moore's son came in our pen with a few young girls. Colonel Moore was commander of the post, his son was a foppish young fellow, and one of the girls overdressed and attracted him. While passing through our ward, with her dainty fingers she tipped up her rustling silken skirts and passed along with an affected air and a disdainful look on her countenance, saying, "Oh, the nasty, dirty, ignorant, beastly Rebels. How filthy they are." On she continued with a peculiar air, while some of the girls gave us kindly words and looks, and were embarrassed by her rudeness. But she was punished for being so unlady-like. One of our number, Bish Fletcher, a daredevil, took the opportunity as the girl passed by him to present her with some body lice, "Grey Backs," we called them. . . . .

"A LAMENTABLE AFFAIR"

Prison "discipline" could be lethal. POWs who violated prison rules were sometimes hanged by their thumbs, beaten, or "bucked and gagged." Guards were also sometimes quick to shoot with little or no provocation. The result could be tragic, as noted in the prison diary kept by Confederate I. W. K. Handy at Fort Delaware in 1864.

July 3, 1864—A lamentable affair occured at "the rear" about dusk this evening. Many persons are now suffering with diarrhea, and crowds are frequenting that neighborhood. The orders are to go by one path and return by the other. Two lines of men, going and coming, are in continual movement. I was returning from the frequented spot and, in much weakness, making my way back when suddenly I heard the sentinel challenge from the top of the water-house. I had no idea he was speaking to me, until some friends called my attention to the order. I suppose my pace was too slow for him. I passed on; and as frequent inquiries

were made in regard to my health, I was obliged to say to friends, "We have no time to talk; the sentinel is evidently restless or alarmed, and we are in danger."

I had scarcely reached my quarters before a musket fired and it was immediately reported that Colonel E. P. Jones had been shot.

The murder of Colonel Jones is the meanest and most inexcusable affair that has occured in the officers' quarters; or that has come under my own observation since my imprisonment at Fort Delaware. I did not see him fall; but I have heard from Captain J. B. Cole, who was an eye-witness

Armed guards walk the walls at Ohio's Camp Chase. Wandering too close could be fatal for Confederate POWs.

to the whole scene, that although he was standing within ten steps of the man that killed him, he heard no challenge and no order to move on. The first intimation he had of the sentinel's displeasure was the discharge of the musket, and the simultaneous exclamation of the Colonel: "Oh, God! Oh, God! My God, what did you shoot me for? Why didn't you tell me to go on? I never heard you say anything to me!" With a few such exclamations, he sank upon the ground; and then fell, or rather rolled, down the embankment.

Colonel Jones had been in the barracks so short a time that I have not had the pleasure of making his acquaintance. I have only learned he is an intelligent physician of considerable property and influence, and he is from Middlesex County, Virginia. Since he came to Fort Delaware, he has been constantly suffering with some affliction of the feet causing lameness.

At the time he was shot, he was hobbling along with one shoe and was carefully stepping down a rough place, near the waterhouse, buttoning his pants. He could not have been more than twenty steps from the point of the musket. It is said that the murderer seemed all day to be seeking an opportunity to shoot someone.

Friday, 8th—The boy who shot Colonel Jones is again on guard this morning; and it is reported that he has been promoted to a corporalcy. He belongs, I think, to an Ohio regiment, is about eighteen years old, and is known as Bill Douglas.

Colonel Jones lingered a few hours, and died in great agony.

"THEN COMMENCED A RACE"

The hardships of life in Northern prisons made most Confederate POWs desperate for freedom, and some tried to escape. At Point Lookout, a sprawling Federal prison on a Maryland peninsula where the Potomac River met Chesapeake Bay, almost 20,000 poorly fed Confederates were imprisoned in an overcrowded, inadequate collection of tents. After five months of confinement, Virginian Simon Seward could stand no more and engineered an escape. His recollection of the event:

The First day of December, 1863, was dark and rainy. I thought this was my time, so just before time to shut the gates I crept out. Not a soul was to be seen. The fence was very strongly built, with very large posts and a parapet on top where the guards were on duty.

After passing out of the gates, I went to the right for several panels. Seeing a squad of soldiers, I hid behind a post until they passed. They were within thirty yards of me. When they returned, they would pass within five feet of me. So I got on the other side of the post when I saw them coming back. I expected to be found and pinned to the wall with a bayonet; but when they came within twenty feet of me their attention was called to a pile of sand on the beach that looked like a grave, piled up during the day by some prisoners. The soldiers went at once to the mound and commenced to stick their bayonets through it. It was owing to this that I escaped detection.

I remained close behind the post until nine o'clock, when all was quiet except the tread of the guards overhead and the murmur of their voices as they conversed with each other. My next move was to go from post to post until I reached the corner. To leave there was to do one of two things—either swim the Chesapeake Bay or go through the 5th New Hampshire Regiment in camp on the only ground there was. I decided on the latter. When inside the camp, I saw some horses tied, and tried to untie one, thinking to ride him through the camp and out; but this was "no go." The horse commenced to move; the men saw it and said: "Who is there?" I said nothing and they came to see.

Then commenced a race for the bay, about one hundred yards off, the soldiers and guards after me. The darkness saved me from being riddled with bullets. I went at once into deep water, and commenced to swim for my life up the bay toward Baltimore—the soldiers being camped on the shore for a mile or more. I had a fair wind and tide, and made good time. When I found I could go no farther, I gave up to drown, bidding farewell to this world, when I found myself in water only three feet deep. I thought at first I had struck a whale, but found afterwards it was a sand bar. After a good rest I commenced again, and continued in the water a distance of six miles, passing outside of what was called the blockhouse, where they had wires connected with bells in a house on shore.

Thinking myself safe, I went ashore. A chill came over me from a sharp wind then blowing. My teeth commenced to chatter so loud I thought I would be heard. So I put my finger between them. My feet then refused to move. I was chilled through; but hard work and a determination to move on brought circulation, and I moved, first slowly, then faster, until I struck a path through the woods. . . .

I walked all night, and at the break of day took a little rest to wait for more darkness. I soon fell asleep but it was a short nap. Some dogs came across me, and made so much fuss that I ran through the woods in an opposite direction from which I was going. This saved me from capture, as a company of cavalry was right after me. The dogs followed me through the woods until I came to a deep break covered with ivy. I frightened something, either a man or deer, I can't say which; but it scared me nearly out of my wits. The dogs left me and ran after it.

I moved on through the woods and fields until I came to a road and started to cross it, when I met a man who said: "If you go up this road, you are caught, for the sheriff is coming." I looked, and there he was, riding a horse, with a double

Confederate prisoners at Point Lookout.

barreled shotgun on his shoulder and a prisoner walking by his side. I walked right by him, and as soon as I could took to the woods, running a mile or more until I found a thicket, where I hid until nearly night.

Being much refreshed but a little hungry, I started off again and reached a small house. Seeing a bucket of water on the porch and wishing for information, I asked for a drink of water. The lady said: "You are the man they are looking for. The soldiers on horses have just left here." I moved on again faster than ever until I heard them coming back. I jumped over the fence and waited until they passed by. As they passed I heard them talking, I suppose about me. It was dark, and I commenced again crossing fields and woods until I gave out. Walking and running twenty-five or thirty miles with nothing to eat was telling on me. I decided to go to the next house and ask for food. This I did, but the lady said: "I can give you nothing; my husband is absent." I asked if I might stay until he returned. She replied: "Yes, we know of you. You may stay in the yard." When her husband came, he said I could eat and sleep in his house if I wished.

That night I had a good supper brought to me and the pleasure of sleeping in a top stack near the house. I stayed for a day or more awaiting "orders." Finally they came, saying a man living on the river had been hired for two barrels of corn to carry me across. I left at once, accompanied by his son, but found that the man's boats had just been destroyed by the soldiers. This was sad news to me. He asked if I had money. I told him I had and gave him fifty cents. He sent off and got a quart of whiskey, and while his wife was gone for the dram we went down to the oyster bed, got a sack full, and such eating and drinking we had that night! I mean, they did the drinking and I did the eating. While at the oyster bed I saw a little log canoe about eight feet long and very narrow. It was so old that one end had rotted off and a plank had been nailed on it. I asked if I could cross in it, but my friend said it would sink. The river was about six miles wide and very rough.

Early the next morning before light I got the boat out of the creek and put it in the river opposite the house and told him I was going to try to make the trip, although he insisted it could not be done. I stood for a few moments with a small paddle in my hand, looking first at the river then at the Virginia shore on the other side. I was so anxious to get there I decided to run the risk, although it was very great. The boat was so small I had to put my feet outside. I started, and never looked back; in fact, never had time.

Several times I thought the boat would fill. When about half a mile out a big wave struck me, and came so near sinking me that I commenced to do what my mother taught me at her knee—which had of late been neglected—I prayed for deliverance. The water seemed to jump out of the boat. The winds calmed and the waves ceased to roll. I rested a little and I now noticed blood dripping from my hands. The rough paddle had rubbed the skin and flesh from them, leaving them perfectly raw; but they did not hurt. Looking up the river, I saw a gunboat under a full head of steam coming down on me. Owing to the shallow water, I "got there first," but it was a close race. I struck a rock about a hundred yards off shore. On reaching the shore I rolled over a ditch bank and was safe. I soon saw the old boat stream back up the river and pass out of sight. I was in Virginia once more. . . .

"CHARLIE BECAME AN OBJECT OF STRICTEST SURVEILLANCE"

Escaping from a well-guarded prison was no easy task. Even the best-conceived escape plots often ended in failure, yet escape attempts persisted. At Johnson's Island, Lt. Charles H. ("Charlie") Pierce of Louisiana earned a reputation in two categories of prison life: He was the prison's champion baseball player, and he was the ruling king of escape attempts.

A gifted athlete and a respected officer, Pierce was a natural leader who even earned the grudging admiration of his captors. Seven times he engineered escapes from Johnson's Island. Each time either his attempt was foiled or he was recaptured. Back in prison, he would resume his plans to escape. After one unsuccessful breakout, a Federal officer confided, "Pierce, I wish you could get away. You certainly deserve to be free."

Despite strict surveillance by prison authorities, Pierce's daring, ingenious escape plots did not cease until war's end. A fellow Confederate, Lt. M. McNamara, preserved this testimony of the plucky escape artist's perseverance.

In all the prison sports, Lieutenant Charlie Pierce was regarded as the leader. His versatile talent, genial humor, sterling manhood and undoubted bravery, together with his kindness of heart, endeared him to all, and even commanded the respect of his captors.

The severity of the wintry season being past, the minds of many of the prisoners naturally reverted to attempts to escape, and no one was more bent on it than the heroic and daring Charlie Pierce. A tunnel had been commenced from Block 8, but the project was deemed abortive, owing to its long distance from the dead-line, and abandoned. Charlie then transferred his operations to Block 1, where he soon organized a working party, who succeeded, by incessant labor, in completing a tunnel to the extreme end of the works. But, alas! When the attempt was made to pass out, they were pounced upon by a guard, and their hopes blasted.

On a less active and vigorous mind, such a signal failure would have had a paralyzing effect. But it only aroused the ambition of our hero to succeed at all hazards, and his thoughts were instantly turned to some plan for the future.

An opportunity soon presented itself, which he eagerly seized. One morning the offal cart was driven in by a soldier under the influence of liquor, who lay down in Charlie's block while the cart was being filled. Quick as thought, Charlie jumped upon the driver's seat, seized the reins, and drove out the cart. He passed the sentinels at the gate, who opened it for his egress, and got beyond the parapet, imagining himself at last free. But the condition of the soldier being discovered by the prison guard, a hue and cry was raised, the ruse detected, and a squad sent in pursuit of the fugitive, who was soon overtaken, and the intrepid Charlie was brought back to his prison quarters.

With a chosen few he conceived the project of scaling the parapet, attacking the sentinels with rocks, and breaking for the Canadian shore, the lake being frozen over. Scaling ladders were made as secretly as possible, and a bright moonlight night selected for the attempt. There was only one pistol obtainable, and this fell, by lot, to the possession of Lieutenant Wheeler, of Morgan's cavalry. The others armed themselves with rocks.

Using handmade ladders, Confederate prisoners scale a prison wall.

Lieutenants Pierce, Wheeler and J. B. Bowles, of Louisville, Kentucky, were the first to get their ladders in position and attempt the ascent. Our hero, however, was the only one who gained the parapet. A rock in his hand was as true as a rifle ball, thanks to his base-ball experience. With it he felled the sentinel. His cousin, Lieutenant Bowles, was shot on the ladder and his body fell inside. His dying words to Charlie were to push on, and leave him to his fate. Lieutenant Wheeler and the sentinel in front of him fired at each other simultaneously, and singularly both missed, when the Lieutenant slid down to avoid a second shot, he having no other means of defense. Lieutenant Pierce speedily pursued his way over the natural bridge of ice on the lake, under a constant fire from the sentinels, until he got beyond the range of their guns. . . .

He gained the strip of land twelve miles distant, and pursued his way through the woods until daylight, when he was halted by some farmers,

with shot-guns. Those fellows, when aroused by the alarm guns, were ever on the alert to capture an escaping prisoner and claim the reward. They had no ordinary one in Charlie Pierce, and hungry, chilled and foot-sore, he was speedily marched back to his old quarters.

It is not to be wondered at that Charlie now became an object of the strictest surveillance on the part of every agent of the enemy. His every movement was watched, so that his sole reliance was upon strategy.

Procuring a Federal uniform (it was supposed from someone connected with the hospital), he carefully concealed it in his bunk. With a piece of wood, of which there was plenty, he manufactured a gun stock; with a lot of fruit cans, which he procured from the hospital, he manufactured a barrel, and a piece of the handle of a camp kettle was wrought into a lock. After five months' incessant labor, he completed his task, and during the time he was exceedingly reticent, confining himself to his bunk as much as possible, keeping his own council, like a good general, but working like a beaver. As a piece of workmanship, it was pronounced by all who saw it a marvel of mechanical ingenuity and skill, He was fortunate enough to find an old rusty bayonet, which he soon made to look like polished steel, and how he stained the gun to make it look real no one but himself knew.

Having everything in readiness, how to put them to use? The guard must be brought into the block at night, so that he could fall in with the men and march out with them. Confiding his intention to only a trusted few of his mess-mates, he requested Lieutenant Michael Long to inform the guard that an attempt would be made to break out that night from Block 8. The Lieutenant was thanked for the information; the sentinel called, "Corporal of the guard" and the Corporal carried the information to the Officer of the Guard. The guard was doubled for the emergency and an inspecting party was soon going round the prison. Charlie, with his Federal uniform and improvised gun, quietly fell in with them. Not finding anything suspicious in that block, they were marched out. All the other blocks were visited without any discoveries being made. The guard was then formed in line for inspection. The Lieutenant in command, examining the accoutrements of the men, discovered that Charlie had no cartridge box, then the following dialogue took place:

Lieutenant of the Guard: "How is it, sir, that you have no cartridge box?"

Charlie: "Well, Lieutenant, we fell in outside in such a hurry, I declare I forgot it."

Lieutenant: "Well, you are a fine soldier! No cartridge box! Suppose the Rebels were to attack us while we were in here among them? Let me see your gun, sir!"

Then the lieutenant proceeded to an inspection of arms, still upbraiding the delinquent soldier.

Charlie, seeing this his last effort was defeated, straightened himself, brought his gun to "in-spection arms," in true military style, and passed it to the officer. Of course, its weight told the tale. The ruse was discovered, and by neglecting the cartridge-box, the easiest of all to make, our hero was again defeated in his plans. . . .

So confident were his comrades that he had been successful in this last attempt, they prepared his bunk to lead the sentinel to believe that he was still there, and was ready to vouch for his sickness at roll call the following morning. But when roll-call came, the intrepid Pierce was there to answer for himself, and there he remained until paroled with the others at the close of the war.

At war's end, Lieutenant Pierce finally walked out of Johnson's Island a free man. He returned home to New Orleans, where he died in a yellow fever epidemic in 1867 at age twenty-six.

"WE HAD CUT THROUGH FORTY-TWO BRICK WALLS"

One of the most extraordinary prison escapes of the war occurred in February of 1865 at Georgia's Fort Pulaski, a coastal fortress captured by the Federals in 1862, and later pressed into temporary service as a prison. After two months of grueling labor under the most adverse conditions, a handful of imprisoned Confederate officers equipped with improvised tools cut through forty-two of Fort Pulaski's thick masonry walls in a determined break for liberty.

The idea for the remarkable escape attempt originated with Maj. J. Ogden Murray. His story:

Christmas eve night, December 24, 1864, was one of the coldest nights I think we had to endure while at Fort Pulaski prison. I was lying in my bunk, praying that God would let me go to sleep and never awake in life. Yes, I was begging God to let me die and end my torture. I was cold and hungry, no blanket to cover me, no fire to warm me. As I turned over in my bunk to warm the side of my body exposed to the cold, one of the boards fell from the bunk, and I got out to replace it, that I might lie down. In fixing the board in its place, by the dim light of the prison lamp, I saw beneath my bunk a trap door. For a few moments I felt dazed and really believed I was but dreaming. Little sleep came to me after this discovery. I laid all sorts of plans, only to brush them aside. At daylight I awoke my comrade, Dave Prewitt, of Kentucky, and communicated to him my discovery. . . .

We got hold of an eighteen-inch stove poker. Prewitt had an old dinner knife of which we made a saw. Billy Funk agreed to watch for the coming of the guard or officer of the day, and that night, December 25, 1864, we began what seemed to be a hopeless task. After taps, every night for a week [we dropped through the trap door and chipped away at the walls below]. Lieutenant Funk would take up his position on my bunk, and if anything moved he notified us by knocking on the floor with his heels. We would then stop work until he gave the signal all was well.

We worked on for one week, getting out but few bricks. We finally concluded to take into our confidence some help, so we organized a working party of Capt. W. W. Griffin, 1st Maryland Battery, C. S. A.; Captain Kent, Georgia; Lieutenant W. H. Chew, Georgia; Lieutenant Hugh Dunlap, Tennessee; Lieutenant Ed Chambers, Alabama; with Prewitt and myself. One night a fellow named Gillispie caught Prewitt coming out of the trap door, so we took him in with us to keep him quiet. Every night we would go down in pairs to work on the wall. Our only tools were the case knife, made into a saw, and the eighteen-inch fire poker.

We worked waist deep in water from the 25th of December, 1864, to February 28, 1865. We never missed one night, and our efforts were finally rewarded. We had cut through forty-two brick walls that were eight feet thick, making a cut through 336 feet of solid brick walls, with that old case knife and poker. At last we were done and fixed upon the night of February 28, 1865, which was Saturday night, to say goodbye to our Yankee captors.

At 11 P.M., February 28, 1865, we began our exit. Captain Griffin was the first man below. Lieutenant Chew followed, then Captain Kent, then Dunlap, Gillispie, Prewitt, then myself. When we had all gotten below, Captain Chambers could not, he said, get through the trap door, so we left him. Poor Lieutenant Billy Funk cried and pleaded to be taken with us, but the poor fellow was unable to get out of the bunk, practically dead with scurvy. . . .

The night was dark, and a drizzling rain was falling. All went well with us through the tunnel until we reached the trapdoor in the casement above. When we attempted to remove the door we found to our consternation that it was weighted down by some very heavy weight. It was a dilemma we had not counted on. We knew we could not cut through another wall by daylight; so we concluded to force up that door at all risk. Four or five of us got under it, pushing with our hands and heads until Dave Prewitt could get the poker under the edge of the door. When he pried down on the poker he started the heavy body on the door to moving. Well, I have heard the artillery of Jackson in the Valley; I heard the roar of the guns at Gettysburg; I have heard the heavenly thunders of the Rocky Mountains; but I say to you, all these sounds combined were but pop-gun reports when compared to the noise those barrels made above our heads rolling over the casemate floor; and, yet, strange as it may be, the noise did not disturb the slumbers of a whole company of the 157th New York Volunteers, asleep in the very next casemate. After waiting for a time, to hear if the noise alarmed the sentinels about the fort, we began to ask each other, "Shall we go back or go on?" The question was put to vote and the majority said, "Let's go on."

Hearing no one moving above, we pushed up the trapdoor and began the ascent to the casemate above. Lieutenant W. H. Chew, of Georgia, being the smallest man in our party, was raised upon our shoulders to the floor. He, with the help of our rope, made of old pieces of clothing, blankets, and such material as we could from time to time get, pulling us up one by one. When we had all reached the casemate we had no trouble in getting out of the casemate window. Groping about the casemate in the darkness, we found an old army blanket. This, cut into strips, materially strengthened our rope. All being ready, we threw out our rope and began our exit from the fort porthole. . . .

Now that we were in the swamp, free from the prison, the problem presented itself, how to get a boat to leave the island. Then came the question, who should go forward and overpower the sentinel over the boats at the wharf, where they were kept moored, constantly guarded. Lieutenant

The Federal garrison at Fort Pulaski parades before casemates housing Confederate prisoners.

Chew suggested that we draw cattails. This was adopted. Chew held the cuts, and the choice fell on Gillispie. He at once objected to going on the ground that a smaller man could get through the swamp better than he. Not having time to discuss the philosophy of his objection, Prewitt said, "Come on, Murray. You and I will go ahead." Off we started, Prewitt in the lead, I next, and Captain Kent, of Georgia, close behind me, with Captain Griffin, Chew, and others following in our wake, some fifty feet behind, so as not to attract the sentinel. We came in sight of the wharf; against the horizon we could see the sentinel walking his beat. We stopped to arrange a plan of attack upon him. Prewitt was to move down on the right of the boats, I on the left, and Kent, direct from the point we halted.

We started; everything was going nicely, and in a very few minutes we would have had the sentinel, and the boats would have been ours. We were slowly getting nearer and nearer to the bridge upon which the sentinel walked, which was built upon piles about two feet above the water. Just as we were ready for the final move, out on the night air rang the voice of Gillispie, howling, "Don't shoot! Don't shoot!" This, of course, alarmed the sentinel on the bridge; he fired his gun and called lustily for the sergeant of the guard. The fort was alarmed, the guard turned out, and our liberty was gone. In a few minutes more we would have been sailing across the mouth of the Savannah River, free men, had not Gillispie howled like a wolf. . . .

Why Gillispie betrayed us has always been a mystery to me. He worked just as hard as any one of our party to cut the tunnel through the walls, and ate his cornmeal and pickle with us. I can only account for his conduct on the ground that when it came to killing the sentinel over the boats, he thought if the escape failed we would all be shot; and this broke his nerve and made him shout as he did. Afterward, shame of his conduct made him take the oath, so that he would not be put in the cell with us.

"NOW FOR CANADA"

Breaking out of prison did not assure freedom. A successful escape could still leave Johnny Reb hundreds of miles from his Southern home, surrounded by the enemy and deep in Northern territory. In fact, the rigors of avoiding capture sometimes made the escape seem easy in comparison. Such was the perilous wintertime trek of four Confederate officers who escaped from Johnson's Island. Their four-day race to freedom was recorded by a survivor of the ordeal.

New Year's day, 1864, was extremely cold; that night the mercury fell to thirty degrees below zero. As the cold north winds beat with cruel violence against the thin weather-boarding, Captains Robinson and Davis of Virginia, Captain McConnell of Kentucky, and Major Winston of North Carolina determined to risk a desperate attempt that night. They came to the conclusion that the boldest and best way to get out of prison was by scaling the wall. So a rude ladder was extemporized by tying with clothesline the legs of a bench across a board at intervals of about three feet, to answer for steps. Our means of escape ready, we made such preparations as we could to protect ourselves against the cold weather. Our chums were exceedingly kind in furnishing all the citizens' clothing that they had. The next thing was, who should go first? The lot fell to Major Winston.

Captain Davis and Major Winston promptly left the room, each placing himself flat on the frozen ground at his end of the ladder. Thus they dragged the ladder up the sewer to the corner of the building, thence across toward the deadline. With great caution we crawl on over the "deadline." Reaching the wall, we stand our ladder against it. Davis holds while Winston mounts. Davis screams in whispers and jerks at the feet of Winston, who, fearing they were discovered, stoops down and asks, "What is the matter?" "Get off my thumb!" says Davis.

The ladder proved to be about four feet too short. However, Major Winston succeeded in pulling himself over on the parapet as silently as possible; and after looking to see if he was seen by either sentinel on his right or left, he let himself down, first on a brace that supported the wall and then on a large stump. Evading the line of sentinels, he sat behind a large oak tree some fifteen steps from the wall. Captain Davis soon joined him. Then came Captain Robinson and next came Captain McConnell, who very nearly lighted on the head of the man on the ground, but fortunately was not discovered.

So our party was all out, ran across the island and, finding the ice firm, ventured on it. About half-way across we found a large air hole, and in our heedless hurry came near being engulfed; but fortunately that night a thin snow whitened the ice, while the water appeared black. After an exciting run, slipping, sliding, and tumbling, we reached the shore almost breathless. It was half-past ten o'clock, and we could hear the soldiers on the distant walls calling out the numbers of their posts and "All's well!"

A short rest, and we started on our long journey, over fences and through fields, toward the west. We found it much warmer in the woods. Two hours before day, foot-sore, chilled, and weary, we sought shelter in a straw stack, but it had been wet and frozen. We went into a farmer's stable, and, groping in the dark, found bridles and two large, fat horses. While the honest man slept and slumbered, each of his spirited animals bore away two Rebels. On they sped over the level country, passing farmhouses and woods. When many miles had fled behind us, just as streaks in the east ushered in another gray, cold morning, Captain McConnell stopped his horse and complained he was freezing. After going a little farther, McConnell repeated, "I am freezing," and fell from his horse, groaning like a dying man. Winston tried by chafing to revive him, but to no effect, as he had on too much clothing. We tied the bridles over the horses' necks and turned their head homeward. They were in a trot the last we saw of them.

Poor McConnell was straightened up and pushed along until his frozen hinges got in working order again. Awhile before sunup we knocked at a door to warm, and if possible, eat breakfast. We passed ourselves off as land speculators walking over the country, prospecting, but our jaded looks, and especially the dilapidated condition of our apparel, excited [the farmer's] curiosity. After such fatigue and exposure to cold, we would go to sleep in spite of ourselves. We gratified our friend's curiosity by reliefs, as soldiers say. Bread, strong coffee, and fat bacon were soon prepared and dispatched. We left the little man standing in the door wondering why land speculators should be too mean to pay for breakfast.

For fear of being overtaken, we shunned the highways. The frost told badly on our ears, fingers, feet, and noses. We heard large oaks bursting about in the woods, I suppose from the moisture in the trees crystallizing. We journeyed on, and a little after midnight Captain McConnell stopped at a house to get some soda for the heartburn. Several hours he continued to grow worse; before sunrise he gave out and begged to be left at the next house. We placed him on the doorstep and gave him one-fourth of our money, and with much sorrow parted.

Toward midnight one of our party asked admittance to a house larger than common on the road. To our great relief, the door was opened and we were invited to the fire. A few questions convinced us that we were in the hands of a "down-Easter." He seemed to suspect something and asked where we were from. "New Bedford, Mass.," replied Captain Robinson. "Ah! that's my old home,"

and he began by naming different residents of that old place to try Captain Robinson. But the Captain, who had been many years in the whaling service, and of course had at least visited New Bedford, was posted.

We crossed the river into Toledo about daylight, and were in time to join the early workmen going to their places of labor. After leaving the city we abandoned the railroad and bore away to the lakeshore road. At noon our treasurer, Captain Davis, purchased some cheese and crackers at a country store, the first food we had eaten, I think, for thirty hours. That night, January 4, we passed through Monroe [Michigan], during a snowstorm, and met people coming from the church. We had walked a long day's journey, but it was ten o'clock before we could find an agreeable roof. This was a French-Canadian, who had moved to Michigan a short time previously. We tumbled all three together on a pallet and were very soon asleep; had no supper, and left very early next morning before breakfast.

We led people to believe that Detroit was our home. We met an officer going to a depot which we had just passed, and we continued on the Detroit road until he was out of sight; we then turned to the right and made for Trenton, a village on the Detroit River near its entrance into Lake Erie.

Just at dusk we entered Trenton, passed down a street, and jumped on the ice. The ice at first seemed as smooth as glass. Captain Robinson was so stunned by a fall that he scarcely recovered that night. We took it to be one mile across to Fighting Island, and two miles across the channel of the river. Briars and marshes made our progress on the island quite slow. We passed one or two dwellings, but were not disposed to stop, as we felt that our troubles were almost ended.

On the ice again, and now for Canada! After going about a mile on, the ice became exceedingly troublesome. A storm a day or two before had broken and blown it about in waves. We clamored over the broken blocks, slipping and sliding at

Federal guards, like these at Indiana's Camp Morton, made escape difficult.

every pull. Major Winston felt the ice giving away and remarked that we were nearing an air hole, and as he turned one foot broke through. Captain Robinson endeavored to get back, but both feet broke through, and he barely saved himself by leaning over on firm ice. Davis and Winston kneeled over and pulled him out; almost instantly his trousers were frozen stiff. This treacherous hole had well-nigh cut short our earthly pilgrimage.

Our situation was a critical one in the extreme. To avoid turning back in our confusion, Davis placed himself about ten feet in advance of the others, and under their direction made toward the north star. Poor Captain Robinson was so worn out and stunned by his fall that he threw his arm over Winston's shoulder, who bore him on. When we felt that we could not dispense with our beacon, clouds suddenly shut out every star. Just then a light immediately before us in Canada rekindled our hopes. Davis said: "If we ever get there, I will kiss the ground." Near the shore another airhole obstructed our way. We concluded, after going up and down the beach trying for firm ice till we grew desperate, to run across one at a time; and if one broke in, the others could save him. The ice did not let us in, but cracked. We were safe!

A few steps drew us to the door of a pleasant woman, a Mrs. Warrior, half French and half Indian. She was glad to see us, gave us some pies—all she had cooked—and laid a pallet for us before the fire and near a large stove, both of which were kept roaring all night. The reader can somewhat appreciate our feelings of relief when he recollects that this was ten o'clock of the 5th of January, four days and four nights to an hour since we had left the prison. In these four days and four nights we had eaten two regular meals and three snacks. Above all, we were safe under the protection of the British flag.

From Canada, where they were supplied with funds by Confederate sympathizers, the three escapees took a steamer to Bermuda, then reentered the Confederacy by blockade runner. Captain McConnell, unavoidably left behind on an Ohio doorstep, was recaptured.

"I WAS ARRESTED AS A SPY"

Some Confederate prisoners of war did not live long enough even to see a prison camp. Declared to be spies or guerrillas, they were shot or hanged soon after capture—sometimes following a hasty court-martial and sometimes without any judicial action. In 1863, Pvt. Sam Davis, a twenty-one-year-old Confederate courier, was charged with spying by Federal authorities in Pulaski, Tennessee. Davis was offered his life in exchange for revealing the source of information he was carrying, but refused and was hanged. Posthumously, he became a Confederate Nathan Hale, praised in print and memorialized in stone throughout the South as a martyr to the Cause.

A lesser-known Confederate who suffered an identical fate under similar circumstances was an Arkansas teenager named David O. Dodd. The seventeen-year-old was living with his family in Little Rock, when the Arkansas capital was captured and occupied by Federal forces in September of 1863. On Christmas Eve of that year, young Dodd was arrested and found to be carrying coded information about Federal troop strength and fortifications in the Little Rock area.

Dodd admitted he was on an intelligence mission for the Confederate army when captured, but rejected the offer of a pardon if he would expose his collaborators. Instead, the youthful courier was publicly hanged by Federal troops in Little Rock on January 8, 1864.

The night before his capture, young Dodd took Mary Swindle Brantly to a dance. Soon afterwards, the Little Rock girl watched Dodd go to his execution. Here is her account of his capture and hanging, followed by Dodd's last letter home—written a few hours before his death.

David O. Dodd, son of Andrew and Lydia Owen Dodd, was born in Texas, but reared in Little Rock, Ark., and educated in St. John's Masonic College in Little Rock. At the time of his execution he was not yet eighteen years old and rather small for his age, but was an unusually handsome and manly, though extremely modest, little fellow.

In September, 1863, Federal troops, about thirty thousand strong, under General Steele, occupied Little Rock, all the male citizens capable of serving in the army withdrawing under General Fagan to the vicinity of Camden and leaving the city occupied only by the old men, women and children. Among the refugees were all the members of David O. Dodd's family, he and his father joining General Fagan, his mother and sisters going farther South. David was sent back into Little Rock on some private business for his family and with instructions to find out what he could about the Yankees, their location, etc., and remained there several weeks.

Having possessed himself with information con-

Confederate courier David Dodd, hanged as a spy at age seventeen.

cerning the enemy's strength and movements, he started south again, and safely passed all the pickets, but was overtaken by a party of Federals, scouts perhaps, who searched him and found secreted on his person documents in telegraphic code, maps of the fortifications, etc. He was imprisoned but was offered his liberty if he would disclose the names of the parties from whom he had received his messages. This he steadfastly refused to do, declaring that he had assumed a man's duties and would abide the consequences.

Every possible effort in his behalf was made by the citizens of Little Rock, but in vain, and on January 8, 1864, he was executed. He asked that he might be shot to death, but this request was refused, and he was hanged on one of the trees of the campus of St. John's College, where he had gone to school. The execution took place in the presence of a full regiment of Federal soldiers, one of whom fainted dead away at the sight, and another, in speaking of it afterwards to my father, wept and declared that he would have refused to be present had he known that a mere boy and not a man was to be hanged.

The remains were taken with the rope still about his neck to the residence of Mr. Barney Knighton and were interred in the presence of only the members of the family and of Rev. Colburn, the Methodist minister. No prayers or funeral services of any kind were permitted.

Military Prison, Little Rock
January 8, 10 o'clock A.M., 1864
My Dear Parents and Sisters:

I was arrested as a spy and tried and was sentenced to be hung today at 3 o'clock. The time is fast approaching, but, thank God! I am prepared to die. I expect to meet you all in Heaven. I will soon be out of this world of sorrow and trouble. I would like to see you all before I die, but let God's will be done, not ours. I pray to God to give you strength to bear your troubles while in this world. I hope God will receive you in Heaven; there I will meet you.

Mother, I know it will be hard for you to give up your only son, but you must remember it is God's will. Goodbye! God will give you strength to bear your troubles. I pray that we may meet in Heaven. Goodbye! God will bless you all.

Your son and brother,
David O. Dodd

"THE HAPPIEST MAN IN THE SOUTHERN CONFEDERACY"

Few escapes from the enemy were more unusual than that of Cap. J. M. Null, a youthful Confederate cavalry officer captured by Federal cavalry in northern Mississippi. Null's story begins as he and four companions pause from a scouting patrol to beg a meal:

It was getting dusk, and thinking we had gotten in front of the command, we rode up to a house for the purpose of getting something to eat. Gates dismounted and gave me his bridle to hold while he went in to prospect. When he had gotten nearly to the steps a lady met him. When he raised his hat and said something about Confederate soldiers, and the lady said: "For God's sake, run! Leave here quick!" Gates jumped up on the veranda, took a look over, jumped back down again, and struck a turkey trot for his horse: but before he could mount, a squad of Federals dashed up to the opposite side of the garden and opened fire on us.

My horse took the bit between his teeth and let out down the road in dead earnest. About four hundred yards from the house the road made an abrupt turn, almost at a right angle, and just at the turn and immediately at the front, stood a tree with a stout projecting limb exactly the right height to catch a man across the stomach. I saw it but could not check or turn my horse. The limb caught me, lifted me up and threw me down in the road on my back.

Of course the other four must pass over me, not having time to go around. I had fallen on my back, and when I turned over on my all fours the first horse, instead of making a clear jump, struck me under the arm with his fore feet, which knocked out the little remaining breath the fall had left in me. I don't know what happened for some time, but felt that the other three horses must have jumped on me with all their feet. I don't know how I got away from there, but I was headed downhill,

and ran into a treetop which had fallen with the leaves on, and this offered me a splendid hiding place, and I remained there until it was quite dark. My horse, baggage, hat, pistols, were all gone; both spurs were broken, my left shoulder and all the ribs on the left side seemed to be broken, the skin torn from the back of one hand, and I was spitting blood. I turned my back upon the enemy, and took up a line of march which carried me to the back yard of a farmhouse. The lady of the house said she heard the firing, and saw four Confederates and a loose horse pass there at dark. This brave lady went off in the dark across the field after her husband, who took me to the house of one of Gholston's cavalrymen, where I took up my quarters.

He had two very nice young lady daughters. One of them was sitting near the front window, and in the course of our general talk remarked that she wished that she could see a Yankee, as she had never seen one. It so happened that in a few minutes she called back to me: "Come to the window, quick. Yonder come some men with blue clothes on and yellow stripes on them. See if they are Yankees!" I went to the window, and sure enough, coming directly toward the house in a gallop were six mounted Federals.

I darted out a back window and toward a thicket in the rear. They saw me, rushed their horses over the fence, drew their sabers, and came upon me like a storm. I faced about and surrendered to six raw Dutchmen, belonging to the Second New Jersey Cavalry. The sergeant, who could speak very little English (the others

Confederate horse soldiers try to elude Federal pursuers.

could not speak a word), said: "Halt dere! you my breesner!" Then he asked: "You von soldier?"

I replied, "I used to be"; and he said, "Ve dakes you to Memphis."

Soon we went back to the house and took seats on the steps. They put up their sabers and ordered the young ladies to get them something to eat. The sergeant continued his examination, translating my answers to the others.

"Who dot men vat runs efer time ven we gooms?"

"Guerrillas."

"Vy dey runs avay, unt no fight?"

"They will fight when night comes. They have nothing but shotguns, and can't shoot as far as you can; but when it gets dark you had better look out; they will slip up close and kill the last one of you, and me too, I am afraid."

I went on to tell them that there were two hundred and fifty or more and pointed their locations as east, west, and south. This brought on another Dutch confab. I told the sergeant I wouldn't mind going with them to Memphis, that I wanted to get out of the war, that my uncle was the mayor of Memphis and a good Union man, and when I got there he would get me paroled and I could make money; but if I went with them the guerrillas would think I belonged to their squad and would kill me as well as them.

This caused any amount of jabber among them. Then the sergeant asked me if I could give them paroles. I told them if I were to capture them and take them to General Forrest, he would parole them and they could go home and stay and draw their pay until the end of the war. More Dutch jabber followed until one of the young ladies came to the door, and calling me "captain," said to tell them that dinner was ready. When she called me "captain," the sergeant saluted me and asked: "You von captain?"

"Yes, I am one of General Forrest's captains." They loosed their belts, took off their sabers, laid them and their carbines down in front of me, assembled before me, took positions of soldiers without arms, and held up their hands. The sergeant said: "Ve your breesners; ve vant barole; ve keep der horses." I showed them into the dining room, and went and sat on the doorstep and wondered what a parole was like. After dinner I wrote paroles for them, stating that guards and pickets should pass them from there to Memphis on good behavior. Then I directed each one to hold up his right hand and take an oath to the truth of the contents.

Before leaving, the sergeant asked me to go behind the smokehouse with him. He produced a half-pint of the best peach brandy I had ever tasted, and we drank to fraternal friendship. We shook hands all round, then they mounted and rode away, leaving me the happiest man in the Southern Confederacy. . . .

"WE LONGED FOR DEATH"

One group of Confederate prisoners was different. It was composed of six hundred captive officers selected by Federal authorities to receive special treatment: They were to be imprisoned in an open stockade under the fire of their own army's artillery.

The six hundred were the unfortunate victims of wartime game of one-upmanship that began in beleaguered Charleston, South Carolina, in 1864. Charleston was a city at war, blockaded by Union batteries that hammered away at its fortifications and routinely shelled civilian neighborhoods. In June of 1864, Charleston's Confederate authorities, protesting the Federal bombardment of the city's noncombatants, moved fifty captured Federal officers into a civilian section of the city that drew frequent fire from enemy batteries.

In retaliation, six hundred Confederate officers imprisoned at Fort Delaware were placed on an overcrowded troopship and transported to Morris Island, offshore Charleston. There they were penned inside a log stockade near Federal artillery positions that drew regular fire from Charleston's Confederate batteries. The helpless six hundred endured the artillery fire for forty-five days before Federal authorities ended the experiment and shipped them farther south to Fort Pulaski near Savannah. There they suffered from hunger and inadequate care until near war's end, when the survivors were finally returned to Fort Delaware.

Their unique ordeal bequeathed a legacy: generations of Southerners would remember the contingent of captives as "The Immortal Six Hundred." One of them, Confederate John J. Dunkle, preserved this account of their peculiar experience.

In the latter part of August 1864, we were paraded in Fort Delaware, and after having packed our baggage—consisting of old clothes and worn out blankets—and bidding farewell to our friends, we were marched in order to the wharf. We took pasage in a steam-ship called the *Crescent*; into her small hold or middle deck we were quickly crowded—huddled and jammed together like swine on a hog car. We were too many for the capacity of the boat, yet she was made to contain us.

About three-fourths of us became very sick shortly after leaving Fort Delaware. We contracted sea-sickness by not being familiar with the sea and sea voyages. And as closely confined as we were, the spectacle was horrid—the entire floor covered with sick men—horribly sick, vomiting to a fearful extent, and groaning in a terrific manner. It presented a sight too sickening to behold, and too repulsive to endure, and too wretched to describe. Even those of us who were not infected by the sickening malady, were made faint by the loathesome spectacle we were obliged to witness.

We suffered very much from the scarcity of water. At one time we had no water for forty hours. Oh, the intense suffering of those forty hours is beyond description! No pen could convey to the mind an idea of the cruel agony of suffering without water, shut out from light and fresh air in the heat of summer, and confined with a heated steam boiler.

Many persons in sound health became pale and sickly, and their parched lips, sallow complexions, and wrinkled faces betrayed, in unmistakable lines, the approach of the destroyer. No agony or pain could have been greater than the agony created by thirst and the dreadful misery of being without light or fresh air. Many of us became so reduced during these sufferings that we were unable to leave the boat. About fifty had to be carried away, being unable to walk. Many suffered severely from disease even before we left the boat. A pen was constructed on Morris Island close to Battery Wagner, in the direct range of our guns at Fort Moultrie, and whenever a shell fell short of Wagner, it would undoubtedly fall among us.

On the inside of the enclosure, about thirty feet from the pine poles, stakes were driven in the sand parallel with the wall. All around, from the gate back again a rope was stretched from one to the other, so as to reach all around the sides and

the ends. Inside of the rope was the place allotted to us. We were not permitted to touch the rope upon pain of being instantly shot. Any one endeavoring to cross the rope was shot without hesitancy. The pen was situated two hundred and fifty yards from Battery Wagner. Every shell thrown from it caused a jar in our pen. We were four hundred yards from Battery Gregg, which kept up a regular fire on Fort Moultrie and Fort Sumter.

We were five hundred yards from Cumming's Point, which kept up day and night, a continuous fire on the town of Charleston. Our situation was twelve hundred yards from Fort Moultrie on Sullivan's Island, which kept up a slow fire upon all the Yankee batteries. It was supposed that the shells from this point would fall among us.

We were not permitted to collect together in our tents. If a sentinel noticed any more than the inmates of a tent collecting together in the same, he would immediately fire into the tent. We were not suffered to talk loud, or halloo, or shout. Fire was not permitted to come within the pen— indeed it was not desirable except of a rainy or foggy morning when the sea-breeze was very chilling. When the sun shone, the heat was very burdensome, and almost intolerable. The sand frequently got so hot that it was impossible to walk upon it in bare feet. The Yankees at no time gave to the prisoners any articles of clothing, bedding, or anything to shelter the person from observation, the chilling blast, or the burning rays of the sun. At 9 o'clock every prisoner was required to go to bed. After that time no one was allowed to talk only in a whisper. If anyone abused this privilege, as it was called, by talking aloud, he was instantly fired upon.

Our food consisted of three small crackers three inches square, one quarter inch thick, two ounces of meat (mule or horse), and a half a pint of warm water imitation of soup. Thus we starved day after day and night after night. The rations were nearly enough for one meal. I usually ate it all at once, that was in the evening, and involuntarily fasted till

Four members of "The Immortal Six Hundred": (top left) Maj. William P. Emanuel of the 4th South Carolina Cavalry; (top right) Maj. L. Clarke Leftwitch of Virginia; (bottom left) Lt. J. W. O. Funk of the 5th Virginia Infantry; and (bottom right) Lt. Col. E. S. M. LeBroten of Louisiana.

the next. We suffered the bitterest and most pinching hunger. The only wonder is that we did not all starve to death in this horrible place.

Vast numbers of shells were thrown every day from the Federal batteries to various points, and from different batteries. Gregg kept up an incessant fire day and night upon Sumter and Moultrie. This fire drew a return for Moultrie, which was executed at long intervals, and only when something was to be accomplished by the action.

Wagner frequently threw shells at Moultrie in order to draw her fire, so that, falling short, it might fall amongst us. This was frequently the case, fragments of shells falling among the prisoners, and, indeed, on every side of the pen, yet no man was seriously injured by any explosion.

Thus day after day and night after night we feasted our longing eyes on the grandeur of these death-bearing scenes, and filled our minds with the horrors attending the same. Our ears were constantly greeted with the roar of artillery, the concussion of shells, the groans of wounded, or the shrieks of the dying.

Thus living on three crackers and two ounces of meat and some warm water, abused, fired upon, shelled, cursed, starved, and rendered miserable in every form, we lingered on for forty-five days in this horrible place, ere we were permitted to bid a final, and I hope an everlasting, farewell to Morris' Island.

"HE IS OF THIS WORLD NO MORE"

Even when paroled and exchanged, a prisoner had no assurance he would safely reach home—as illustrated by this letter to Mary Gaston of Monroe County, Tennessee. Her husband, Sgt. David Gaston of the 59th Mounted Tennessee Regiment, was among the Confederate troops who were surrendered and paroled at Vicksburg in 1863.

Coopers Well, Mississippi
September 12, 1863

Mrs. David Gaston:
Dear Madam:

Hard as it may be for me to pen these few lines to you, it is best you should know. It is in relation to your husband. He is of this world no more. But let it be a comfort to you to know that he died believing in his God. He prayed to God that he might see his wife and children before he died. He said he was happy and ready to go.

He was a paroled prisoner from Vicksburg and was on his way home, but being too ill to travel he stayed at my house in Byram. He was with us a week when he died on the 22nd of August at 6 o'clock P.M. We buried him in Byram about 10 miles below Jackson, Mississippi.

It may be gratifying to you to know that his last wants were attended to and everything was done to prolong his life, but of no avail. Some letters and papers which he had and a piece of his hair I cut, and if I ever have a chance I will send to you.

It is a sad office I have had to perform, but when you reflect how much better off he died than many a poor soldier on the battlefield, with no one to give them a little water, I know you will be comforted.

Hoping Madam, that you will receive this, I am yours respectfully.

Mrs. M. E. Jackson

Corp.Calvin H. Hill of the 26th South Carolina Infantry survived imprisonment at Point Lookout and was eventually reunited with his wife Harriet. Many Confederate POWs were not so fortunate.

"FATHER RAN TO MEET ME"

When freedom finally came, most Southern prisoners faced a long trek home to an uncertain future in a war-torn land. Still, if they were well enough to withstand the journey, most could look forward to a warm homecoming down South.

Georgia Confederate John Bowden emerged from Point Lookout relatively healthy and happily free. He left a terse memoir of his return home.

I got out of prison about twenty days before the surrender at Appomattox. I went on an old boat across the bay, and up the James River to Richmond. When I reached there I had on most of the same clothes I had worn for eight or ten months. The underclothing was pretty well worn out. I went at once to the quartermaster's department and drew some underclothes made of osnaburg. I put them on over the old ones, for it was very cold and sleeting. I went to the depot to take the first train that might leave for Georgia, the Confederate Government paying for my transportation.

Upon reaching the depot I came upon a boy about sixteen years of age whom I had never seen before. He was shivering, and seemed to be very cold. I said, "Son, what's the matter?" He replied, "I'm freezing." I said, "Why you seem to be as well clad as I am." "Maybe not," said he. I walked

Safely home and the center of attention.

coming toward Georgia. It was noised around among the soldiers that Richmond would surrender to the Federals within the next few hours. I was anxious to leave on the first train. . . .

As soon as the train stopped I went down with great haste, ran to the first empty boxcar and crawled into it. Stock had been hauled in it until it was a very undesirable place to ride, but it was much better than on top in the cold. We continued the ride during the night, nothing of special interest occuring. The sleet continued to fall, and the wind howled outside, and, though without any covering, I slept sweetly as we rode on through Dixie.

After going as far as the cars could carry us, the Yankees having torn up the railway tracks, we began a long march, and finally reached Washington, Georgia. From here we walked across country to Covington. Here we took the cars again for Atlanta, thence to Grantville, where I again walked across country, via Greenville, to my home.

My father and mother did not know that I would ever come home, for they had heard from me but once in six months. During this period throughout our land what must have been the anxious thoughts and watchful waiting of many a fond parent! The anxious father, as he went about his daily work, wondering if his brave soldier boy would ever return; for he feared that even then his bones might lie bleaching upon the field of battle. The tearful mother, as she lay upon her bed at night, prayed fervently that her boy might come home.

I shall never forget when I first came upon my Father. He was in the field at work, directing a number of his hands. Seeing who it was, Father ran to meet me, and caught me in his arms. . . .

up to him, pulled open his roundabout, and discovered he had on no shirt. I at once said, "Follow me." I carried him into a room at the depot, removed my new osnaburg shirt, and had him put it on. He went on his way trying to earn enough bread for his mother and her younger children. He told me his father was in the Confederate army. I was always glad I did this, though I had no other shirt left save the old, dirty ragged one I had worn so long.

A long freight train carrying cars in which stock had been hauled was about to leave Richmond

6

In Sherman's Path

Never had so great an army unleashed such devastation against so many Americans. From Atlanta to Savannah, and from Columbia, South Carolina, to central North Carolina, Gen. William T. Sherman's 62,000 battle-hardened troops cut a fiery, destructive swath across the heart of the South. When the terrible march ended, much of the Confederacy lay in smoldering ruins, and the South had been terrorized and ravaged on a scale never experienced elsewhere in America.

Today, for many Southerners, knowledge of Sherman's March is vague and impersonal, but Southerners who experienced it never forgot what it was like to be caught in Sherman's path.

The last train out of Atlanta stands ready to roll, its car piled high with the household goods of Atlanta's refugees.

"DEAR, DEAR ATLANTA!"

"I have deemed it to the interest of the United States that the citizens now residing in Atlanta should remove, those who prefer it to go South and the rest North." With this official proclamation Gen. William T. Sherman ordered the entire civilian population of Atlanta relocated, evacuated by Federal order.

Never before had an American military commander forcibly emptied such an important American city of its resident population, but nothing would change Sherman's mind: not pleas from Atlanta's citizenry nor protests from the Confederate government. He intended to destroy Atlanta's importance as a Southern supply and transportation center, and he deemed evacuation of the city to be a necessary first step.

Atlantans decried Sherman's edict and proclaimed him "the Nero of the nineteenth century," but the evacuation order was mandatory, and the city's residents began packing. Atlantans willing to leave the South would be provided free transportation to any Northern destination. Those unwilling to go north would be sent to a neutral location outside the city and passed under a flag of truce into Confederate lines. Atlanta would be abandoned.

The exodus soon began. The roads leaving the city eventually filled with refugees and their wagons, packed high with bureaus and bedding, cooking pots and family heirlooms—the salvaged belongings of a displaced people. At the city's railroad depot, Federal officers and railroad officials told many panicky refugees that each departing train would be the last, and thus solicited outrageous bribes in exchange for seating. After tearful farewells with relatives and friends, the refugees were wedged into overpacked trains, which carried them away from home toward uncertain futures.

Among Atlanta's dispossessed families, which included the old and the ill, nursing mothers, excited children, and pregnant women, was a Confederate officer's wife named Mary Rawson, who evacuated Atlanta with her parents and recorded the event in a wartime diary.

Thursday [September 8, 1864]

The order compelling all persons to evacuate the city was today plainly written out; we could not misunderstand it. All those whose husbands were in the service were to leave on Monday, while the remainder were given fifteen days to pack and leave.

Tuesday [September 13, 1864]

This morning Father concluded to go himself to see Gen. Sherman and ask if he could get a written order permitting him to sell his provisions.

About ten o'clock he came back bringing the papers signed by the General. Then came a long conversation with Mother which terminated in the resolve to brave the severities of the cold North West, so we immediately prepared to emigrate to the prairies of Iowa. We had no time to spare and now began the work of packing in earnest, and from morning till night we were running up and down stairs assisting Mother in her work.

Thursday [September 15, 1864]

The evening set in and this was to prove to be our last night in our dear sweet home. As I lay in bed long after all quiet, the house and cheerful paper on the wall seemed to find utterance and sorrowed audibly for their departing occupants. The entire room appeared [to talk]. I, said the wall, have many, many times protected you from the piercing wind and cold of the winter. And had it not been for me, said the roof, your bed would not have afforded you the comfort which it has been so many, many years. I have prevented the cold rain from trickling through and soaking both you and your property. So one by one the room and pieces of furniture gave vent to their feelings in words.

No, my loved home, never shall [I forget] the pleasant hours spent with friends and classmates before the open windows in summer . . . in winter the happy hours spent with kindred clustering around the cheerful fire. Oh, how bright will the meeting with kindred be if after this separation we ever again meet in the dear old home.

Friday [September 16, 1864]

Morning dawns. And as if in sympathy with our feelings the clouds shut out the genial light of the sun. A Capt. Seymore has just come and with him he has brought almost a regiment of Federal soldiers to sweep the yards. This they immediately proceed to accomplish while the Capt. hurried to and fro giving orders and receiving the furniture of Gen. Geary, for he has concluded to establish his headquarters on our hill. In front of the house

there is already a large tent stretched. After continued labor in the forenoon we finally made the last preparation on dressing preparatory to the journey. I found I had still a short time which would be unoccupied. This I determined to pass among the flowers.

So wandering among the familiar walks and beds. I gathered some favorite roses. But it was not long ere a call came from the house and recalled me from my reflections. Going in, I found Mr. Rawlings and Penny were there to bid us good-bye. And Charlotte had prepared supper in our little sitting room. This meal was partaken of in sadness and after it, everything was in confusion. The wagons had arrived and the baggage was being rapidly stowed away for transportation. Then came the parting from loved home servants and kindly associations. There was Mammy, who had been living with us since I can remember. Mother used to leave me in her care when I was a wee child and her kind ebony face looked down upon me then. Charlotte with her little ones around her tearfully shook my hand. There were many others with whom it proved a hard trial to part, and it shall be my earnest prayer that this shall not be a lasting separation, but if we are not allowed to meet again on earth may we join our voices together in singing praises to Him who has redeemed us in the mansion Jesus has gone to prepare for his children.

Taking a sad farewell from servants and friends, we seated ourselves in the ambulance which slowly moved out of the yard. In a few minutes we found ourselves on the hill on which stood our schoolhouse and from which a fine view of our place could be obtained. Never, never did this hill look so pleasant in the setting sun as it now did, and now as I looked upon the groups of oaks and hedges . . . I for the first time could appreciate the words of the song "the dearest spot of earth to me is home sweet home."

Dear, dear Atlanta! City of hills, with your bright blue sky, southern constellations, innumerable bright flowers and birds and clear sparkling water, your wells of which are never insufficient. When, oh when, shall I again tread your pavement and breathe your exhilarating atmosphere.

It seems so sad that our beautiful stores and the fine passenger depot, where so many gay companies of young persons on pleasure parties have been accomodated . . . and where so many poor sick soldiers have found shelter and kindness, should be leveled to the ground. Father goes right away to see about the car that had been promised us, but finds the train full and no box reserved. He now goes to the manager of the train and complains that he did not keep his word. He then said he would have one brought directly. We waited some half hour when we received the intelligence that the box was made fast to the train and they were storing the baggage in the two ends of it. Then we left the ambulance and walked under the shed.

The word was finally given for us to get on board, and one by one we were placed in our rough temporary home. There were ten of us, then came Mr. Andrew's family of six and lastly a little pet dog. Sixteen refugees in a box car. We were scarcely seated when the shrill whistle of the engine told us we were about leaving. Then, in a few seconds, we received a sudden jerk that nearly seated us on the floor. Then we went dashing and clattering along, and soon Atlanta and with it, home, was not distinguishable in the distance. . . .

"THE HEART WAS BURNING OUT OF BEAUTIFUL ATLANTA"

Sherman left Atlanta in flames. The city was the Deep South's most vital rail junction, and Sherman believed it was too important to leave intact in his rear. Officially, only the city's military resources were to be destroyed, but due either to the inability of the Northern officers to control their troops or to deliberate disregard of orders, much of Atlanta was gutted. It was a fiery omen for other Southern communities in Sherman's path. As the March to the Sea began, David P. Conyngham, a New York Herald *correspondent attached to the Federal army, reported the destruction of Atlanta.*

Sherman's orders were that Atlanta should be destroyed by the rearguard of the army, and two regiments were detailed for that purpose. Although the army, cantoned along the Chattanooga line of railroad towards Kingston and Marietta, did not pass through until the 16th, the first fire burst out on the night of Friday, the 11th of November, in a block of wooden tenements on Decatur Street, where eight buildings were destroyed.

Soon after, fires burst out in other parts of the city. These certainly were the work of some of the soldiers, who expected to get some booty under cover of the fires.

The fire engines were about to be shipped to Chattanooga, but were soon brought in, and brought to bear on the burning districts.

The patrol guards were doubled, and orders issued to shoot down any person seen firing buildings. Very little effort had been made to rescue the city from the devouring elements, for they knew that the fiat had gone forth consigning it to destruction. Over twenty houses were burned that night, and a dense cloud of smoke, like a funeral pall, hung over the ruins next morning.

General Slocum offered a reward of five hundred dollars for the apprehension of any soldier caught in the act of incendiarism. Though Slocum knew that the city was doomed, according to his just notions of things it should be done officially. No officer or soldier had a right to fire it without orders.

It was hard to restrain the soldiers from burning it down. With that licentiousness that characterizes an army, they wanted a bonfire.

The last train for Chattanooga left on Saturday night, November 12. Next morning, the 14th, 15th, and 17th corps commenced their march from Kingston and Marietta, where they had been resting ten days, while Sherman was making preparations for his new campaign. They destroyed Rome, Kingston, and Marietta, on their march, and tore up the track, setting on fire sleepers, railroad depots, and stores, back to the Etowah.

An immense amount of government property, which we could not transport to the rear or carry

Atlanta's railroad depot: reduced to smoldering rubble by Sherman's troops.

along with us, had been destroyed at the different depots. Coffee sacks, cracker boxes, sugar and pork barrels, bales of blankets and boxes of clothing were burst open and strewn about and burned. Soldiers were loaded with blankets and supplies, which they got tired of before night and flung away. It is said that about three million of dollars worth of property had been destroyed in this way.

On Sunday night a kind of long streak of light, like an aurora, marked the line of march and the burning stores, depots, and bridges in the train of the army.

The Michigan engineers had been detailed to destroy the depots and public buildings in Atlanta. Everything in the way of destruction was now considered legalized. The workmen tore up the rails and piled them on the smoking fires. Winship's iron foundry and machine shops were early set on fire. This valuable property was calculated to be worth about half a million of dollars.

An oil refinery nearby next got on fire and was soon in a fierce blaze. Next followed a freight warehouse, in which were stored several bales of cotton. The depot, turning-tables, freight sheds, and stores around, were soon a fiery mass. The heart was burning out of beautiful Atlanta.

The few people that had remained in the city fled, scared by the conflagration and the dread of violence.

Some ruffians ran with brands to fire the churches, which were considerably retired. The Roman Catholic minister, Father O'Reiley, who was the only minister that remained in town, met them and upbraided them for their impious sacrilege. Even these hardened men of war shrank before virtue and truth, and the good priest not only saved his own church, but also those of his fellow-Christians.

The Atlanta Hotel, Washington Hall, and all the square around the railroad depot, were soon in one sheet of flame. Drug stores, dry goods stores, hotels, negro marts, theatres, and grog shops were all now feeding the fiery element. Worn-out wagons and camp equipage were piled up in the depot and added to the fury of the flames.

A store warehouse was blown up by a mine. Quartermasters ran away, leaving large stores behind. The men plunged into the houses, broke windows and doors with their muskets, dragging out armfuls of clothes, tobacco, and whiskey, which was more welcome than all the rest. The men dressed themselves in new clothes and then flung the rest into the fire.

The streets were now in one fierce sheet of flame; houses were falling on all sides, and fiery flakes of cinders were whirled about. Occasionally shells exploded, and excited men rushed through the choking atmosphere, and hurried away from the city of ruins.

At a distance the city seemed overshadowed by a cloud of black smoke, through which, now and then, darted gushing flames of fire or projectiles hurled from the burning ruin. The sun looked, through the hazy cloud, like a blood-red ball of fire; and the air for miles around felt oppressive and intolerable. The Tyre of the south was laid in ashes, and the "Gate City" was a thing of the past.

"THE VANDALS LEFT SUFFERING AND DESOLATION"

A mighty fear swept across Georgia that November: Sherman's legions were coming, and terrible was their vengeance. Moving southeast across the state in two implacable wings, the 62,000 Federal troops quickly established the standard practices of the march, leaving twisted rails, blazing homes, and empty pantries in their wake.

An early target was Milledgeville, Georgia's capital. The city's defenders— youthful military school cadets and paroled convicts—were easily brushed aside by Sherman's veterans, who entered the capital on November 22, Milledgeville's railroad depot was destroyed, factories and warehouses were burned, and the state library was sacked. Then drunken Federal officers and troops held a mock session of the legislature in the Georgia Statehouse, which had been abandoned in panic by the real legislators.

Twenty-year-old Anna Maria Green lived in Milledgeville, where her father served as superintendent of the state asylum for the mentally ill. Although at this stage of the march Sherman's army generally behaved with a measure of restraint, Anna Maria's journal describes the fear awaiting a host of other Southerners.

Saturday evening November 19th—Again we are in a state of excitement caused by the near approach to our town of the enemy. Last night they were two thousand strong at Monticello. Cobb having ordered the cadets and other troops we had for local defence to Macon there to meet the yankees, Gov. Brown ordered the evacuation of Milledgeville, and today has been one of intense excitement, families moving and the cadets and the other troops. Minnie came in to call me to look at a fire in the west. My heart sank, and almost burst with grief as I beheld the horizon crimson and the desolation our hated foe was spreading. Great God! Deliver us, oh! Spare our city--Papa thinks the fire is Clinton, as that place was not burned before as we supposed. It may be.

Yesterday morning there was much excitement in the legislature. . . . The scene at the State

House was truly ridiculous, the members were badly scared. Such a body of representatives made my cheeks glow with shame—what a time it was too for the display of cool, wise, legislation, and undaunted courage and exalted patriotism. Instead of that, they passed a law levying troops in masse, excepting the legislature and judiciary. The

Carrying what they can, Southern civilians flee from Sherman's march.

men paid three thousand dollars for the conveyance to move with speed from this place of danger, when the enemy were approaching. They could [not] stand for the defence of their own capital.

Sister Mattie was at the depot this evening and saw Drs. Bell and Thomson leave and on another train, quite late, the cadets passed and one hundred and fifty convicts pardoned by the governor. Tomorrow will be Sunday, how I may spend it I now have little idea. No train arrived.

Nov. 25th Friday evening . . . Last Sunday morning dawned upon us amid excitement. There was no rest on Sunday—the day was forgotten, even so entirely that Fanny and Mary went after persimmons. Dr. Powell was going to Sparta. Mrs. P. was too unwell to go with him as she had expected and they were all here. About sunset

Olivia came running in from town excited and crying and said the yankees were in town. We then were terribly frightened and listened over and over again to her account and I ran to put on the bag of jewelry I had made in the morning. Olivia said there were five or six and gave a terrible account of them. There was little sleep for us that night. From twelve to three I sat in Aunty's room. She and Dr. Powell, Brother Charley and Papa had been engaged all night hiding valuables. They had buried our silver service and plate beneath the reservoir on the Avenue.

Monday we saw nothing of the yankees and almost concluded the men seen Sunday were deserters. However, on Tuesday William Cotting brought intelligence of their arrival in reality, and soon after five horsemen dashed up to the gate creating no little excitement. Papa went out to meet them and expressed a desire to see their commanding officer. They told him General [Slocum's] headquarters were at the Capital Square. Papa went in at once to see him. He treated him very gentlemanly and volunteered a guard for the institution.

All day Wednesday they were here in crowds and the asylum would have suffered much loss of property but for the efficiency of one of our guards, a Mr. Evelyn. Thursday we had another guard, but before they reached us some of them had taken two of the mules, we think at the instigation of Tom, who had gone to them.

This morning the last of the vandals left our city and burned the bridge after them—leaving suffering and desolation behind them, and embittering every heart. The worst of their acts was committed to poor Mrs. Nichols—violence done, and atrocity committed that ought to make her husband an enemy unto death. Poor woman. I fear she has been driven crazy. Nearly every family has [lost] all their provisions and the poor are left I fear to perish.

"WE LOOKED OUT UPON A SCENE OF DESOLATION AND RUIN"

By the time they left Milledgeville, if not sooner, Sherman's troops knew their officers would make little attempt to restrict destruction merely to railroads, military factories, and Confederate stores. Instead, every family living on Sherman's route was a potential target. Bands of foragers, known as Sherman's Bummers, scoured the countryside for livestock and foodstuff for the army, stripping the land and its people of all sustenance within reach—and anything else they wanted.

Even worse were the hordes of common soldiers intent on booty. Some Federals displayed military discipline, and a few even defended helpless civilians and their property, but marauders were legion. Unrestricted plundering was commonplace and wanton vandalism was widespread. Georgians living in Sherman's way suffered terrors generally unknown to civilians in the North.

Nora M. Canning, wife of a Georgia judge, watched the blue-clad army swarm over the family plantation, which lay midway between Milledgeville and Savannah.

About the 24th of November we heard that Sherman's army was in possession of Milledgeville and was on its way to Savannah, burning and destroying everything in its course. Our home being directly on the wagon road from Milledgeville to Savannah, we of course expected them to lay everything in ashes that they could find.

On Sunday, the 28th of November, we heard that the destroyers were encamped just above our upper plantation, about four miles from our home. That night the heavens looked as if they were on fire from the glare of hundreds of burning houses. About noon, just as we were ready to sit down to dinner, a little negro boy came running in half breathless from fright.

"Marster," he cried, "dey's coming down de lane."

"Who is coming?" asked his master.

"Two white man's wid blue coats on," the little negro answered.

Hundreds of the "Bluecoats" could be seen everywhere. One could not look in any direction without seeing them. They searched every place. Some of the men insisted that my husband should go down to the swamp with them to show them where some syrup was hidden. He told them he was old and feeble and was not able to walk so far. One of them thereupon went and brought a mule to put him on it and three of them started with him to the swamp.

While my husband was absent the destroyers set fire to the ginhouse, in which were stored over two hundred bales of cotton and several bales of kersey, which we had hidden between the bales of cotton. The granary, in which were several hundred bushels of wheat, was also set on fire.

One man, who had been particularly insulting, came up to me and laughed harshly. "Well, madam," he said, sneeringly, "how do you like the looks of our little fire? We have seen a great many such within the last few weeks."

Just then I saw my husband coming up on a bareback mule with a Yankee soldier on each side of him holding him on. He was brought up to the

Sherman's Bummers sack a plantation on the line of march.

piazza, lifted from the mule and brought into the house. They took him into a small room and I followed. He turned to me and requested me to give the men his watch.

"Why?" I asked. "They have no business with your watch."

"Give it to them," he repeated with a gasp, "and let them go. I am almost dead."

I got my husband to his room as soon as possible. Imagine my horror, when he revived sufficiently to talk, to hear that the fiends had taken him to the swamp and hanged him. He said he suspected no harm until he got about two miles from the house when they stopped the mule, and said, "Now, old man, you have got to tell us where your gold is hidden." He told them he had no gold. They cursed him and told him that story would not do, then they said they had brought him to the swamp to make him tell where it was. He repeated his first statement, and told them he had no gold. They then took him to a tree that bent over the path, tied a rope around his neck, threw it over a projecting limb and drew him up until his feet were off the ground. He did not quite lose consciousness when they let him down and said: "Now, where is your gold?" He told them the same story, whereupon they raised him up again, and that time, he said, he felt as if he was suffocating. They again lowered him to the ground and cried out fiercely: "Now, tell us where that gold is or we will kill you, and your wife will never know what has become of you." "I have told you the truth. I have no gold," he again repeated. "I have a gold watch at the house but nothing else."

They then lifted him up and let him fall with more force than before. He heard a sound as of water rushing through his head and then a blindness came over him, and a dry choking sensation was felt in his throat as he lost consciousness. . . . When he was able to sit up they placed him upon the mule and brought him to the house to get his watch.

Oh! the horror of that night! None but God will ever know what I suffered. There my husband lay with scorching fever, his tongue parched and swollen and his throat dry and sore. He begged for water and there was not a drop to be had. The Yankees had cut all the well ropes and stolen the buckets, and there was no water nearer than half a mile.

Saturday morning we looked out upon a scene of desolation and ruin. We could hardly believe it was our home. One week before it was one of the most beautiful places in the state. Now it was a vast wreck. Gin-houses, packing screws, granary— all lay in ashes. Not a fence was to be seen for miles. The corn crop had not been gathered, and the army had turned their stock into the fields and destroyed what they had not carried off. Burning cotton and grain filled the air with smoke, and even the sun seemed to hide its face from so gloomy a picture.

I remember well the distress of one of the negro women. She was sitting on her doorsteps swaying her body back and forth. . . and making a mournful noise, a kind of moaning, a low sorrowful sound, occasionally wringing her hands and crying out. As we approached her, she raised her head.

"Marster," she said, rolling her eyes strangely, "What kind of folks dese here Yankees? Dey won't even let de dead rest in de grave."

"What do you mean?" he asked.

"You know my chile what I bury last week? Dey take em up and left em on top of de groun for de hog to root. What you tink of dat, sir?"

Her story was true. We found that the vandals had gone to the graveyard and, seeing a new-made grave, had dug down into it and taken up the little coffin containing a dead baby, no doubt supposing treasure had been buried there. When they discovered their mistake, they left it above ground, as the poor mother had expressed it, "for the hog to root."

We soon discovered that almost everything we had hidden had been found, and either carried off or wantonly destroyed. All around the grove were carcasses of cows, sheep, and hogs, some with only the hind quarters gone and the rest left to spoil. There were piles of carcasses all around where the army had camped. Some of them had been killed and left without being touched. The question of getting anything to eat was a very serious one. The stores were all burned, not one being left within thirty-five miles. The mills were all destroyed, or partially so, railroads were torn up, bridges broken, all our stock carried off and our fences burned. There seemed to be nothing left to live on during the winter. Oh! the first of December, 1864, is indelibly impressed upon my mind.

"MADE TO FEED THE FLAMES"

Sherman's soldiers cheered when they entered South Carolina. It was February of 1865, and the march-hardened veterans had fulfilled Sherman's promise to "make Georgia howl." They called South Carolina "the hellhole of Secession," and they intended to make South Carolinians suffer even more than the citizens of Georgia.

"We can punish South Carolina as she deserves," Sherman had vowed. "I almost tremble for her fate, but feel she deserves all that seems in store for her."

What was in store for the Palmetto State was destruction unimagined by even the most fearful of the state's residents. Sherman's 62,000 troops were opposed by a drastically inferior Confederate force unable to mount a serious defense; and in little more than a month, Sherman's army turned much of the state into ashes. Later that year, after the war ended, Northern journalist John Townsend Trowbridge inspected South Carolina and described the desolation he found.

No language can describe, nor can any catalogue furnish, an adequate detail of the wide-spread destruction of homes and property. Granaries were emptied, and where the grain was not carried off, it was strewn to waste under the feet of the cavalry, or consigned to the fire which consumed the dwelling. The negroes were robbed equally with the whites of food and clothing. The roads were covered with butchered cattle, hogs, mules, and the costliest furniture. Valuable cabinets and rich pianos were not only hewn to pieces, but bottles of ink, turpentine, oil, whatever could efface or destroy, were employed to defile and ruin. Horses were ridden into the houses. People were forced from their beds to permit the search after hidden treasures.

The beautiful homesteads of the parish country, with their wonderful tropical gardens, were ruined; ancient dwellings of black cypress, one hundred years old, which had been reared by the fathers of the Republic, men whose names were famous in Revolutionary history, were given to the torch as

Sherman's army moves onward, leaving the South Carolina village of McPhersonville in flames.

recklessly as were the rude hovels. Choice pictures and works of art from Europe, select and numerous libraries, objects of peace wholly, were all destroyed. The inhabitants, black no less than white, were left to starve, compelled to feed only upon the garbage to be found in the abandoned camps of the soldiers. The corn scraped up from the spots where the horses fed has been the only means of life left to thousands but lately in affluence. The villages of Buford's Bridge, of Barnwell, Blackville, Graham's, Bamberg, Midway, were more or less destroyed; the inhabitants everywhere were left homeless and without food. The horses and mules, all cattle and hogs, whenever fit for service or for food were carried off, and the rest shot. Every implement of the workman or the farmer, tools, ploughs, hoes, gins, looms, wagons, vehicles, was made to feed the flames.

"A VISIT FROM THE FIRE FIENDS"

The frightening news of Sherman's approach usually preceded his army. Those living on his expected line of march had to decide whether to remain at home or flee. Leaving might be safer, but might ensure destruction: Sherman's soldiers were especially quick to fire deserted houses, owned, they assumed, by ardent Confederates trying to dodge the Federal army.

Southerners who chose to face the enemy sometimes managed to save their homes from the torch, but almost certainly had to undergo an ordeal of terror. Among the first South Carolinians to experience the horrors of Sherman's March were the citizens of little Barnwell, located near the Georgia state line. This letter from an anonymous Barnwell resident described the trial many South Carolinians would soon undergo.

Barnwell C. H.

My Dear Tody:

Can I possibly picture to you all the horrors we have undergone since I last wrote you? I will try, for I know your dear heart is bleeding to hear from the home folks, and of course you have seen from the papers that Sherman's men have been here. What that means, dear child, you cannot know without feeling it as we have.

On the first of this month they entered the village, and of course we could not hope to miss them, but our house being so far away from the main road we did half hope they might pass by. Of course most of the negroes on the place just took short leave when the Yankees came near, but Delia and Ann remained true to the end. It was at the suggestion of the latter that I stored quite a supply of meat, corn and potatoes in the loft over our bed-rooms. I had very little idea that the provisions would be safe there, but concluded that one place would suit about as well as another and even allowed Ann to take up a lot of bedding and some of our old family silverware. When the things were all satisfactorily put away she came down and told me she was "not done yet." She lighted a huge fat splinter and holding it close to the aperture smoked the edges all around.

When asked her idea for this freak, she replied, "Why, Missis, ain't you see de big tags of smoke that is settled on de edges? Dey wont tink anybody been frough dere lately."

I smiled, for I had heard of them digging four or five feet under some freshly stirred earth, in the belief that valuables had been buried there, and I did not think that Ann's trick would stop them. Here we were, three helpless women, and four

On the march, Sherman's "fire fiends" camp in a Carolina pine forest.

little frightened children clinging to us and every moment expecting to see that avalanche of terror sweep down on us. You may imagine that we did not sleep much those four nights following, and we all huddled together in my room, half crying as we talked in whispers of them.

Then the beautiful Sabbath sun rose on our still troubled vision. This day, the holy day of days, was to be desecrated by those brutal creatures called men. We had just risen from our hastily gotten breakfast when Ann came running to us. "Oh! Missis, dey is comin', sure enough."

Our first impulse was to flee, but we thought of our old home, which would certainly be burned did we leave it, and so we stood there, the children crying and Delia and Ann trying to quiet them, while Addie, Lizzie and I stood silently waiting the entrance of the men. We could now very plainly hear their heavy tread and an occasional loud, coarse laugh, followed by a general uproar. Then we heard the short, sharp bark of little Fido and Carlo's low growl, but in an instant both were hushed, two sharp pistol reports followed the last growl as the faithful dogs bounded forward only to fall in their tracks, dead. A horrible oath rang out as the brutes entered the yard and came to the house.

I don't know how they came in, but in a

moment the whole house was full of the dirtiest, most villainous set of men it has ever been my lot to see. "Look here, madam, we want a hot breakfast! Quick, too!" said a man who seemed to be the leader of the mob. Ann was up in a moment hurrying to help Delia with the meal, while the men were going into every room searching bureaus, closets and trunks with a vim.

I was glad to learn that breakfast was to be prepared only for the head men, and hoped they would leave us enough for dinner. In this I was disappointed, however, as the other wretches completely cleared out the smokehouse and pantry. They stored all they could carry on their wagons, and then seeing that a good deal was left they destroyed it, breaking open a large barrel of syrup and letting it run on the ground and scattering the corn and the rice so that it could not be gathered. They shot a great many of the chickens and the rest they carried off. Of course they took the two horses. They also burned the stable and the fodderhouse.

We, of course, then expected they would burn the dwelling house, but one of the most decent-looking officers told us they would spare the house, as we had not "sassed" them. When the men had eaten, Ann and Delia came in to us and stayed by us all the time. We all went into my room and closed the door. A moment after a brute pushed it open, with the injunction, "Let that d——d door stay open. We want no secret conferences here."

Then another one came in and took the bed covering away, and a third seeing the aperture, remarked that "something might be up there," and three or four advanced into the room. This aroused Ann's temper and she gave them her mind.

"I 'clar," she said. "I nebber een my life seen such a ting. . . . Yes, climb up een de loft ef you wants to, en you'll clean de place of smoke en spider web, anyhow. Put dat table here, Delia, en

let's help dese white gentlemen to git de rats outen de loft."

Ann's tirade had the desired effect, and glancing up at the smoked edges one remarked that "nothing had been through there lately," and went out, leaving Ann triumphant. It was late in the evening before they left us, and we heard their wagons rumbling down the avenue and saw the last straggling couple disappear we only thought then to look around at the wreck they had made.

Poor old Carlo lay dead between the house and gate and Fido, also stiff and cold, lay under the jessamine bush close by. Not a solitary chicken was to be seen, they having shot all they could not catch. We had a fine sow and six pigs in a pen near the barn. The sow they carried off and the pigs, being very young, they killed with an axe right in the pen. You don't know how pitiful it looked to see those poor little creatures butchered up just for spite. Outside the smokehouse door lay a great puddle of black stuff, which we saw was the hogshead of syrup they had broken open, and being fearful that we might be able to gather some of it, had afterwards taken a hoe and throughly mixed in dirt with it. From the kitchen they had taken every utensil except an old one-legged oven and a frying pan.

When we re-entered the house we went from room to room, finding them almost bare. In one of the bedrooms, the mattress was gone, the feather bed cut open and the feathers piled on the floor, the mirror smashed and the door broken from its hinges. In another the bedstead was destroyed, and some of the furniture cut into by axes, completely ruining it, of course. In the parlor the pictures were either broken or stolen, and the furniture defaced, and some of it completely destroyed. The dining-room was bare and desolate with the exception of the table and a broken dish. This is a mere shadow of the desolation we saw that day.

I hope dear Tody, you will not have a visit from the fire fiends.

"THE BEDS WERE ON FIRE"

Specifically targeted by Sherman's forces was the property of prominent Confederates. In South Carolina, state leaders who had signed the 1860 Ordinance of Secession found their homes to be especially vulnerable.

As Sherman's army approached Columbia in February of 1865, a detachment of Federal troops came to destroy nearby Pinarea, the country home of South Carolinian Paul Quattlebaum, a brigadier general in the state militia and a signer of the Ordinance. Quattlebaum was away in service, so his wife and children had to deal with the invaders. Quattlebaum's grandson and namesake, Dr. Paul Quattlebaum, later recorded how the family home was set ablaze— and saved.

Pinarea was out of the line of march, but the people at home felt uneasy. Bombardment of Columbia could be heard even at that distance. Grandma knew that Wheeler's Cavalry that had been in the neighborhood was falling back before the might of Sherman's Army. Musketry could be heard to the south. Wagons were loaded with valuables and supplies and directed to drive north.

Not being in the line of march did not save the place. A detachment of soldiers, under the command of a major, was sent to burn the house. As they came down the lane, they met an old negro woman and asked if any "Rebels" had been there. She did not understand what they meant, so they asked if any Confederate soldiers had been there. She replied, "Yes, some have just left."

They rode on into the spacious backyard. Standing on the back steps to the house was a negro boy. The first Yankee soldier to ride up threw him his reins and told him to hold the horse. Each man in the outfit did likewise, so the boy was left holding the reins of all the horses.

The men scattered throughout the house. The children were all playing on the floor in the parlor. A soldier stuck his head in the door and with a deep down eastern voice demanded, "Where are the folks?" Seeing only children, he slammed the door behind him.

The children all ran for the previously prepared

hideout in the woods. That is, all except my father, Perry, then a young boy. When he reached the back porch, he met an officer, whom he addressed as captain, though he later learned from a description of his insignia that he was a major. He said, "Captain, there are only women and children here. Don't burn the house." The officer patted him on the head and said, "No son, we will not burn the house."

The same officer met my grandmother and asked her if any "Rebels" had been there. She gave him the same answer the old negro woman had given him: "Yes, some have just left." She purposely said "some." The fact was, that morning three of Gen. Wheeler's men had stopped there. Grandma had fed them and had given them supplies for their saddlebags. She had gladly fed for several days Gen. Wheeler's men who had come her way. She had also given them food for their horses.

The table was set for dinner. One Yankee soldier went around the table and gathered up all the silver. Another was sacking the sideboard. Grandma called him to wait that she would unlock the door. Instead he slammed his boot through the panel and smashed the mahogany door.

It was a cold February day in 1865. Fire was in the fireplaces throughout the house. The major went from bedroom to bedroom, took a stick of word to the boy holding the horses: "Yankees," which sent the boy running for the woods. Believing the child had been sent to alert nearby Confederate cavalry, the officer commanded his men to mount. One soldier who had been busy with his loot said, "What's the hurry?" The officer stamped his foot on the floor and yelled, "I command you to mount." They all mounted and rode off.

The beds were on fire. My father ran to the negro quarter and called for help. Help came running—men and women. The beds, though blazing, were carried out of the house.

Grandma said to Martin, a fine young negro. "I saw them carry fire upstairs and they did not bring it back." Martin ran up the stairs and opened the first door he came to. A cloud of smoke came out. He slammed the door shut, filled his lungs with fresh air, ran through the room and butted the window out. He again caught a breath of air, grabbed the bed in his arms, and down the stairs he went. He did not stop until he threw the blazing bed in the millpond a short distance from in front of the house. By the heroic work of all under the direction of my father, then only a lad, and the direction of Grandma, a frail little woman, the house was saved.

Nor did the squad of Yankee troops escape without casualty. They were met by an outfit of Confederate troops and one Federal soldier was killed in the skirmish that ensued. This also meant that Grandma's flour mill, evidently on the list to be burned, escaped the Yankee torch.

Militia general Paul Quattlebaum: His signature on South Carolina's Ordinance of Secession made his home a special target.

firewood from each fire, placed it in the bed, and pulled the cover over the blazing log. Grandma protested, but he cursed her and rudely pushed her aside saying that he could run his own business.

Grandma went to the back porch and said one

"YOUR CITY IS DOOMED"

As they marched into Columbia, the soldiers of Sherman's army sang a corrupt version of "Hail, Columbia":

> *Hail Columbia, Happy land*
> *If I don't burn you, I'll be damned.*

Gracefully rising from a high bluff over the Congaree River, Columbia was a young city compared to venerable Charleston. It had been established seventy-

nine years earlier as South Carolina's capital. Wide, shady streets, named for Revolutionary War heroes, led to a high hill at the center of the city, where an impressive new statehouse was under construction.

Gusting winds were sweeping the city on February 17, 1865, as Sherman's army entered Columbia unopposed. Mayor T. J. Goodwyn met the enemy troops at river's edge, officially surrendered the city, and requested protection for its inhabitants and property.

"Go home and rest assured that your city will be as safe in my hands as if you had controlled it," Sherman told the anxious official. That evening Columbia was in flames. During the day's widespread plundering of the city's stores, the Federals had discovered and consumed plentiful stocks of liquor. After dark, gangs of soldiers—many of them drunk—roamed the city streets, waving firebrands, kicking in doors, smashing windows, and setting fire to homes and businesses. Fanned by the strong winds and fed by a large quantity of abandoned cotton, the conflagration gutted the city. By morning, most of Columbia was rubble and ashes.

Sherman publicly blamed Columbia's destruction on Confederate Gen. Wade Hampton, whose cavalry, Sherman claimed, had fired cotton bales left in the city streets as they retreated. Years later, Sherman admitted he had accused Hampton falsely, hoping to discredit the general.

"Though I never ordered it and never wished it," Sherman eventually testified, "I have never shed any tears over the event, because I believe it hastened what we all fought for, the end of the war." Despite his disclaimers, Sherman was responsible for the burning of Columbia, argued the victims of the flames, who recalled their night of horror to Northern journalist John Townsend Trowbridge.

Early in the evening [of February 17] as the inhabitants, quieted by General Sherman's assurances, were about retiring to their beds, a rocket went up in the lower part of the city. Another in the center, and a third in the upper part of town, succeeded. Dr. R. W. Gibbes was in the street near one of the Federal guards, who exclaimed on seeing the signals, "My God! I pity your city!" Mr. Goodwyn, who was mayor at the time, reports a similar remark from an Iowa soldier. "Your city is doomed! These rockets are the signal!" Immediately afterwards fires broke out in twenty different places.

The dwellings of Confederate Treasury Secretary George A. Trenholm and General Wade Hampton were among the first to burst into flames. Soldiers went from house to house, spreading the conflagration. Fireballs, composed of cotton saturated with turpentine, were thrown in at doors and windows. Many houses were entered and fired by means of combustible liquids poured upon beds and clothing, ignited by wads of burning cotton, or by matches from a soldier's pocket. The fire department came out in force, but the hose-pipes were cut to pieces and the men driven from the streets. At the same time universal plundering and robbery began.

The burning of the house of Dr. R. W. Gibbes, an eminent physician, well-known to the scientific world, was thus described to me by his son: "He had a guard at the front door; but some soldiers climbed in at the rear of the house, got into the parlor, heaped together sheets, poured turpentine over them, piled chairs on them, and set them on fire. As he remonstrated with them, they laughed at him. The guard at the front door could do nothing, for if he left his post, other soldiers would come in that way.

"The guard had a disabled foot, and my father had dressed it for him. He appeared very grateful for the favor, and earnestly advised my father to save all his valuables. The house was full of costly paintings, and curiosities of art and natural history, and my father did not know what to save and what to leave behind. He finally tied up in a bedquilt a quantity of silver and gems. As he was going out the door the house was already on fire behind him—the guard said, 'Is that all you can save?' 'It is all I can well carry,' said my father. 'Leave that with me,' said the guard; 'I will take charge of it, while you go back and get another bundle.' My father thought he was very kind. He went back for another bundle, and while he was gone, the guard ran off on his lame leg with all the gems and silver.''

The soldiers, in their march through Georgia, and thus far into South Carolina, had a wonderful skill in finding treasures. They had two kinds of

Columbia, South Carolina, as it appeared the morning after Sherman's arrival.

"divining-rods," negroes and bayonets. What the unfaithful servants of the rich failed to reveal, the other instruments, by thorough and constant practice, were generally able to discover. On the night of the fire, a thousand men could be seen in the yards and gardens of Columbia by the glare of the flames, probing the earth with bayonets. "Not one twentieth part of the articles buried in this city escaped them," Mr. Gibbes assured me.

The dismay and terror of the inhabitants can scarcely be conceived. They had two enemies, the fire in their house and the soldiery without. Many who attempted to bear away portions of their goods were robbed by the way. Trunks and bundles were snatched from the hands of hurrying fugitives, broken open, rifled, and then hurled into the flames. Ornaments were plucked from the necks and arms of ladies, and caskets from their hands. Even children and negroes were robbed.

Fortunately the streets of Columbia were broad, else many of the fugitives must have perished in the flames which met them on all sides. The exodus of homeless families, flying between walls of fire, was a terrible and piteous spectacle. Some fled to the parks; others to the open ground without the city; numbers sought refuge in the graveyards. Isolated and unburned dwellings were crowded to excess with fugitives.

Three-fifths of the city in bulk, and four-fifths in value, were destroyed. The loss of property is estimated at thirty millions. No more respect seems to have been shown for buildings commonly deemed sacred, than for any others. The churches were pillaged, and afterwards burned. St. Mary's College, a Catholic institution, shared their fate. The Catholic Convent, to which had been confided for safety many young ladies, not nuns, and stores of treasure, was ruthlessly sacked. The soldiers drank the sacramental wine, and profaned with fiery draughts of vulgar whiskey the goblets of the communion services. Some went off reeling under the weight of priestly robes, holy vessels and candlesticks.

Not even the Masonic and Odd Fellows lodges were spared. Afterwards tipsy soldiers were seen about the streets dressed up in regalias of these orders. The sword of state, belonging to the Grand Lodge of South Carolina, a massive, curious, two-edged weapon of considerable antiquity, was among the objects stolen.

Yet the army of Sherman did not in its wildest orgies forget its splendid discipline. "When will these horrors cease?" asked a lady of an officer at her house. "You will hear the bugles at sunrise," he replied; "then they will cease, and not till then." He prophesied truly. "At daybreak, on Saturday morning," said Gibbes, "I saw two men galloping through the streets, blowing horns. Not a dwelling was fired after that; immediately the town became quiet."

Some curious incidents occurred. One man's treasure, concealed by his garden fence, escaped the soldiers' divining-rods, but was afterwards discovered by a hitched horse pawing the earth from the buried box. Some hidden guns had defied the most diligent search, until a chicken, chased by a soldier ran into a hole beneath the house. The soldier, crawling after and putting in his hand for the chicken, found the guns.

A soldier, passing in the streets and seeing some children playing with a beautiful little greyhound, amused himself by beating its brains out. Some treasures were buried in cemeteries, but they did not always escape the search of the soldiers, who showed a strong distrust of new-made graves.

Of the desolation and horrors our army left behind it, no description can be given. Here is a single instance: At a factory on the Congaree, just out of Columbia, there remained for six weeks a pile of sixty-five dead horses and mules, shot by Sherman's men. It was impossible to bury them, all the shovels, spades, and other farming implements of the kind having been carried off or destroyed.

Columbia must have been a beautiful city, judging by its ruins. The streets were broad and well shaded. Many fine residences still remain on the outskirts, but the entire heart of the city is a wilderness of crumbling walls, naked chimneys, and trees killed by the flames. The fountains of the desolated gardens are dry, the basins cracked; the pillars of the houses are dismantled, or overthrown; the marble steps are broken. All these attest to the wealth and elegance which one night of fire and orgies sufficed to destroy.

"HELL ON EARTH"

"No pen can adequately depict the horrors of the burning of Columbia," recalled a victim of the blaze. "Every hearthstone was an altar on which the Yankees sacrificed to their gods—Vengeance and Hatred. . . ."

Generation after generation would arise and pass away before the terrible legacy of that cataclysmic night in February would soften and become dim history for South Carolinians. The personal tragedy that befell numerous Columbia residents was preserved in an unsigned letter written by a survivor to her daughter soon after Sherman's army left the devastated capital.

Columbia March 3, 1865

My dear Gracia

Doubtless your anxiety is very great to hear something about us after the great calamity that has befallen our town. We have lost everything, but thank God, our lives have been spared. Oh Gracia, what we have passed through no tongue can tell, it defies description! Such a scene as was witnessed on the day and night of 17 February. God grant that we may never see the like again!

The enemy entered the city about nine o'clock in the morning; passed our street about ten, and at dark were still passing. The first regiment sent into the city was what Sherman calls his "Tigers." Whenever he sends these men ahead, he intends to do his worst. He says he would not be afraid to go to the lower region with this regiment in the lead. They had the toes of their boots covered with steel and would kick in the strongest locks.

The first thing they did was break open the stores and distribute the goods right and left. They found liquor and all became heartily drunk. The very elements seemed to conspire against us, for the wind blew a perfect gale. Bags of cotton were cut open in the streets and the wind carried it even into the trees. The streets looked as if they were covered with snow. When night came on, the soldiers went about with matches, turpentine and cotton, with which they fired the houses. It was a fearful sight, in whatever direction you turned your eyes, they met the flaming fire. At one time I thought there was no way of escape left for us—we seemed to be enveloped on every side. About nine o'clock I took your Grandmother to Mrs. Bronson's. I returned to try to save something. When I got back the fire had nearly reached the house, and all that I saved was three blankets, a comforter and a bundle of clothes, scarcely a change for each. Charley Pinckney's trunk was rifled and all his clothes taken. Everything in the way of provisions is gone. While I was getting some things out of a trunk, there were three men in the room rifling another, but I felt no fear, tho' alone. One Yankee was burned to death on our own lot. I can compare that night to nothing but hell on earth, yet I walked back and forth without the slightest fear.

We stayed all night in the street, protected by a Yankee Captain from Iowa who was very kind to us. He carried my bundle on his back, and about twelve next day we moved to the Seminary, where there were fourteen of us, white and black, in one room. Your sister saved a feather bed on which we laid the children, but we did not take off

When Sherman's troops left Columbia, the heart of South Carolina's capital was a wasteland.

our clothes from Thursday till the following Wednesday. All day Sunday they were playing the fiddle outside our window, where they were encamped and the full band was playing at Geri Preston's, just opposite. Such a Sabbath! We had nothing to eat but a little meal and rice. Mary said to one of the soldiers, "All our provisions have been burned, and are we to starve?" He took up a stone and struck a pig nearby, then cut its throat and gave it to her, saying "You shall have something to eat, take that." We had it cooked, and it lasted two days. We are now drawing rations, and Mr. Windsor offered to share with us meat, flour, clothes and offered us a house which he owns. What kindness!

I saved our watches by wearing them in a quilted belt about my person, but carrying the silver almost broke me down. Many persons have lost all their silver, watches and jewelry. Mrs. Frazier lost everything, even her thimble and spectacles and Mrs. Hughes' wedding ring was taken from her! Mrs. J. L. was taken sick at D. H.'s—was confined, and died on the floor without ever having her clothes taken off. Mrs. Robinson, Mrs. Heyward and three gentlemen were all that followed her to the grave.

We have two rooms on the first floor of the seminary. What we are to do for clothes I know not, but God will provide. Rich and poor are drawing rations alike. There is not a house left on Marion Street. The new State House is standing but all the work which was ready to put up is destroyed. I cannot be too thankful you were not here—and your father and brothers also.

Your ever affectionate
Mother

"AUNT PENNY RAIDED THE YANKEES"

When Sherman's army passed, it was usually trailed by swelling ranks of Contraband—slaves who ran away from their masters to join "Mr. Lincoln's Army." Many never returned. Others, bewildered by their newfound liberty or unnerved by unfamiliar surroundings, eventually drifted back home. Some made no attempt to join Sherman's forces, and at least a few boldly defended their owners.

When Sherman's troops raided the MacQueen plantation near the South Carolina hamlet of Cheraw, the head of the house, Lt. Alexander MacQueen, was away in Confederate service. Left to face Sherman's dreaded torch bearers were MacQueen's wife, Marjory, a handful of small children, and a slave nursemaid named Aunt Penny, who provided unexpected assistance.

MacQueen's granddaughter, Alexia Marlowe, described the day the Yankees came.

Grandpa's home was a beautiful old house about five miles from Cheraw on Cabin Branch. The house had immense pillars, dormer windows, high ceilings, and a wide hall extending from the front door to back door. The kitchen was set apart from the house and meals were cooked in the kitchen and brought into the house on large silver trays.

Grandpa was not yet back from the war, so Grandma Marjory MacFarlan MacQueen gave the orders. Meat was placed in a lined box and secreted in a hole nearby with a generous cover of pinestraw. Valuables were hidden between the box-lined hedges and under the high back porch—the children's playhouse—then the chickens were turned in to leave tracks in the sand. The overseer went with two horses and a cow to the swamps.

And then the Yankees came.

Grandma was told to get out of the house with the children because the house was to be burned. Grandma was from Scotland, and she replied, "I am still a sovereign subject of Great Britain and you would have to answer to them."

They didn't burn the house, but just for meanness one soldier stuck a lighted candle under my Uncle Johnny's nose—he was just a little boy.

Attired in turban and white apron, Aunt Penny holds one of the MacQueen children on her lap.

Grandpa and Grandma were good to their servants—Grandma taught the children to read—and most of the servants stayed loyal. But some just went crazy and told of the hidden meat. The Yankees found the meat and took it all, and they also took everything out of Grandpa's pantry—the flour and sugar and all. Then they went out in the yard and poked their sabers in the ground, looking for valuables. They found one big silver tray that had been buried, but they did not find the other valuables.

On their tour of the house they slashed a large painting of Grandma's father hanging in the parlor. They also cut places in the velvet drapes and slashed places on the Brussels carpet.

While the Yankees were chasing and killing the chickens and the turkeys, Mama's nursemaid, dear old black Aunt Penny, went out and raided the Yankees' collection of stolen things. The family loved Aunt Penny. She had looked after all the children, and she was so loyal. She always wore a big white apron and she came back with an apron full of things the Yankees had taken from the pantry. It's a wonder they didn't catch her, but they were busy with the fowls.

They shot all the chickens and turkeys and took them with them when they left. They took everything that had not been taken to the swamp. The only livestock saved were the two horses and the cow that the overseer had taken to the swamp. Later on a hen which had a nest in the swamp arrived with her little biddies in the rear. That furnished the family with chicken. That old hen was the only one the Yankees didn't get. Besides that, all that was left was what Aunt Penny had gotten back from the Yankees.

"A RECKLESS DEMON . . . READY FOR ANY ATROCITY"

Sherman's March kindled special fears for Southern women. Among the horror stories whispered nervously throughout Georgia and the Carolinas was the rumored mistreatment of Southern women by Sherman's soldiers. In nineteenth-century America, rape was a relatively uncommon crime, even among the worst plunderers of Sherman's throng. Yet it did occur—especially among the female slaves along Sherman's route. Tragically, an unknown number of black women, including some of those who cheered Sherman's army as liberators, were victimized by brutal, undisciplined Federal soldiers.

After Sherman's army had left his area, Dr. Daniel Heyward Trezevant, a prominent Columbia physician, penciled a brief report of what most Southerners discussed only in hushed confidence. His account:

The Yankees' gallantry, brutality and debauchery were afflicted on the negroes. . . . The case of Mr. Shane's old negro woman, who, after being subjected to the most brutal indecency from seven of the Yankees, was, at the proposition of one of them to "finish the old Bitch," put into a ditch and held under water until life was extinct. . . .

Mrs. T.B.C. was seized by one of the soldiers, an officer, and dragged by the hair and forced to the floor for the purpose of sensual enjoyment.

She resisted as far as practical—held up her young infant as a plea for sparing her and succeeded, but they took her maid, and in her presence, threw her on the floor and had connection with her. . . .

They pinioned Mrs. McCord and robbed her. They dragged Mrs. Gynn by the hair of her head about the house. Mrs. G. told me of a young lady about 16, Miss Kinsler, who . . . three officers brutally ravished and who became crazy from it. . . .

Details of the mistreatment Trezevant outlined were seldom reported in the South of the 1860s. Victims kept their injuries and humiliation quiet, although less violent offenses against women were widely reported: In their search for hidden treasure, Sherman's troops sometimes coarsely searched Southern women, ripping open dresses and hoisting skirts. Accounts of rape, however, appear to have been voluntarily suppressed. Such assaults were regarded as the worst fate that could befall a lady. Clara MacLean, a rural North Carolina homemaker, was one who openly discussed her experience when the worst nearly occurred. Her story begins near the end of Sherman's march, as the blue-clad invaders approached her home on one of their last looting expeditions.

For several days I had been wearing my dagger. As the danger seemed delayed, I laid it on the dressing-table with watch, jewelry, etc. Thus one may sleep on the very crest of Vesuvius. A few days after, about three o'clock in the afternoon, I was sitting quietly in my room reading. There came a tap at the door, and a girlish face appeared. "The Yankees are coming," she said.

Going to the window, I looked out and saw a half-dozen horses fastened to the palings. As usual, these unwelcomed visitors had made themselves at home, and entered by the back gate. We had reached the door when I returned, found the dagger under a lot of feminine small-wear and thrust it into [its scabbard]. Very deliberately we two advanced to the charge.

At the foot of the stairs a man was standing, as if uncertain where to proceed.

"Who are you?" I asked. "Do you belong to Johnston's command?"

"Yes," he replied very promptly.

"And this uniform?"

The fellow hesitated a moment and then burst out laughing. "Well, we is what you call the Yankees," he allowed.

Mrs. DeG. now appeared, bathed in tears and wringing her hands pitifully. Her mother-in-law, an elderly lady—and an invalid—was lying in a small bed when the invaders arrived. They had forced her to rise, suspecting some ruse to protect valuables in or under the bedding. Then thrusting in their sabres they literally disemboweled the mattress and feather bed, the debris of which now was strewn far and wide. The poor old lady was deeply distressed at the indignity of their treatment, but she opened not her lips, but surveyed the ruins with Roman fortitude. I spoke a few encouraging words to her, gave a glance at the side-board with doors broken off their hinges, and empty decanters and a sugar bowl laying about; then hastened back to watch, and, if possib prevent the work of destruction.

Sounds of discordant music issued from the parlor, and thither I went. One of the blue-coats was seated at the piano, strumming away quite complacently, while another, in some seeming embarrassment at my sudden appearance, dropped a plated water-pitcher which had at-

Federal raiders loot a Southern home.

tracted his artist eye. At this moment my little sister rushed up from some unexpected quarter, crying wildly: "Oh, where is mamma's picture? They will get mamma's picture!"

"Hush!" I whispered, grasping her arms, "or they will get it just to provoke you."

The silver connoisseur, relieved by the diversion, made a hasty exit from the parlor and dashed by me up the stairs. The investigating Federal proceeded to open drawers and wardrobes upon reaching my room. After watching him a few moments, I asked quietly what he wished.

"We have come looking for arms," was his somewhat sullen reply. Then in a tone of abrupt harshness, he added, "Open these trunks!" indicating one by a kick of his foot.

I felt the better policy was to obey. So, taking out my keys and drawing up a chair, I deliberately sat down, unlocked the trunk and began taking out one little dainty after another, shaking each one carefully. "You can perceive," I said, inviting scrutiny of each bit of ribbon and lace, "that there is no mounted cavalryman or loaded cannon in here."

He turned off with a horrid oath and drawing an immense navy revolver from his boot—there was one in each Hessian-top—he presented it to my head. "Be in a hurry!" was his order, evidently warming to his work.

I was just excited enough to be utterly reckless of consequences. "I am not used to such commands," I said, and therewith folded my hands. He advanced to the other trunk, and was about to break it open when I left off my dignity and came forward with the keys. The first object that met his eye—well trained in such service—was a tiny morocco purse. "Ha! what's that?"

I took it up and unclasped it tenderly. There lay one poor little silver sixpence, my only remaining bit of specie, which I had kept "for luck." There also nestled a miniature Confederate flag that had been wont to adorn my toilette as a breast-knot in happier days, and was endeared by a thousand sweet memories.

"This is all the money I have in the world," I said, holding up the sixpence, "but you can have it if you wish."

He threw it aside with an impatient gesture and another oath and walked off. Before I was aware of his intention, he had locked the door. I rose and walked toward it. "Come," I said, "and I will show you the trunks in the other room, as there is nothing here, you see, in the way of arms."

But he had stationed himself in front of the door, his back toward it. For a moment, nay, a long minute—centuries it seemed to me—we stood thus. There he was, a stalwart blonde of perhaps twenty-three or four, over six feet in height; his breath hot with the peach brandy they had unearthed on this raid; his eyes blood-shot, a reckless demon looking out of their grey-green depths, ready for any atrocity. I measured him from cap to boots, then fixed my eyes steadily on his, not fearful in the least, calm to petrification almost, only as I pressed my left hand against my side I felt there a strange, wild fluttering, as of an imprisoned bird. With the other I slowly and stealthily unloosed the stiletto from its sheath, for it stuck tightly in the silver scabbard, and still gazed at him with unflinching nerves and tense muscles.

Whether he saw and divined the movement, or whether he heard his companions galloping away, I know not; or if indeed any "means" were necessary in this wonderful intervention of a protecting Providence. I only spoke these words very low, and my own voice was strange to me in its vibrating intensity: "What do you mean, sir? Open that door!"

One moment more his eye retained its fiendish brightness, then drooped. He turned, unlocked the door, and went down, I following. As the big blonde threw himself into his saddle I remarked, "I think I see some of Wheeler's men coming down the lane." This dashing corps had been lingering in our vicinity for several weeks, and were in some sort "household troops" for us.

"Who's afraid of Wheeler's men?" he cried, adding an oath that made one's blood curdle. Then he sped after his comrades.

I was sitting in the back porch when they returned. The first soldier to dismount and enter was one I had not observed before, a dark, wiry, middle-aged man, with a brigandish face and air, a sort of American "Devilshoof." "Say, old woman," he began, addressing Mrs. DeG., "where is that watch I told you to hide when I was here two or three weeks ago?"

In vain the poor lady protested she had no watch, did not recollect ever having a watch, and would not have hidden it if she had ever had a watch! The fellow laughed at her incoherency and iteration with demoniacal sarcasm.

"You wouldn't, hey? Well, let's see if your memory is better than mine," and deliberately putting his hand to her pocket he drew forth a small tin box of snuff, stick-brush, a knife, and—a watch! Without a word, but with a gesture of infinite mockery, and a leer I have never before or since seen on a human face, he transferred the two latter articles to his own pocket.

At this moment, my attention was distracted by the striking of matches in the inner room, and I saw only with divided mind the next outrage—the same man tearing open the dress-neck of the dignified old mother, and drawing thence a silk handkerchief in which was wrapped sixteen golden dollars. My blood boiled at the sight, but I dared not speak. The consciousness of my own heavy-laden pocket weighed upon me and fastened me to my seat. No attempt, however, was made to search either V. or me, and the little poniard rested quietly in its hiding place.

The sun was setting when the horrible comedy ended, and the order to mount was given. Somehow the matches had gone out which were thrown on beds and into closets. But they imagined and hoped that a dozen incipient fires had been left burning which would effectually destroy what

could not be carried off. So mounting in hot haste, . . . the dreaded enemy fled away through the falling twilight to death and destruction.

A few miles off they were intercepted by a half-dozen "home-guards" led by a disabled Confederate officer. A skirmish ensued, and the big blonde dragoon was wounded—John Miller, of the [10th] Ohio Cavalry. He and a comrade made their way across the river to a farm-house, and there stopped, unable to proceed. Captain C. kept them in view, while the others were followed and dispatched by his men. Only one escaped to tell the tale.

Captain C. traced his two men to their lurking place. In the dim moonlight he saw that one stood sentry at the front door. Following their example, he made a detour and entered from the rear.

"Surrender!" he cried. But before the poor wretch had time to speak, he was ushered into eternity.

Passing swiftly to the inner room, the Confederate officer found John Miller in bed, the woman of the house bending over him with a bottle of camphor, or spirits of some kind, in her hand. He had heard the report and was struggling violently to rise. But it was too late. In another moment his soul had sped to join those of his companions in evil-doing, and an untold list of atrocities and cruelties was at last avenged.

Within two hours, I held in my hand the little morocco purse, which I had not even missed. The tiny flag was still there; the silver sixpence gone! The sides of the purse had been burst open as if too tightly packed. Some of Mrs. DeG.'s gold had no doubt filled it; but it, too, had disappeared.

The gallant Captain offered me the huge revolvers, one of which had presented its cold muzzle to my head. Shudderingly, I refused. They were stained with human blood—associated with nameless crimes.

When I went to my room that night it was not to sleep. In the flickering fire-light, which did duty as lamps and candles in those make-shift days, I lived again, over and over a hundred times, the fearful experiences of that brief afternoon. Not until then, in the silence and loneliness of midnight, did I realize the unutterable peril with which I had been threatened. As the ghostly shadows danced over the wall, I seemed to see the athletic frame looming up out of the darkness, the fierce fair face, pallid, yet lit up with a baleful glare, staring at me till I was turned to stone. For many weeks and months this fearful vision filled my waking hours as it did my dreams; and not even the distance of twenty years has dimmed a memory so fraught with horror.

7

Legends in Gray

The War Between the States produced a remarkable handful of great Southern chieftains. Extraordinary achievements or dramatic, colorful personalities caused them to rise above the ordinary. They were a diverse group: the profane, tempestuous Forrest contrasts starkly with the taciturn, devout Jackson. Yet they had much in common. All were men of strong will; all were gifted with superior leadership abilities; all were zealously devoted to the South; and all were made famous by the war.

Most were native Southerners, although some were not. A few were products of the Southern aristocracy, but most came from more ordinary backgrounds. All were commanders and almost all ended the war as generals—although only one began the war as such. One enlisted in Confederate service as a private. A few were West Pointers. Several were cavalry commanders, and one was a political leader. Many knew each other, but some had never met.

While battling for Southern independence, each acquired a larger-than-life reputation. Afterward, they were viewed by generations of Southerners—and others—as figures of almost mythical stature.

They were legends in gray.

NATHAN BEDFORD FORREST

As Gen. Braxton Bragg's Confederate army passed her home in retreat, a distraught Tennessee housewife hurried from her doorstep and confronted the hapless Bragg, anxiously urging him to stand and fight. The general ignored her pleas and sullenly plodded onward. Angrily, the woman shook her fist at Bragg's departing back and yelled loudly, "Oh, you big cowardly rascal! I only wish old Forrest was here; he'd make you fight!"

Such was Nathan Bedford Forrest's reputation. The eldest son of a Tennessee blacksmith, Forrest assumed support of his large family at age sixteen, when his father died. Although he had received practically no formal education, Forrest swapped and sold his way to affluence as a businessman, cotton planter, and slave trader. When the war began, he organized and outfitted a troop of cavalry at his own expense and entered Confederate service as a private. He was soon appointed lieutenant colonel and, as the war progressed, experienced a rapid rise in rank from private to lieutenant general.

Forrest had no military training, but he was a natural leader and displayed a single-minded understanding of the fundamentals of warfare. "War means fightin'," he would say, "and fightin' means killin'."

He did not care for West Pointers, thrashed several in battle, and had nothing but contempt for fighting by the book. "Whenever I met one of them fellers that fit by note," he once said, "I generally whipped h–ll out of him before he got his tune pitched." His unconventional, unpredictable tactics made him an unnerving opponent to Federal forces in the Western Theater. (A favorite Forrest practice was to surround an enemy, then demand surrender with a threat of no quarter if the offer was refused. Usually, the offer was accepted.) His reputation as a ferocious fighter acquired an even more controversial edge after the Battle of Fort Pillow, in which Forrest's troops were accused of slaughtering a Federal garrison after it surrendered. Gen. William T. Sherman, who later described Forrest as "the most remarkable man our Civil War produced," referred to him during the war as "that devil Forrest" and urged that he be "hunted down and killed if it costs ten thousand lives and bankrupts the Federal treasury."

When Forrest's superiors dismissed his advice and submitted to the disastrous surrender of Fort Donelson in 1862, he took a large force of troops and slipped through the encircling enemy to freedom. He distinguished himself at the Battle of Shiloh, whipped a superior force of Federal cavalry into an embarrassing, panicky retreat at Brice's Crossroads; inflicted a humiliating defeat on the Federal navy near Johnsonville, Tennessee; and conducted a series of spectacular cavalry raids that made him famous as the Wizard of the Saddle.

Although his remarkable military success was undoubtedly due to his native genius for command and his eagerness to do battle, the force of his personality also must have contributed to his accomplishments. Forrest was normally mild-mannered, affable, and untalkative. In battle or when angry or excited, however, he could be wild, profane, and terrifying—although he always managed to maintain the self-control and judgment necessary for effective command. His personality softened dramatically near the end of his life, when he reportedly became a Christian, but those who met him during the war—in battle or otherwise—generally remembered the encounter.

A descriptive profile of Forrest's wartime personality was preserved by an enemy—a staff officer under one of Forrest's primary antagonists, Gen. James H. Wilson. The officer chanced to meet the Wizard of the Saddle during a temporary truce. His account:

I was at the time struck by what then seemed the aristocratic mien of General Forrest. Our present meeting was in the dim light of common tallow candles on a dark, rainy night, in the living room of a somewhat rude country residence.

Forrest is a man fully six feet in height, rather waxen face, handsome, high full forehead, and a profusion of light gray hair thrown back from the forehead and growing down rather to a point in the middle of the same. The lines of thought and care, in an upward curve receding, are distinctly marked and add much to the dignity of expression. The general effect is suggestive of notables of the Revolutionary times, with powdered hair as we see them in the portraits of that day; and to our unaccustomed eyes the rich gray uniform with its embroidered collar (a wreath of gold on black ground enclosing three silver stars) added much to the effect produced.

I could not but observe the quickness of apprehension and decision displayed by Forrest in seizing the entire thought intended to be conveyed from the introductory expressions. To think quickly and concretely, and to decide likewise, seemed to be his mental habit. There was about his talk and manner a certain soldierly simplicity and engaging frankness and I was frequently lost in real admiration.

I could not, in the dim light of tallow candles, observe the color of his eyes, but they seemed to be brown and pleasant-looking, lit up occasionally by a gleam of soldierly bravery. His expression, both pleasant and striking, is given to his physiognomy by the slightest possible elation of the eyebrows.

The latter are black with a tinge of gray, and a black moustache and chin whiskers, both cut short, add to the military bearing of the man. His face is long and cheekbones rather prominent, eyes large, though not noticeably so, and the head full above the eyes and ears. His habitual expression seemed subdued and thoughtful, but when his face is lighted up by a smile, which ripples all over his features, the effect is really charming. Forrest expressed great admiration for soldierly qualities and especially for personal courage and was evidently pleased at our recognition of the fame of his exploits at the head of his cavalry.

His language indicates a very limited education, but his impressive manner conceals many otherwise notable defects. The choice of words too plainly evidences early associations, unfortunately, and one feels sometimes disappointed at errors palpable to any school boy. He invariably omits the final "g" in the termination "ing," and many words are inexcusably mispronounced, and he always uses the past particle in place of the past tense of such words as "see"—as "I seen" instead of I saw, and "hep tote," meaning to help carry. . . .

In a very short time, however, these pass unnoticed. He speaks of his success with a soldierly vanity, and expresses the kindest feelings toward prisoners and wounded. I told him that I had the honor to present the compliments of my general, our cavalry Murat—Wilson—to him, in the hope of meeting him upon some future occasion. He at once accepted this as a challenge which the friendly message might be construed to convey, and with a curl of his lip he said: "Jist tell General Wilson that I know the nicest little place down below here in the world, and whenever he is ready, I will fight him with any number from one to ten thousand cavalry, and abide the issue. Gin'ral Wilson may pick his men, and I'll pick mine. He may take his sabers and I'll take my six-shooters. I don't want nary a saber in my command—haven't got one." At parting we shook hands all around, and just as we were leaving, the General took my hand in his own a second time, and holding it in a cordial grasp, said in a friendly and courteous manner, "Don't git too far away from your command when you come down into this country—some of our boys may pick you up."

J. E. B. STUART

On the evening of May 12, 1864, Maj. Gen. James Ewell Brown Stuart was dying. He lay on a bed in a relative's house on Richmond's Grace Street, his life slowing draining away from a bullet wound in his right side. He had been shot by an unhorsed Yankee cavalryman the day before in a minor engagement at Yellow Tavern near Richmond. While his wife raced across the Virginia countryside in a futile attempt to reach her husband before he died, Stuart's friends and fellow officers stood at his bedside and looked for the last time at the pale, bearded young man who had been transformed by war into a Southern hero.

Stuart—called Jeb from his initials—was thirty-one years old. Although bright, flamboyant, energetic, and good-humored, he was not naturally handsome: as a joke on his homeliness, classmates at West Point had ironically dubbed him Beauty. Yet, he was dashing. A reddish brown beard disguised his common face, and he enhanced his appearance with careful grooming and a colorful military costume: a red-lined cape, a yellow sash, thigh-high boots, gold spurs, and a plumed hat. Southerners loved his romantic attire and cavalier image. They were also cheered by his military exploits, and they respected his personal character. Like Stonewall Jackson, Stuart was a devout Christian.

While still in his twenties, he had become commander of all the cavalry forces in Robert E. Lee's Army of Northern Virginia. His wartime rise in rank and command had been meteoric. After a seven-year tour of prewar cavalry duty on the wide-open prairies of Texas and Kansas, he had resigned his commission in the U.S. Army just three weeks after a long-awaited promotion.

Motivated by a desire to defend his native Virginia from Federal invasion, he had entered Confederate service as a captain, a rank he would hold only briefly. By the Battle of First Manassas he was a colonel of cavalry, and following the Confederate victory, which he aided with a well-timed cavalry charge, he was promoted to brigadier general. Within a year he was a major general and commanded all of Lee's cavalry.

Under Stuart's training and leadership, his cavalry became an invaluable asset to the Army of Northern Virginia. Lee called him the eyes of the army, and except for his performance during the Gettysburg campaign—when he allowed his troops temporarily to lose contact with the rest of the army—Stuart played a principal role in Lee's skillful maneuvers. After Stuart fell at Yellow Tavern, Lee was unable to find a cavalry commander of comparable ability. "I can scarcely think of him without weeping," he said.

J. E. B. Stuart died at 7:38 P.M., Thursday, May 12, 1864. The Richmond Examiner *chronicled the final moments in the life of the heralded Dixie Cavalier.*

We learn from the physicians in attendance upon the General, that his condition during the day was very changeable, with occasional delirium and other unmistakable symptoms of speedy dissolution. In the moments of delirium the General's mind wandered, and, like the immortal Jackson (whose spirit, we trust, his has joined), in the lapse of reason his faculties were busied with the details of his command. He reviewed in broken sentences all his glorious campaigns around McClellan's rear on the Peninsula, beyond the Potomac, and upon the Rapidan, quoting from his orders and issuing new ones to his couriers, with a last injunction to "make haste."

About noon, Thursday, President Davis visited his bedside, and spent some fifteen minutes in the dying chamber of his favorite chieftain. The President, taking his hand, said, "General, how do you feel?" He replied, "Easy, but willing to die, if God and my country think I have fulfilled my destiny and done my duty." As evening approached, the General's delirium increased and his mind again wandered to the battlefields over which he had fought, then off to wife and children, and off again to the front. A telegraphic message had been sent for his wife, who was in the country, with the injunction to make all haste, as

the General was dangerously wounded. . . .

As the evening wore on, the paroxysms of pain increased, and mortification set in rapidly. Though suffering the greatest agony at times, the General was calm, and applied to the wound with his own hand the ice intended to relieve the pain. During the evening he asked Dr. Brewer how long he thought he could live, and whether it was possible for him to survive through the night. The Doctor, knowing he did not desire to be buoyed by false hopes, told him frankly that death, that last enemy, was rapidly approaching. The General nodded and said, "I am resigned if it be God's will; but I would like to see my wife. But God's will be done." Several times he roused up and asked if she had come.

To the Doctor, who sat holding his wrist and counting the fleeting, weakening pulse, he remarked, "Doctor, I suppose I am going fast now. It will soon be over. But God's will be done. I hope I have fulfilled my destiny to my country and my duty to God."

At half-past seven o'clock it was evident to the physicians that death was setting its clammy seal upon the brave, open brow of the General, and they told him so; asked if he had any last messages to give. The General, with a mind perfectly clear and possessed, then made dispositions of his staff and personal effects. To Mrs. General R. E. Lee he directed that his golden spurs be given as a dying memento of his love and esteem of her husband. To his staff officers he gave his horses. So particular was he in small things, even in the dying hour, that he emphatically exhibited and illustrated the ruling passion strong in death. To one of his staff, who was a heavy-built man, he said, "You had better take the larger horse; he will carry you better." Other mementoes he disposed of in a similar manner. To his young son he left his glorious sword.

His worldly matters closed, the eternal interest of his soul engaged his mind. Turning to the Rev. Mr. Peterkin, of the Episcopal Church, of which he was an exemplary member, he asked him to sing the hymn commencing—

> "Rock of ages cleft for me,
> Let me hide myself in thee,"

he joined in with all the voice his strength would permit. He then joined in prayer with the ministers. To the Doctor he again said, "I am going fast now; I am resigned; God's will be done." Thus died General J. E. B. Stuart.

PATRICK R. CLEBURNE

On the march that took him to his death at the Battle of Franklin, Maj. Gen. Patrick R. Cleburne and his staff rode past St. John's Episcopal Church in Ashwood, Tennessee. Pausing to gaze at the quaint, ivy-covered Gothic-style church and its well-kept, pastoral-looking cemetery, Cleburne mused aloud that it would be "almost worth dying for, to be buried in such a beautiful spot." Soon his body would lie buried in that very churchyard, placed there by comrades who remembered his admiration of the little church and its handsome graveyard.

He was called the Stonewall of the West. Born in Ireland in 1828, Cleburne apprenticed as a pharmacist and planned a medical career, but failed the language portion of his medical examination. Disappointed, he joined the British army and served three years in the 41st Regiment of Foot before emigrating to the United States. He worked awhile as a pharmacist in

Cincinnati, then moved to Arkansas, where he became a partner in a drugstore and later, after studying law, also became a practicing attorney.

A popular and prominent citizen of Helena, he cast his lot with his adopted South when the war began and organized the Yell Rifles. He was elected captain and was soon promoted to colonel, serving first in the 1st Arkansas Infantry and later in the 15th Arkansas. As a brigadier general he displayed extraordinary personal valor and obvious command ability at the Battle of Shiloh. He survived a serious facial wound at the Battle of Richmond in Kentucky, and served with distinction in many of the major engagements of the war's Western Theater: Chaplin Hills, Murfreesboro, Chickamauga, Atlanta. Promoted to major general in late 1862, he was considered by some to be as irreplaceable in the West as was Stonewall Jackson in the East.

On November 30, 1864, at the Battle of Franklin, Cleburne's division led the assault against the heavily fortified Federal position—a charge made across an open field twice the distance of Pickett's charge at Gettysburg. Typically, Cleburne was at the head of his troops and two horses were killed under him during the charge. When his second mount went down, Cleburne placed his kepi atop his sword, held it aloft so his troops could follow him, and disappeared on foot into the smoke of battle, leading his bloodied division in a futile final push toward the enemy entrenchments. He was killed a few moments later.

After the fighting ended, his body was found on the field within fifty yards of the Federal lines. He was buried in the churchyard he had admired, and was widely mourned by the troops of his division. Few officers commanded as much respect and affection from the soldiers in the ranks as did Cleburne. Three decades after he fell at Franklin, one of his soldiers, T. O. Moore of the 7th Texas Infantry, recalled two wartime incidents that illustrate the rapport Cleburne shared with his men.

In the fall of 1864, Cleburne's division was thrown with a portion of the army across the Coosa River above Rome, Georgia, and started across the mountains of North Georgia to the railroad leading to Atlanta. We were cut off from our supply trains and had to live off the country through which we passed. Apples, chestnuts and persimmons were plenty, so we did pretty well. Strict orders had been issued that we must not depredate upon private property.

One morning on leaving camp, General Cleburne's brigade led the column. I was badly crippled from sore feet and could not keep up with the command, so on this particular morning had special permission to march at the head of the brigade. I was trudging along the best I could just in the rear of General Granbury's horse, when I saw down the road General Cleburne sitting on top of a rail fence smoking a cob pipe. Below, on the ground, were five or six bushels of fine red apples. Nearby stood one or two of his aides; also five or six "web-foot" soldiers, who looked as mean as they well could look.

As we drew near, General Granbury saluted General Cleburne, who in his turn said: "General Granbury, I am peddling apples today."

General Granbury said: "How are you selling them, General?"

General Cleburne replied: "These gentlemen (pointing to the web-feet, who had stolen the

Patrick R. Cleburne.

This was done. In the meantime, the boys were hurrahing for old Pat. When the apples gave out, General Cleburne made each man who had stolen the apples carry a rail for a mile or two. Old Pat enjoyed the thing as much as did his men. . . .

During the campaign around Atlanta our company was out on picket. Just before we were relieved in the morning our company killed a fat cow, and we managed to bring a quarter into camp. As we were expecting to move at any time, we cut up the beef in chunks, built a scaffold and spread the meat on it, then built a fire and were cooking it so we could take it with us. We were all busy working at it when one of the company looked up and saw old Pat coming down the line on a tour of inspection. We had no time to hide the beef, and knew we were in for it.

One of the company stepped out and saluted the General, and said: "General, we have some nice, fat beef cooking, and it is about done; come and eat dinner with us." "Well," he replied, "it does smell good. I believe I will." He sat down on a log, one of the boys took a nice piece of beef from the fire, another hunted a pone of corn bread and handed it to him. The General ate quite heartily, thanked us for the dinner, took out his cob pipe, filled it and began to smoke, chatting pleasantly with us, asking what we thought of our position, and if we thought we could win the fight if we had one, and then passed on down the line, while we cheered him. How could we help admiring him?

apples) have been very kind. They have gathered the apples for me and charged nothing. I will give them to you and your men. Now, you get down and take an apple, and have each of your men pass by and take one—only one, mind—until they are all gone."

RAPHAEL SEMMES

Raphael Semmes, destined to become famous as captain of the Confederate cruiser Alabama, *began the war peacefully enough—as head of the Confederate Lighthouse Service. A career officer in the U.S. Navy, he had become a midshipman at age sixteen. By the time he saw action in the Mexican War, he had long been a naval lieutenant, and in 1855, he was promoted to commander. By then, he had managed to establish a home in Mobile, Alabama, and to write a book about his service in the Mexican War. When*

Alabama seceded in 1861, he resigned from the U.S. Navy and entered Confederate service.

In June of 1861, Semmes took the Confederate cruiser Sumter to sea and for the next six months plagued Northern merchant shipping in the Atlantic, capturing and in some cases burning eighteen Northern vessels before the Sumter was decommissioned at Gibraltar. His success with the Sumter was merely a prelude for the blow he dealt the enemy with the C.S.S. Alabama. In August of 1862, Semmes assumed command of the newly built Alabama, constructed at Great Britain's Laird shipyards, and in the next twenty-two months he made the Alabama the most successful—and most feared— Confederate raider of the war. From August of 1862 until June of 1864, the Alabama took sixty-four Northern vessels worth more than $6.5 million, battled and sank the Federal warship Hatteras, and seriously disrupted Northern merchant shipping. (In postwar international arbitration, the United States was awarded $15.5 million in compensation from Great Britain for the wartime damage inflicted by the Alabama.)

The Alabama's exploits ended on Sunday, June 19, 1864, when the raider was sunk in combat with the U.S.S. Kearsarge, commanded by Capt. John A. Winslow, a Federal naval officer from North Carolina, who had been a prewar messmate and friend of Semmes's. The battle occurred in the English Channel off the French port of Cherbourg, where the Alabama had gone to make repairs. After the sinking, Semmes was rescued by the British yacht Deerhound, which had been taken out for a good view of the battle. Semmes returned to the Confederacy, was promoted to rear admiral, and commanded Richmond's James River squadron until the fall of the Confederate capital. At war's end, he was detained for three months on piracy charges by the Federal government. Afterward he returned to civilian life, engaged in publishing and teaching, and wrote a classic memoir of his service in the Confederate Navy. His accomplishments as captain of the Alabama brought lasting fame, and by the time of his death in 1877, Semmes was already viewed as one of the most notable figures produced by the war.

Below, Semmes's official report to Confederate Secretary of the Navy Stephen R. Mallory details the combat with the Kearsarge that resulted in the sinking of the C.S.S. Alabama.

Hon. S. R. Mallory,
 Secretary of the Navy, Richmond, Va.
  Southampton, June 21, 1864.
Sir: I have the honor to inform you, in accordance with my intention as previously announced to you, I steamed out of the harbor of Cherbourg between 9 and 10 o'clock on the morning of June 19 for the purpose of engaging the enemy's steamer Kearsarge, which had been lying off and on the port for several days previously. After clearing the harbor we descried the enemy, with his head offshore, at a distance of about 9 miles. We were three-quarters of an hour in coming up with him. I had previously pivoted my guns to starboard, and made all my preparations for engaging the enemy on that side. When within about a mile and a quarter of the enemy he suddenly wheeled, and bringing his head inshore presented

Raphael Semmes.

his starboard battery to me. By this time we were distant about 1 mile from each other, when I opened on him with solid shot, to which he replied in a few minutes, and the engagement became active on both sides. The enemy now pressed his ship under a full head of steam, and to prevent our passing each other too speedily, and to keep our respective broadsides bearing, it became necessary to fight in a circle, the two ships steaming around a common center and preserving a distance from each other of from a quarter to half a mile. When we got within good shell range, we opened upon him with shell. Some ten or fifteen minutes after the commencement of the action our spanker gaff was shot away and our ensign came down by the run. This was immediately replaced by another at the mizzenmast-head. The firing now became very hot, and the enemy's shot and shell soon began to tell upon our hull, knocking down, killing, and disabling a number of men in different parts of the ship. Perceiving that our shell, though apparently exploding against the enemy's sides, were doing but little damage, I returned to solid shot firing, and from this time onward alternated with shot and shell. After the lapse of about one hour and ten minutes our ship was ascertained to be in a sinking condition, the enemy's shell having exploded in our sides and between decks, opening large apertures, through which the water rushed with great rapidity. For some few minutes I had hopes of being able to reach the French coast, for which purpose I gave the ship all steam and set such of the fore-and-aft sails as were available. The ship filled so rapidly, however, that before we had made much progress the fires were extinguished in the furnaces, and we were evidently on the point of sinking. I now hauled down my colors to prevent the further destruction of life, and dispatched a boat to inform the enemy of our condition. Although we were now but 400 yards from each other, the enemy fired upon me five times after my colors had been struck, dangerously wounding several of my men. It is charitable to suppose that a ship of war of a Christian nation could not have done this intentionally. We now turned all our exertions toward the wounded and such of the boys as were unable to swim. These were dispatched in my quarter boats, the only boats remaining to me, the waist boats having been torn to pieces.

Some twenty minutes after my furnace fires had been extinguished, and the ship being on the point of settling, every man, in obedience to a previous order which had been given to the crew, jumped overboard and endeavored to save himself. There was no appearance of any boat coming to me from the enemy until after the ship went down. Fortunately, however, the steam yacht *Deerhound,* owned by a gentleman of Lancashire, England (Mr. John Lancaster), who was himself on board, steamed up in the midst of my drowning men and rescued a number of both officers and men from the water. I was fortunate enough myself thus to escape to the shelter of the neutral flag, together with about forty others, all told. About this time the *Kearsarge* sent one and then, tardily, another boat.

Accompanying you will find lists of the killed and wounded, and of those who were picked up by the *Deerhound.* The remainder there is reason to hope were picked up by the enemy and by a couple of French pilot boats, which were also fortunately near the scene of action. At the end of the engagement it was discovered by those of our officers who went alongside the enemy's ship with the wounded that her midship section on both sides was thoroughly iron-coated, this having been done with chains constructed for the purpose, placed perpendicularly from the rail to the water's edge, the whole covered over by a thin outer planking, which gave no indication of the armor beneath. This planking had been ripped off in every direction by our shot and shell, the chain broken and indented in many places, and forced partly into the ship's side. She was most effectually guarded, however, in this section from penetration. The enemy was much damaged in other parts, but to what extent it is now impossible to tell. It is believed he was badly crippled.

My officers and men behaved steadily and gallantly, and though they have lost their ship they have not lost honor. Where all behaved so well it would be invidious to particularize; but I can not deny myself the pleasure of saying that Mr. Kell, my first lieutenant, deserves great credit for the fine condition in which the ship went into action, with regard to her battery, magazine, and shell rooms; also that he rendered me great assistance by his coolness and judgment as the fight proceeded.

The enemy was heavier than myself, both in ship, battery, and crew; but I did not know until the action was over that she was also ironclad. Our total loss in killed and wounded is 30, to wit, 9 killed and 21 wounded.

I have the honor to be, very respectfully, your obedient servant,

R. Semmes,
Captain.

JOHN SINGLETON MOSBY

Officially, they were known as the 43rd Battalion of Partisan Rangers; unofficially, they were known as Mosby's Rangers—an irregular force of Confederate cavalry often operating behind Federal lines, frequently with dramatic results. Their leader, John Singleton Mosby, a young Virginia lawyer, was a scout for Gen. J. E. B. Stuart, when granted permission to organize the Partisan Rangers. Ironically, Mosby had been a prisoner of war a few months earlier, and his success as a leader of irregular troops would make Federal officials sorry he was ever released.

Mosby launched his rangers in January of 1863, with a handful of horsemen. His ranks grew quickly, however, and at one time numbered about 800, although normal strength was about 200. The rangers harassed Federal troops, raided behind enemy lines, and may have diverted 30,000 Federals, who otherwise would have strengthened Federal forces on the front lines. To the frustration of the enemy, Mosby's Raiders, using guerrilla tactics, assembled for raids and dispersed afterward. It was dangerous service: Mosby was wounded seven times. He recovered from each injury, and eventually rose to colonel. So effectively did his partisan force dominate Northern Virginia's Loudoun County that the region became known as Mosby's Confederacy.

What was perhaps Mosby's most daring feat occurred in the morning darkness of March 8, 1863. Mosby and a small force of rangers, led by a Federal deserter named Ames, raided Fairfax Court House and captured Federal Gen. Edwin H. Stoughton from a warm bed at his headquarters. In postwar memoirs, Mosby recalled the event.

On the evening of March 8, 1863, in obedience to orders, twenty-nine men met me at Dover, in Loudoun County. None knew my objective point, but I told Ames [the Federal deserter] after we started. . . .

The weather conditions favored my success. There was a melting snow on the ground, a mist, and about dark, a drizzling rain. Our starting point was about twenty-five miles from Fairfax Court House. It was pitch dark when we got near the cavalry pickets at Chantilly—five or six miles from the Court House. At Centreville, three miles away on the Warrenton pike and seven miles from the Court House, were several thousand troops. Our problem was to pass between them and Wyndham's cavalry without giving the alarm. Ames knew where there was a break in the picket lines between Chantilly and Centreville, and he led us through this without a vidette seeing us. After passing the outpost the chief point in the game was won. I think no man but me, except Ames, realized that we were inside the enemy's lines. But the enemy felt secure and was as ignorant as my men. The plan had been to reach the Court House by midnight so as to get out of the lines before daybreak, but the column got broken in the dark and the two parts travelled around in a circle for an hour looking for each other. After we closed up, we started off and struck the pike between Centreville and the Court House. But we turned off into the woods when we got within two or three miles of the village, as Wyndham's cavalry camps were on the pike.

We entered the village from the direction of the railroad station. There were a few sentinels about the town, but it was so dark that they could not distinguish us from their own people. . . .

When the squads were starting around to gather prisoners and horses, Joe Nelson brought me a soldier who said he was a guard at General Stoughton's headquarters. Joe had also pulled the telegraph operator out of his tent; the wires had been cut. With five or six men I rode to the house, now the Episcopal rectory, where the commanding general was. We dismounted and knocked loudly at the door. Soon a window above was opened, and someone asked who was there. I answered, "Fifth New York Cavalry with a dispatch for General Stoughton." The door was opened and a staff officer, Lieutenant Prentiss, was before me. I took hold of his nightshirt, whispered my name in his ear, and told him to take me to General Stoughton's room. Resistance was useless, and he obeyed. A light was quickly struck, and on the bed we saw the general sleeping as soundly as the Turk when Marco Bozzaris waked him up. There was no time for ceremony, so I drew up the bedclothes, pulled up the general's shirt, and gave him a spank on his bare back, and told him to get up. As his staff officer was standing by me, Stoughton did not realize the situation and thought that somebody was taking a rude familiarity with him. He asked in an indignant tone what all this meant. I told him that he was a prisoner, and that he must get up quickly and dress.

I then asked him if he had ever heard of "Mosby," and he said he had.

John Singleton Mosby.

"I am Mosby," I said. "Stuart's cavalry has possession of the Court House; be quick and dress."

Stoughton had the reputation of being a brave soldier, but a fop. He dressed before a looking-glass as carefully as Sardanapalus did when he went into battle. He forgot his watch and left it on the bureau, but one of my men, Frank Williams, took it and gave it to him. Two men had been left to guard our horses when we went into the house.

There were several tents for couriers in the yard, and Stoughton's horses and couriers were ready to go with us, when we came out with the general and his staff.

When we reached the rendezvous at the courtyard, I found all the squads waiting for us with their prisoners and horses. There were three times as many prisoners as my men, and each was mounted and leading a horse. To deceive the enemy and baffle pursuit, the cavalcade started off in one direction and soon after it got out of town, turned in another. We flanked the cavalry camps, and were soon on the pike between them and Centreville. As there were several thousand troops in that town, it was not thought possible that we could go that way to get out of the lines, so the cavalry, when it started in pursuit, went in an opposite direction. . . .

Our safety depended on our getting out of the Union lines before daybreak. We struck the pike about four miles from Centreville; the danger I then apprehended was pursuit by the cavalry, which was in camp behind us. When we got near the pike, I halted the column to close up. Some of my men were riding in the rear, and some on the flanks to prevent the prisoners from escaping. I left a sergeant, Hunter, in command and rode forward to reconnoitre. As no enemy was in front, I called to Hunter to come on and directed him to go forward at a trot and to hold Stoughton's bridle reins under all circumstances. Stoughton no doubt appreciated my interest in him.

With Joe Nelson I remained some distance behind. We stopped frequently to listen for the hoofbeats of cavalry in pursuit, but no sound could be heard save the hooting of owls. My heart beat higher with hope every minute. . . .

After we had passed the forts and reached Cub Run, a new danger was before us. The stream was swift and booming from the melting snow, and our choice was to swim, or to turn back. In full view behind us were the white tents of the enemy and the forts, and we were within cannon range. Without halting a moment, I plunged into the stream, and my horse swam to the other bank. Stoughton followed and was next to me. As he came up the bank, shivering from his cold morning bath, he said, "Captain, this is the first rough treatment I have to complain of."

Fortunately not a man or a horse was lost. . . . We crossed Bull Run at Sudley Ford and were soon on the historic battlefield. From the heights of Groveton we could see that the road was clear to Centreville, and that there was no pursuit. . . .

I could not but feel deep pity for Stoughton when he looked back at Centreville and saw that there was no chance of his rescue. Without any fault of his own, Stoughton's career as a soldier was blasted.

There is an anecdote told of Mr. Lincoln that, when it was reported to him that Stoughton had been captured, he remarked, with characteristic humor, that he did not mind so much the loss of a general—for he could make another in five minutes—but he hated to lose the horses. . . .

JOHN HUNT MORGAN

On December 22, 1862, Gen. John Hunt Morgan and a force of more than 3,000 Confederate cavalry splashed across the Cumberland River near Carthage, Tennessee, and thundered north into Union-held Kentucky. Their objective: the tiny railroad village of Muldraugh Hill, where they would destroy two principal railroad trestles on the Louisville & Nashville Railroad and thus disrupt the vital supply line supporting the U.S. Army of the Cumberland. When the two-week dash behind enemy lines ended, Morgan would have *captured almost 2,000 prisoners, burned the targeted trestles, lured 20,000 enemy troops from the front, and destroyed almost $2 million of Federal property.*

It would become known as Morgan's Christmas Raid, and it was typical of the Confederate raider's bold, sometimes reckless forays behind enemy lines. A native of Alabama, raised in Kentucky, Morgan was a tall, glamorously attired cavalry officer with an affection for French-style whiskers and good horseflesh.

In 1862–63, he conducted a series of bold and risky cavalry raids through Tennessee and Kentucky, then unnerved Northerners with a final, daring raid across Indiana and Ohio. Morgan moved rapidly on his famous rides, cutting Federal supply lines, tearing up railroads and bridges, destroying large quantities of enemy supplies, and rounding up thousands of Federal prisoners. He monitored pursuing enemy forces by tapping telegraph lines, avoided unnecessary combat, and dispersed his command to elude capture. His famous Ohio Raid of July 1863 was the longest Confederate cavalry raid of the war, covering more than 700 miles in about three and a half weeks; however, he and his troops were surrounded and captured. Morgan was imprisoned in the Ohio State Penitentiary, but he and some accomplices tunneled out and escaped back to Dixie.

Morgan was a superb cavalry officer and an expert leader. His raids had mixed results, but they undeniably disrupted Federal operations in Kentucky and Tennessee, and provided a much-needed boost to Southern morale in the Western Theater. Like Stuart, Morgan was killed by hostile fire in a minor action in 1864. In preparation for an attack on Federal forces at Knoxville, Tennessee, Morgan halted his command overnight in nearby Greeneville, where, on September 4, 1864, he was surprised and killed by enemy cavalry.

A memoir of life in the saddle on a raid with John Hunt Morgan was recorded after the war by Dr. John Allen Wyeth, who left his Alabama home as a seventeen-year-old to join Morgan's troops on their famous 1863 Christmas Raid.

Early on December 22, we started on what turned out to be an exciting experience and one of the most trying of my life. Neither men nor horses on that wild sweep through Kentucky were spared, until we reached Liberty, Tennessee, not far from our starting point, fifteen days later; not withstanding the cold and fatigue and loss of sleep, I would not have missed it for any consideration. There was something contagious in the spirit, the élan of Morgan's troopers I never met with in other commands in which I became a veteran. Their enthusiasm was an epidemic which spared no one, not even the independent scout. They idolized John H. Morgan, who at the successful termination of this expedition reached the zenith of his glory. This was my first experience in sleeping on the ground in the open air in winter. As it was not very cold, with an abundant supply of wood which had been cut and corded long enough to become well seasoned (seemingly for our use), we made great fires, and Lieutenant Brady and I snuggled up between our oilcloths and blankets, with our saddles for pillows, and slept the sleep of the weary. On the 23rd we rode appearance an ideal soldier, with light blue or gray eyes and a strikingly handsome face, partly concealed by a brown or sandy mustache and imperial. He impressed me as being above average in size, and, as usual with Southerners, at home on horseback.

As we approached a small settlement known as Bear Wallow one of the videttes came tearing back at full speed and shouted out as he drew near: "Yankees thick as hell up the road!" We were quickly told to load and cap our guns, and then rode briskly forward to a rise in the road, and there, some four or five hundred yards in front of us, in a line of battle which extended a hundred yards or more on either side of and across the pike, were at least two hundred men mounted in blue. Captain Quirk yelled out, "Charge 'em, d——'em!" and down the road we fifty rode at full tilt. Our warlike approach did not seem to disconcert the men in blue, who were now in plain view, horses aligned and carbines ready and glinting in the Christmas sunlight. Their attitude evidently had made an impression on our captain; for when about two hundred yards from them, as we reached a slight depression in the road, he halted us, called off his horse holders, and ordered us to dismount and advance on foot. As we reached the top of the rise the forty-odd of us bent over, and, advancing in a lane which had a high worm fence on either side, the Federal line blazed away at us, and such a whizzing of bullets I had never before heard.

Company C, 5th Indiana Cavalry, which had been hidden from view in a hollow to our right, charged up to within a few yards of the road, right abreast of our position, and gave us a volley at almost muzzle range. One of our men, Old Hutch by nickname, was shot in the hand and announced the fact with a loud oath; and our doughty captain received two scalp wounds and was not in the best of humor. At this fusillade the horse holders and horses stampeded to the rear, and to add to the seriousness of our predicament, the Yankees in front charged down on us. The rest

John Hunt Morgan and wife.

all day at good speed, camped again under the sky, and the next day, Christmas eve, just at dark, were in sight of Glasgow, the county seat of Barren County, Kentucky.

On the 25th we started North at daybreak on the Munsfordsville Turnpike, and stopped an hour at noon to feed and wait for the main column to come up. The sun was shining and the temperature unusually warm for Christmas day in this section. General Morgan had overtaken us earlier in the forenoon and rode some distance with our company, which gave me an excellent opportunity of seeing the famous cavalryman. He was in of us scrambled over the opposite fence and made strides for a black-jacket or scrub oak thicket, which seemed to me a long way off, but really wasn't. The run for this copse was expedited by the pot shots from the Hoosier cavalrymen, who never let up on us until we had disappeared from view in the tangled thicket. Just as I reached the edge and turned to see if we were being closely followed, I encountered Captain Quirk, bareheaded, his face streaked with blood running from two scalp wounds. The part which had no blood on it was almost as red with anger and he was swearing like a trooper at his own men for running like cowards. Fortunately for us the Yankees stopped; for had they pressed us closely, few could have escaped.

We hurried through the brush in the direction of our advancing column, recovered our horses, and as the advance guard arrived formed with them, and this time made a sure enough charge. The enemy broke, and in the pursuit Tom Quirk, off in front as usual, got close enough to one of the hindmost Hoosiers and killed him with his pistol. The excitement being over, we marched on toward the Green River crossing, near which we overhauled a huge sutler's wagon, the contents which were unceremoniously appropriated even to a box of women's shoes, which the boys gallantly distributed to the houses on the line of march. That night we camped in the woods a few miles from Upton Station, on the Louisville & Nashville Railroad.

Here General Morgan overhauled the scouts, and I witnessed a very interesting incident. Attached to the General's staff was a telegraph operator, an attractive, quick-witted, clever young man, apparently about twenty-five years old, named Ellsworth, better known in the command as Lightning. He acquired this sobriquet when on a former occasion, having tapped a wire and interposed his instrument (which being a pocket affair, did not always give the most perfect satisfaction), its wobbling and uncertain "tick" aroused the suspicion of the operator he was calling. "Who

are you, and what's the matter with your office?" came over the wire. Quick as a flash Ellsworth broke in and replied, "O.K., lightning," which meant, "Go ahead; storm and lightning here interfering." This restored confidence, and Ellsworth got all the information his general wanted, and also got his nickname.

Our company took up its march toward Nolin, where there was another bridge guarded by a stockade. Before we reached there the garrison had surrendered to a detachment under Colonel Duke, and the bridge was burned. By night the weather had cleared, and we camped in the open a few miles from Elizabethtown. This place was captured after a slight resistance. The garrison, some eight companies of an Illinois regiment, six hundred and fifty-two men and officers, surrendered about 10 A.M.

On December 28 we were up and away early, bound for the two great trestles on the Louisville & Nashville Railroad at Muldraugh's Hill, the destruction of which was the most important object of the expedition. They were each from sixty to seventy-five feet high, seemingly six or seven hundred feet in length, and constructed then entirely of wooden beams. They were deemed of such importance that two strong wooden stockades or forts had been built, and were then garrisoned by an Indiana regiment (I think the 47th Infantry). Dividing his command, Morgan assailed both strongholds at the same time, the artillery doing most of the execution. In less than two hours the garrison of seven hundred men were prisoners.

For the next few hours we were hard at work gathering wood, fence rails, lumber from the shanties which had sheltered the garrison, and anything combustible, which we piled about the bases of the trestle timbers, and it was dark when we began to light the fires. The destruction of this immense network of timber made the most brilliant display of fireworks I have ever seen. When at last they were burned through, the flaming beams began to fall, and as the whole structure came down the heavens were brilliant with the column of sparks, which shot skyward. . . .

I never appreciated General Morgan's great ability as a soldier until I studied the official reports of the various Federal commanders who were trying to destroy him at this time. He was beset on all sides by detachments outnumbering him four to one. Nothing saved him but the genius of leadership, which divined the plans and movements of the enemy in time to elude him, and the devotion of the men who followed his fortunes and believed in him implicitly.

JAMES LONGSTREET

Robert E. Lee fondly referred to him as "My Old War Horse"; and after the death of Stonewall Jackson, he became the most distinguished of Lee's lieutenants. Yet, when he disagreed with orders, James Longstreet was slow to obey, and as a result, he was held accountable by many Southerners for the defeat at Gettysburg and the loss of Southern independence.

A native South Carolinian who grew into manhood in Alabama, Longstreet graduated from West Point in 1842 in the same class as Grant, Sherman, Halleck, McDowell, and other future adversaries. He emerged from the Mexican War with a battle wound and a promotion for valor in combat. Commissioned as a Confederate brigadier general early in the war, he maneuvered troops so skillfully at First Manassas that he was promoted to major general. Despite one of his slow starts at the Battle of Fair Oaks in 1862, Longstreet redeemed himself in the Seven Days Campaign that followed, participated in the Southern victory at Second Manassas and the bloody Sharpsburg campaign, after which he was promoted to lieutenant general on Lee's recommendation.

Viewed as a superb corps commander and a competent tactician, Longstreet was a vigorous, effective commander if he agreed with his orders, but could stall cautiously in carrying out a command he disliked. At Gettysburg, he entered battle with personal misgivings: He had urged Lee to direct an offensive in the Western Theater instead of invading Pennsylvania, and when overruled, he had also argued unsuccessfully in favor of battling the enemy from a defensive position. Whatever his reasons, his performance at Gettysburg was disastrously slow on both the second and third days of battle. Although Lee refrained from blaming him for the crucial defeat, other Southerners were less charitable.

Dispatched to the Western Theater in the fall of 1863, Longstreet contributed to the Confederate victory at Chickamauga, but accomplished little in the campaign to retake Knoxville, and he was soon summoned back East. Wounded at the Battle of the Wilderness, he recovered to command forces in the final, futile defense of Richmond, and was with Lee at Appomattox.

After the war he became an insurance executive and a cotton merchant; then fanned the controversy over his actions at Gettysburg by joining the Republican party—an act that earned him the enmity of many postwar Southerners. The rest of his life was spent in a variety of Federal appointments, including a stint as U.S. minister to Turkey. He defended himself in postwar writing, but despite his best explanations, many Southerners continued to blame Longstreet for the defeat at Gettysburg. Yet, despite his controversial acts, James Longstreet was one of a select handful of officers in whom Robert E. Lee placed his deepest trust. Although far more controversial than the other great Southern chieftains, Longstreet too emerged from the war as a legend in gray. Here, in his carefully chosen words, are excerpts from his official report on Gettysburg.

Report of Lieutenant General James Longstreet, C.S. Army, commanding First Army Corps.

HDQRS. 1st Army Corps,
        Dept. of Northern Virginia Near
        Culpepper Court-House, July 27, 1863

Colonel: In obedience to orders from the commanding general, my command marched from Fredericksburg, on June 3. . . .

On the morning [of July 3, 1863] our arrangements were made for renewing the attack by my right, with a view to pass around the hill occupied by the enemy on his left, and to gain it by flank and reverse attack. This would have been a slow process, probably, but I think not very difficult. A few moments after my orders for the execution of this plan were given, the commanding general joined me, and ordered a column of attack to be formed of Pickett's, Heth's, and part of Pender's divisions, the assault to be made directly at the enemy's main position, the Cemetery Hill. The distance to be passed over under fire of the enemy's batteries, and in plain view, seemed too great to insure great results, particularly as two-thirds of the troops to be engaged in the assault had been in a severe battle two days previous, Pickett's division alone being fresh.

Orders were given to Major-General Pickett to form his line under the best cover that he could get from the enemy's batteries, and so that the center of the assaulting column would arrive at the salient of the enemy's position, General Pickett's line to be the guide and to attack the line of the enemy's defences, and General Pettigrew, in com-mand of Heth's division, moving on the same line as General Pickett, was to assault the salient at the same moment. Pickett's division was arranged, two brigades in the front line, supported by his third brigade, and Wilcox's brigade was ordered to move in rear of his right flank, to protect it from any force that the enemy might attempt to move against it. . . .

About 2 P.M. General Pickett, who had been charged with the duty of arranging the lines behind our batteries, reported that the troops were in order and on the most sheltered ground. Colonel Walton was ordered to open up the batteries. The signal guns were fired, and all the batteries opened very handsomely and apparently with effective fire. The guns on the hill at the enemy's left were soon silenced. Those at the Cemetery Hill combated us, however, very obstinately. Many of them were driven off, but fresh ones were brought up to replace them. Colonel Alexander was ordered to a point where he could best observe the effect of our fire, and to give notice of the most opportune moment for our attack.

Some time after our batteries opened fire, I rode to Major James Dearing's batteries. It appeared that the enemy put in fresh batteries about as fast as others were driven off. I concluded, therefore, that we must attack very soon, if we hoped to accomplish anything before night. I gave orders for the batteries to refill their ammunition chests, and to be prepared to follow up the advance of the infantry. Upon riding over to Colonel Alexander's position, I found that he had advised General Pickett that the time had arrived under it, but the advance was resumed, and with some degree of steadiness. Pickett's troops did not appear to be checked by the batteries, and only halted to deliver a fire when close under musket-range.

Major-General Anderson's division was ordered forward to support and assist the wavering columns of Pettigrew and Trimble. Pickett's troops, after delivering fire, advanced to the charge, and entered the enemy's lines, capturing some of his batteries, and gained his works. About the same moment, the troops that had before hesitated, broke their ranks and fell back in great disorder, many more falling under the enemy's fire in retiring than while they were attacking. This gave the enemy time to throw his entire force upon Pickett, with a strong prospect of being able to break up his lines or destroy him before Anderson's division could reach him, which would, in its turn, have greatly exposed Anderson. He was, therefore, ordered to halt. In a few minutes the enemy, marching against both flanks and the front of Pickett's division, overpowered it and drove it back, capturing about half of those of it who were not killed or wounded. General Wright, of Anderson's division, with all of the officers, was ordered to rally and collect the scattered troops behind Anderson's division, and many of my staff officers were sent to assist in the same service. Expecting an attack of the enemy, I rode to the front of our batteries, to reconnoiter and superintend their operations.

The enemy threw forward forces at different times and from different points, but they were only feelers, and retired as soon as our batteries opened upon them. These little advances and checks were kept up till night, when the enemy retired to his stronghold, and my line was withdrawn to the Gettysburg road on the right, the left uniting with Lieutenant General A. P. Hill's right. After night, I received orders to make all the needful arrangements for our retreat. . . .

James Longstreet.

for the attack, and I gave the order to General Pickett to advance to the assault. I found then that our supply of ammunition was so short that the batteries could not reopen.

The order for this attack, which I could not favor under better auspices, would have been revoked had I felt that I had that privilege.

The advance was made in very handsome style, all the troops keeping their lines accurately, and taking the fire of the batteries with great coolness and deliberation. About halfway between our position and that of the enemy, a ravine partially sheltered our troops from the enemy's fire, where a short halt was made for rest. The advance was resumed after a moment's pause, all still in good order. The enemy's batteries soon opened on our lines with canister, and the left seemed to stagger

STONEWALL JACKSON

Following rumors of a major battle, a throng of worried townsfolk crowded around the little post office in Lexington, Virginia—Stonewall Jackson's hometown—where they anxiously awaited news from the front. When the mail arrived, Dr. W. S. White, the pastor of Lexington's Presbyterian church, was handed a letter from Jackson, who was a deacon in White's congregation. "Now we will have the news!" the preacher proclaimed. "Here is a letter from General Jackson himself!" The crowd hushed as White tore open the envelope from Lexington's now-famous son and listened intently as the pastor began to read aloud. To everyone's dismay, however, Jackson had written not a word about the battle, although he had played a key role in the action. Instead, the general had written to inquire about the status of his church and a Sunday school class he had established for Lexington's black community. The envelope contained an enclosure—a $50 check to buy books for the class.

This wartime correspondence may have disappointed his former neighbors, but it reflected Jackson's primary interests: Biblical theology and Christian discipleship. Like so many other Southerners of his day, Jackson was a deeply committed Christian. His well-defined devotion to duty and a disciplined life-style was the product of his Bible-based personal theology. Not long after he joined the local Presbyterian church, for instance, he was encouraged by the pastor to pray aloud at a prayer meeting. Jackson was reluctant to do so because he tended to stammer, but relented at Pastor White's urging. He did indeed stammer and hesitate—so much that White sympathetically offered to relieve Jackson of the obligation.

"Major," the pastor said to Jackson one day, "we do not wish to make our prayer meetings uncomfortable to you, and if you prefer it, I will not call on you to lead in prayer again."

"My comfort has nothing in the world to do with it, sir," Jackson promptly replied. "You, as my pastor, think that it is my duty to lead in public prayer— I think so too—and by God's grace I mean to do it. I wish you would please be so good as to call on me more frequently."

Thomas Jonathan Jackson's devotion to biblical discipline began early. Orphaned as a young child, he was raised by an impoverished uncle and was unable to obtain a quality childhood education. Thus he was academically handicapped when he entered the U.S. Military Academy in 1842. Determined to make the best of his opportunity, Jackson pursued academic improvement with single-minded devotion, zealous determination, and relentless study. When he graduated in 1846, he had risen to seventeenth in a class of fifty-nine.

Such personal discipline undoubtedly contributed significantly to the feats of military precision that made Jackson famous. Admittedly, he rarely looked like the personification of discipline—sitting at the head of his troops astride a common-looking nag, attired in a plain, mud-flecked uniform with a battered kepi pulled low over his eyes, sucking on a lemon. Yet his rapid-moving Foot Cavalry became the most celebrated of all Confederate commands, and Jackson himself became a military legend in his own lifetime.

From the moment at First Manassas when Brig. Gen. Barnard E. Bee dubbed him "Stonewall" to the untimely, fatal accident at Chancellorsville, Jackson's name was feared by his enemies and adored by his troops. His record of military accomplishments indisputably places him among the greatest captains in American history. After his death, on May 10, 1863, no commander could be found to replace him.

"The Army of Northern Virginia was never the same after Jackson's death," observed historian Douglas Southall Freeman, "and, though Lee conducted in 1864 some of his most brilliant maneuvers, he did not find another lieutenant who so well understood him or could execute his orders with such powerful, perfectly coordinated, hammer-strokes of attack."

There was but one Stonewall.

Jackson was a professor at Virginia Military Institute when the war erupted. He was ordered to Richmond and left Lexington on Sunday, April 21, 1861, leading his VMI cadets. The Sunday departure was ironic: Jackson held a high view of the Sabbath; he loathed doing battle on Sunday and would normally avoid even writing home on the Lord's Day. Nevertheless, he left behind his beloved Presbyterian church and his cherished black Sunday school class, not knowing, of course, that he would never return to either. Yet he was prepared for that possibility. "My religious belief teaches me to feel as safe in battle as in bed," he would say. "God has fixed the time for my death. I do not concern myself about that, but to always be ready, no matter when it may overtake me."

An account of Jackson's last day at home was chronicled by a friend and fellow believer, the Rev. J. William Jones, who recorded Professor Jackson's final peacetime acts before he marched away to war—and the glory that awaited Stonewall Jackson.

The day before he left home for the war was Saturday, and he was very busy all day long making preparations to leave at a moment's warning. He paid all outstanding accounts, and settled up as far as possible his worldly affairs, while his devoted wife was busily plying the needle to prepare him for the field.

At the supper-table Mrs. Jackson made some remark about the preparations for his expected departure, when he said, with a bright smile: "My dear, tomorrow is the blessed Sabbath day. It is also the regular communion season at our church. I hope I shall not be called to leave until Monday.

Let us then dismiss from our conversation and our thoughts everything pertaining to war, and have together one more quiet evening of preparation for our Sabbath duties."

Accordingly, the dark cloud of war was pushed aside. He read aloud to her for a while from religious magazines and newspapers, and then they went to their accustomed study of the Bible lesson, which was to be taught on the morrow to the colored Sunday-school. It was such a bright, happy Saturday evening, as is only known in the well-regulated Christian home. Alas! it proved the last which he ever spent under his own roof.

Stonewall Jackson and family.

Early the next morning a telegram from the Governor of the Commonwealth ordered him to march the corps of cadets for Richmond at 12:30 o'clock that day. Not waiting for his breakfast, he hurried to the institution and spent the morning making necessary preparations for the departure of the cadets, not forgetting to send a request to his pastor that he should be present to hold with them a brief service before they marched forth at the call of their sovereign State.

At 11 o'clock he came home to take a hurried breakfast and make a few personal arrangements, and the last thing he did before leaving home was to retire with his wife into their chamber and read a part of the fifth chapter of Second Corinthians—beginning, "For we know that if the earthly house of this tabernacle were dissolved, we have a building of God, a house not made with hands, eternal in the heavens"—and then made a humble, tender, fervent prayer, in which he begged that the dark cloud of war might even then be dissipated; that the God of Peace might calm the storm and avert the calamity of war, or that He might at least go forth with him and with the young men under his command to guide, guard, help and bless them.

At 12 o'clock the venerable pastor was present to make to the corps an appropriate address of Christian counsel, and to lead in a fervent, tender prayer.

At the appointed hour, to the exact minute, Major Jackson gave the order: "Attention! Forward! March!"

And thus the loving husband bade adieu to his home, the faithful church-member turned away from his communion service, the earnest Sunday-school teacher left his lesson untaught, the peerless soldier marched forth from the parade-ground to win immortal fame, to not come back again until his body was borne to its burial in the beautiful cemetery at "Lexington, in the Valley of Virginia," and two continents were bursting with the fame of "Stonewall" Jackson.

JEFFERSON DAVIS

Even at the very end, with the Confederacy defeated and the South in ruins, Confederate President Jefferson Davis refused to discard his vision of an independent Southern nation. On May 2, 1865, Davis presided over what would prove to be his final war council, held in a borrowed house in the little town of Abbeville, South Carolina. Richmond—once the proud capital of the Confederacy—now lay conquered, gutted by fire and occupied by Northern troops. After four years of determined resistance, Robert E. Lee's Army of Northern Virginia had surrendered and was now disbanded and dispersed. In North Carolina, Gen. Joseph E. Johnston had directed his army to lay down its arms, and in Mobile, Alabama, Gen. Richard Taylor was preparing to surrender the last Confederate army east of the Mississippi.

President Davis and the Confederate cabinet had evacuated Richmond, heading into the Deep South, and the Confederate government had dissolved along the way. Davis, his entourage, and military escort had retreated to Danville, Virginia, then south to Charlotte, North Carolina, and finally to Abbeville. There, hoping to plan a strategy for conducting the war from somewhere west of the Mississippi, Davis assembled his last war council: Secretary of War John C. Breckinridge, Gen. Braxton Bragg, and five brigadier generals.

Faced with the reality of defeat, Davis was still determined to do all in his power to keep the Confederacy alive. Refusal to admit defeat was characteristic of Davis. Revered by many Southerners, reviled by some, he was a forceful, determined leader motivated by a remarkable reserve of energy and self-confidence. Opponents, who viewed him as stubborn, dogmatic, and inflexible, accused him of mishandling the war and overestimating his abilities as commander in chief. Supporters, however, championed Davis as a man of high character who faced an almost impossible task, yet with consummate skill and tireless devotion had directed the new nation through the greatest war ever fought in the Western Hemisphere.

"His slender, tall and erect figure, his spare face, keen eyes and fine forehead—not broad, but high and well-shaped—presented the well-known strong American type," recalled Northern statesman Carl Schurz, who had known Davis in the prewar U.S. Senate. "There was in his bearing a dignity which seemed entirely natural and unaffected—that kind of dignity which does not invite familiar approach, but will not render one uneasy by lofty assumption. His courtesy was without any condescending air. His conversation ran in easy, well-chosen and sometimes even elegant phrases, and the timbre of his voice had something peculiarly agreeable."

When captured by Federal forces near Irwinville, Georgia, on May 10, 1865, Davis was subjected to public ridicule in the Northern press and spent two years in prison without trial, including a period of time in shackles. Imprisoned, he became a symbol of the Lost Cause—a martyr for the shattered dream of an independent South—and thus regained the unified respect and devotion of the Southern people. Until his death on December 9, 1889, at age eighty-one, Jefferson Davis remained a cherished hero to the people of the fallen Confederacy.

Twenty-six-year-old Brig. Gen. Basil Duke was a member of that final council of war at Abbeville. Like the other officers present, Duke believed the war was lost and further resistance was useless. Davis alone would not relinquish the dream of the Confederate nation, and for the rest of his days, the young general would remember the unyielding personal determination of the Confederate president. Duke's account:

We were shown into a room where we found Mr. Davis and Generals Breckinridge and Bragg. No one else was present. I had never seen Mr. Davis look better or show to better advantage. He seemed in excellent spirits and humor; and the union of dignity, graceful affability, and decision, which made his manner usually so striking, was very marked in his reception of us. After some conversation of a general nature, he said: "It is time that we adopt some definite plan upon which the further prosecution of our struggle shall be conducted. I have summoned you for consultation. I feel that I ought to do nothing now without the advice of my military chiefs." He smiled rather archly as he used this expression, and we could not help thinking that such a term addressed to a handful of brigadiers, commanding altogether barely three thousand men, by one who so recently had been the master of legions was a pleasantry, yet he said it in a way that made it a compliment.

After we had each given, at his request, a statement of the equipment and condition of our respective commands, Mr. Davis proceeded to declare his conviction that the cause was not lost any more than hope of American liberty was gone amid the sorest trials and most disheartening reverses of the Revolutionary struggle; but that energy, courage and constancy might yet save all. "Even," he said, "if the troops now with me be all that I can for the present rely on, three thousand

brave men are enough for a nucleus around which the whole people will rally when the panic which now affects them has passed away." He then asked that we should make suggestions in regard to the future conduct of the war.

Jefferson Davis.

We looked at each other in amazement and with a feeling of little akin to trepidation, for we hardly knew how we should give expression to views diametrically opposed to those he had uttered. Our respect for Mr. Davis approached veneration, and notwithstanding the total dissent we felt, and were obligated to announce, to the program he had indicated, that respect was rather increased than diminished by what he had said.

I do not remember who spoke first, but we all expressed the same opinion. We told him frankly that the events of the last few days had removed from our minds all idea or hope that a prolongation of the contest was possible. The people were not panic-stricken, but broken down and worn out. We said that an attempt to continue the war, after all means of supporting warfare had all gone, would be a cruel injustice to the people of the South. We would be compelled to live in a country already impoverished, and would invite its further devastation. We urged that we would be doing a wrong to our men if we persuaded them to such a course; for if they persisted in a conflict so hopeless they would be treated as brigands, and would forfeit all chance of returning to their homes.

He asked why then we were still in the field. We answered that we were desirous of affording him an opportunity of escaping the degradation of capture, and perhaps a fate which would be direr to the people than even to himself, and still more embittering the feeling between the North and South. We said that we would ask our men to follow us until his safety was insured, and would risk them in battle for that purpose, but would not fire another shot in an effort to continue hostilities.

He declared, abruptly, that he would listen to no suggestion which regarded only his own safety. He appealed eloquently to every sentiment and reminiscence that might be supposed to move a Southern soldier, and urged us to accept his views. We remained silent, for our convictions were unshaken; we felt responsible for the future welfare of the men who had so heroically followed us; and the painful point had been reached, when to speak again in opposition to all that he urged would have approached altercation. For some minutes not a word was spoken. Then Mr. Davis rose and ejaculated bitterly that all was indeed lost. He had become very pallid, and he walked so feebly as he proceeded to leave the room that General Breckinridge stepped hastily up and offered his arm.

ROBERT E. LEE

Marching through the Pennsylvania countryside on the invasion that would end at Gettysburg, Robert E. Lee's Army of Northern Virginia passed the front terrace of a handsome mansion, where a party of well-dressed Northern women had gathered to watch the passing Confederate troops. One of the party, an attractive young woman, defiantly waved a small United States flag at the dust-covered gray columns as they marched by the house. The troops passed silently, offering no rebuke, and the flag-waver brandished the banner even more boldly.

Then Gen. Robert E. Lee appeared, moving slowly on horseback alongside his troops. When in front of the young woman, Lee paused momentarily and looked calmly into her face, saying nothing. The young woman slowly dropped the flag to her side. Lee then rode on, and the young woman turned back to her friends, exclaiming, "Oh! I wish he was ours!"

Such was the influence of Robert E. Lee's presence upon those who personally encountered him, including enemies. Even posthumously, the quality of his character and the caliber of his accomplishments produced a lasting influence. Upon completing his definitive four-volume study of Lee, historian Douglas Southall Freeman, who would win a Pulitzer Prize for R. E. Lee, A Biography, *recalled the multitude of obstacles and challenges he had encountered in producing the monumental work. Yet he proclaimed with satisfaction, "I have been fully repaid by being privileged to live, as it were, for more than a decade in the company of a great gentleman."*

Few public figures in any age have bequeathed such an enduring legacy of national respect and affection, and seldom has any military commander so infused his troops with the love and esteem displayed toward Lee by his heralded Army of Northern Virginia. So ardent was their devotion that a battle-hardened Johnny Reb, in the anguish of Appomattox, could shout with a conviction no doubt shared by his comrades, "I love you just as much as ever, General Lee."

When they chanced to encounter their former commander after the war, veterans would automatically emit the fabled Rebel yell in recognition or, hat in hand, would stand transfixed in silent salute. Children of the postwar South who had the opportunity to shake Lee's hand at some rare public appearance would still marvel decades later—as white-headed old men—at the power of Lee's presence.

More than a century after his death, amid the vastly different life-style of modern American society, literate Americans who discovered anew the life of Robert E. Lee would often be affected with the same awe and admiration experienced by Lee's contemporaries. Despite the best efforts of the most jaded revisionists, generation after generation of Americans and others would encounter the Lee of history and, as did so many before them, would marvel at his character and conduct. Today he remains the embodiment of all that was good and noble in the Old South. Despite the passage of time and the ever-changing whims of popular culture, Robert E. Lee retains his position as the foremost Southern hero.

A measure of the common soldier's devotion to Lee was demonstrated at the Battle of the Wilderness on May 6, 1864, when Lee attempted to go into battle at the head of his troops. He was confronted and dissuaded by a determined brigade of Texans, who put the general's safety ahead of their own. This account of the event was recorded by a veteran of the battle, Col. Charles S. Venable.

General Lee soon sent a message to Longstreet to make a night march and bring up his two divisions at daybreak on the 6th. He himself slept on the field, taking his headquarters a few hundred yards from the line of battle of the day. It was his intention to relieve Hill's two divisions with Longstreet's, and throw them farther to the left, to fill up a part of the great unoccupied interval between the Plank Road and Ewell's right, near the old turnpike, or use them on his right, as the occasion

Robert E. Lee.

might demand. It was unfortunate that any of these troops should have become aware they were to be relieved by Longstreet. It is certain that owing to this impression, Wilcox's division, on the right, was not in condition to receive Hancock's attack at early dawn on the morning of the 6th, by which they were driven back in considerable confusion. In fact some of the brigades of Wilcox's division came back in disorder, but sullenly and without panic, entirely across the Plank Road, where General Lee and the gallant Hill in person helped to rally them. The right of his line was thrown back several hundred yards, but a portion of the troops still maintained their position.

The danger, however, was great, and General Lee sent his trusted adjutant, Colonel W. H. Taylor, back to Parker's store to get the trains ready for a movement to the rear. He sent an aide also to hasten the march of Longstreet's divisions. These came the last mile and a half at a double-quick, in parallel columns, along the Plank Road. General Longstreet rode forward with that imperturbable coolness which always characterized him in times of perilous action, and began to put them in position on the right and left of the road. His men came to the front of the disordered battle with a steadiness unexampled even among veterans, and with an élan which presaged restoration of our battle and certain victory.

When they arrived, the bullets of the enemy on our right flank had begun to sweep the field in the rear of the artillery pits on the left of the road, where General Lee was giving directions and assisting General Hill in rallying and reforming his troops. It was here that the incident of Lee's charge with Gregg's Texas brigade occurred. The Texans cheered lustily as their line of battle, coming up in splendid style, passed by Wilcox's disordered columns, and swept across our artillery pit and its adjacent breastwork.

Much moved by the greeting of these brave men and their magnificent behavior, General Lee spurred his horse through an opening in the trenches and followed close on their line as it moved rapidly forward. The men did not perceive that he was going with them until he had advanced some distance in the charge; when they did, there came from the entire line, as it rushed on, the cry, "Go back, General Lee! Go back!" Some historians like to put this in less homely words; but the brave Texans did not pick their phrases. "We won't go on unless you go back!" A sergeant seized his bridle rein. The gallant General Gregg (who laid down his life on the 9th October, almost in General Lee's presence, in a desperate charge of his brigade on the enemy's lines in the rear of Fort Harrison), turning his horse toward General Lee, remonstrated with him.

Just then I called his attention to General Longstreet, whom he had been seeking, and who sat on his horse on a knoll to the right of the Texans, directing the attack of his divisions. He yielded with evident reluctance to the entreaties of his men, and rode up to Longstreet's position. With the first opportunity I informed General Longstreet of what had just happened, and he, with affectionate bluntness, urged General Lee to go farther back. I need not say the Texans went forward in their charge and did well their duty. They were eight hundred strong, and lost half their number killed and wounded on that bloody day. The battle was soon restored, and the enemy driven back to their position of the night before.

QUOTATIONS FROM GENERAL LEE

The Army of Northern Virginia

The world has never seen nobler men than those who belonged to the Army of Northern Virginia.

Slavery

So far from engaging in a war to perpetuate slavery, I am rejoiced that slavery is abolished.

Why the South Fought

All that the South has ever desired was that the Union—as established by our forefathers—should be preserved, and that the government—as originally organized—should be administered in purity and truth.

States' Rights

I consider it as the chief source of stability to our present system; whereas the consolidation of the states into one vast republic, sure to be aggressive abroad and despotic at home, will be the certain precursor of that ruin which has overwhelmed all those that have preceded it.

The Constitution

I trust that the constitution may undergo no change, but that it may be handed down to succeeding generations in the form we received it from our forefathers.

Duty

Do your duty in all things. . . . You cannot do more; you should never wish to do less.

Joining the Confederacy

I did only what my duty demanded. I could have taken no other course without dishonor. And if it all were to be done over again, I should act in precisely the same manner.

War

But what a cruel thing is war; to separate and destroy families and friends, and mar the purest joys and happiness God has granted us in this world; to fill our hearts with hatred instead of love for our neighbors, and to devastate the fair face of this beautiful world.

Salvation

I can only say that I am nothing but a poor sinner, trusting in Christ alone for salvation.

The War Between the States

It was an unnecessary condition of affairs, and might have been avoided if forebearance and wisdom had been practiced on both sides.

History and the South

The reputation of individuals is of minor importance [compared] to the opinion posterity may form of the motives which governed the people of the South in their late struggle for the maintenance of the principles of the Constitution. I hope, therefore, a true history will be written, and justice done them.

8

The Wages of War

In 1861–65, a violent whirlwind of war swept across the South with fearsome destruction. At no time in American history has any other section of the United States suffered such devastation. Cities were gutted. Homes lay in ashes and rubble. Crops were destroyed, livestock lay slaughtered, businesses were ruined. The South's economy was shattered. Its people were defeated, and its future was uncertain. Worst of all, the cream of young Southern manhood lay beneath the earth of battlefields, campgrounds, and prison camps. While some sections of the defeated Confederacy had been spared the torch of warfare, none was spared the ghastly loss of life.

The wages of war had been issued to the South—and had been dispensed on a scale of destruction unknown to any other generation of Americans.

Richmond, once the proud capital of the Confederate States of America, was a defeated city at war's end, gutted and ravaged by the flames of war.

Much of Richmond had been transformed into a community of ashes and rubble. Here, victorious Northern soldiers survey the skeletal ruins of a once-busy city street.

Richmond's war machine, which had supplied the South with the tools of war for four years, had ceased production forever.

A rebuilt Richmond would eventually arise from the ashes, but memories of the war's devastation would endure for generations.

Fredericksburg, Virginia's graceful city on the Rappahannock, endured some of the bloodiest fighting of the war and was left battered and scarred.

The South's small towns and rural areas also felt the harsh brutality of war—although most were too small or too remote to attract photographers. In Virginia's Tidewater town of Hampton, for instance, the war left little more than a lonesome-looking line of chimneys.

In Vicksburg, Mississippi, residents faced the peacetime task of repairing the damage caused by the prolonged Federal siege, which left the river port scarred by artillery fire and pockmarked with makeshift bombproofs.

Knoxville, Tennessee—the site of bitter, bloody combat—was left encircled by a perimeter of earthworks and surrounded by torn and ugly landscape.

Throughout the former Confederacy, the Southern railway system lay in ruins: bridges had been burned, depots had been razed, tracks had been destroyed, and rolling stock had been wrecked. At Bridgeport, Tennessee, above, the remains of a major railroad span were left starkly isolated in midstream.

On Atlanta's Peachtree Street, wagon traffic moved again, but Sherman's torch bearers had left an ugly mark on the city.

Atlanta would rise from the destruction to become a Southern metropolis, but in 1865 much of the city consisted of charred timbers and mounds of debris.

The scorched wreckage of Southern rolling stock was left in a blackened, stationary parade on Atlanta's broken tracks.

In South Carolina, a destructive fire had engulfed Charleston during the war and Federal artillery had pounded the city for years. At war's end, Charleston's classic beauty was severely marred.

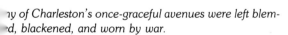

ny of Charleston's once-graceful avenues were left blem-
d, blackened, and worn by war.

Founded almost 200 years earlier, historic Charleston had been robbed of much of its charm by the forces of war.

Perhaps no city in the South suffered as much punishment as did South Carolina's capital. At war's end, the blackened remains of Columbia's business district surrounded the unfinished state capitol in a gruesome circle of ruin.

Under construction when Sherman's army arrived, the new capitol was pitted by shellfire but left standing. However, Columbia's original capitol, adjacent to the construction site, was transformed into a mass of charred bricks.

countless homes along Sherman's route, Columbia's Hunt Hotel emerged from the war as nothing but a collection of ʰed chimneys. To Southerners, the houseless chimneys became known as Sherman's Sentinels, and would serve for ; to come as gloomy reminders of the South's suffering.

Southerners like Columbia photographer Richard Wearn, seen here amid the ruins of his city, faced a grim and uncertain future at war's end. Most would accept the challenge with determination, but for some the impact of the war was overwhelming. Unable to recover his losses, photographer Wearn reportedly committed suicide.

By far the South's worst destruction was the awful loss of life. Almost 290,000 sons of the South, like these Confederates killed at Sharpsburg, would never go home again.

Like these Confederates, killed at Spotsylvania, many of the Southern dead were mere youngsters. They were the rising generation, and their loss to the South and the reunited nation could never be measured.

Row upon row, the Confederate dead were laid beneath the Southern soil. On battlefields and campgrounds, in cities and towns throughout the South, graveyards like Richmond's Hollywood Cemetery marked the wages of war paid in pain by the Southern people.

9

The Thin Gray Line

They were the war's young men grown old—the thin gray line of Confederate veterans. Most were united by a futile dream of Southern nationhood, an abiding love for the South, and the common experiences of soldiers who had worn Confederate gray. Southerners did not neglect them or forget them. As they grew older and their numbers fewer, their deeds and sacrifices glowed brighter aqnd dearer to their children and grandchildren. They were memorialized in monuments and verse; honored at reunions; feted and eulogized on Confederate memorial Day; respected by former foes, and revered by the last generation of Southerners to know them.

For a half century after the war, they dominated the social, business, and political life of the South. Through the efforts of the United Confederate Veterans and the United Daughters of the Confederacy, they reassembled for reunion events, pursued common objectives, lobbied for fair treatment by historians, and—eventually—happily joined their former foes for joint encampments on the battlefields of history. Each year the thin gray line grew thinner. At the turn of the century their numbers were still legion, but their ranks diminished rapidly in the years that followed. By the 1930s few remained. In 1951, the year of their final reunion, only a frail handful were left. In 1959 the last was gone.

The thin gray line marched only in history.

*Within days of Lee's surrender, former Johnny Rebs were reentering the South's civilian society. On a sunny spring
week after Appomattox, ex-Confederates in Richmond mingled with victorious Federal troops beneath Washington's st*

Bound by wartime friendships and a common experience, Confederate veterans began to reassemble within months of war's end. In early 1866, these former members of the 4th Texas Infantry reunited for a photograph. Some, like the disabled veterans seated in front, would carry reminders of the war with them for the rest of their lives.

Eventually, the war-torn South was rebuilt. In Atlanta, a new railroad terminal was erected—bigger and more modern than the depot Sherman had destroyed—and Atlanta became the business center of the South.

In rebuilt Charleston, the port city's once battered and fortified Battery became a peaceful place where veterans' sons could enjoy a recess from military school alongside warlike relics of the past.

Former battlefields like Fredericksburg's Sunken Road, site of some of the war's worst carnage, reverted to peaceful uses, marked by modern improvements like the telephone.

Once formidable military sites like Virginia's Fortress Monroe became favorite spots for Sunday afternoon outings.

torical markers went up at former battlefields Chattanooga's Lookout Mountain, right. ought there. . . . We camped here," visiting nfederate veterans could tell their families.

By the late 1870s, Reconstruction had ended and Southerners began to honor their wartime heroes, hoping the children of the South would revere the best traditions of the Lost Cause.

The wartime symbols of the Confederacy became treasured relics. Years after it was last unfurled in battle, the 10th Virginia's Starry Cross was reverently unfolded for a photographer.

In 1889, the South's aging soldiers established the United Confederate Veterans, which eventually organized 1,855 local posts, or camps, with more than 150,000 members. Beginning in 1890, the UCV sponsored regular veterans' reunions, established soldiers' homes, aided needy veterans, erected monuments throughout the South, produced a voluminous history of the war, and published a monthly magazine, Confederate Veteran. Here, the Robert E. Lee Camp of the UCV assembles in Charleston, West Virginia.

The eager young Johnny Rebs of 1861 gradually became gray-headed old men with vivid memories of a war that was quickly receding into the past. In South Carolina's rebuilt capital, members of a veterans' reunion posed for a group portrait beneath a string of new electric lights. Behind them is the capitol building Sherman had battered decades before.

Linked by the common bond of wartime experiences, the South's veterans reassembled despite the inconveniences of advancing age. Here, elderly survivors of the famed Raccoon Roughs gather in reunion around their former commander, Gen. John B. Gordon, standing at center with a raccoon skin on his chest.

One by one, the veterans joined the ranks those who had fallen on distant battlefields who had died in camp and prison. By Decer ber of 1889, when former President Jefferso Davis's funeral procession paraded solemr down this New Orleans avenue, thousands Confederate veterans were already gone.

Throughout the South, in small towns and large cities alike, a Southern renaissance was celebrated with flags, crowds, and the erection of stone soldiers—usually facing north. Here citizens of LaGrange, Georgia, pay tribute to Johnny Reb.

In 1898, the Spanish-American War ignited a unified spirit of nationalism in the South and North, and lured old soldiers of the blue and the gray back into uniform—this time on the same side. Confederate veterans like these would parade down Southern boulevards holding aloft patriotic banners pointedly denouncing any citizen "who ain't for his country."

Eventually, old animosities—like so many old wounds—healed for most veterans, and were replaced by mutual respect and even affection for the former foe. At joint reunions, Johnny Reb and Billy Yank became genuine, handshaking friends.

No matter how much time passed, some sites would always be identified with Southern valor and sacrifice. On July 13, 1913, a half-century after the smoke had cleared at Gettysburg, these aging Johnny Rebs retraced their famous route in Pickett's Charge.

For many veterans, life would be marked and measured by their wartime deeds and experiences; and for them the battlefields of the conflict would hold an irresistible attraction. Here a group of Confederate veterans join former adversaries on a pilgrimage to the site where Stonewall Jackson was shot in 1863. Standing second from the right with straw hat in hand is an aging Gen. James Longstreet.

By the dawn of the new century, interest in the war was popular enough to create tourist attractions. In 1907, veterans and their families who visited the 350-acre Jamestown Exposition at Hampton Roads, Virginia, could follow the boardwalk to flag-bedecked cycloramas depicting great battles of "the late unpleasantness."

In turn-of-the century Richmond, a well-organized 1907 reunion produced a human version of the Starry Cross beneath the equestrian statue of Robert E. Lee.

Not all reunions were patriotic extravaganzas. Some were casual affairs—like dinner on the grounds after Sunday preaching. In tiny Lake City, South Carolina, an informal reunion of old Confederates was highlighted by a souvenir photograph taken outside a local church building.

Every year there were more widows. Their dark garments made them conspicuous at public ceremonies like this one in Lexington, Kentucky, where members of the United Daughters of the Confederacy joined white-headed veterans in 1911 to dedicate a statue to Gen. John Hunt Morgan.

As their numbers diminished, the aging Johnny Rebs became the cherished heroes of the South, treated with honors and saluted for their wartime deeds. At the 1916 Confederate reunion in Birmingham, Alabama, the city's residents flew the Starry Cross alongside the Stars and Stripes; packed the downtown sidewalks, and staged a memorial parade in honor of the South's old soldiers.

Veterans of General Nathan Bedford Forrest's command mustered a proud but thinning line at the Birmingham reunion. They were frail and gray in 1916, but their name alone had once been enough to throw a scare into the Yankees.

Throughout the South, grateful citizens established soldiers' homes to care for aging veterans. At the Confederate Home of Missouri, in Higginsville, old warriors of the Confederacy paused for a photograph outside a readied dining hall. Eventually, their home would become a state historic site.

To young Southerners of the early twentieth century, the War Between the States was history. It must have been difficult for them to associate wartime deeds of glory with the stooped and fragile old men for whom the conflict was memory. Here, elderly veterans of Mosby's Rangers sit for a photograph at a reunion in Warrenton, Virginia.

What wartime scenes their aging eyes had surveyed a half-century earlier: the Peach Orchard at Shiloh, the numbing slaughter of Franklin, a cornfield of carnage at Sharpsburg, the winter agony of Camp Douglas. Elderly veterans like these undoubtedly hoped admiring youngsters of their day would never know the reality of war.

Gradually, quietly, the thin gray line marched into history.

Notes and Picture Credits

Chapter 1. Soldiers of the South

Lt. Laurie M. Anderson
  Compiled Service Records of the 1st Florida Infantry, National Archives.
  Laurie M. Anderson Papers, Florida State Archives.
  Picture Credit: Florida State Archives.

Pvt. John Bagnel Brogdon
  Compiled Service Records of the 7th South Carolina Cavalry, National Archives.
  Picture Credit: Barbara Thomas, Myrtle Beach, S.C.

Bugler John Washington Payne
  Compiled Service Records of the 2nd Kentucky Mounted Infantry, National Archives.
  Picture Credit: Kentucky Military History Museum.

Pvt. Andrew F. Skidmore
  Compiled Service Records of the 17th Virginia Infantry, National Archives.
  Picture Credit: Library of Congress.

Sgt. David Grey Parker
  Compiled Service Records of the 14th North Carolina Infantry, National Archives.
  Picture Credit: J. Keith Parker, Charlotte, N.C.

Lt. Andrew H. Ramsey
  Compiled Service Records of the 1st South Carolina Rifles, National Archives.
  Picture Credit: South Caroliniana Library, University of South Carolina.

Capt. Edward Currie
  Compiled Service Records of the 1st Texas Infantry, National Archives.
  Simpson, Harold B. *Hood's Texas Brigade, A Compendium.* Hillsboro, Texas: Hill Junior College Press, 1977.
  Picture Credit: Confederate Research Center, Hill Junior College.

John Rhodes
  Compiled Service Records of the 5th Virginia Infantry, National Archives.
  Picture Credit: Library of Congress.

Capt. Thomas R. Love
  Compiled Service Records of the 8th Florida Infantry, National Archives.
  Thomas R. Love Papers, Florida State Archives.
  Picture Credit: Florida State Archives.

Benjamin G. Liddon
  Compiled Service Records of the 3rd Georgia Infantry, National Archives.
  Benjamin G. Liddon Papers, Florida State Archives.
  Picture Credit: Florida State Archives.

Drummer Charles E. Mosby
  Compiled Service Records of the 6th Virginia Infantry, National Archives.
  Picture Credit: *Confederate Veteran,* Vol. XII, no. 4 (April 1904), p. 18.

Corp. James Parker Boswell

Compiled Service Records of the 3rd South Carolina Light Artillery, National Archives.
Picture Credit: Gwynn Meroney, Mocksville, N.C.

CAPT. AMOS WHITEHEAD
Compiled Service Records of the 2nd Florida Infantry, National Archives.
Amos Whitehead Papers, Florida State Archives.
Picture Credit: Florida State Archives.

W. F. JONES
Richard Bacot Papers, Manuscripts Collection, South Caroliniana Library, University of South Carolina.
Picture Credit: Richard Bacot Papers, South Caroliniana Library, University of South Carolina.

PVT. FERDINAND BERRY
Compiled Service Records of the 1st Tennessee Infantry, National Archives.
Picture Credit: Tennessee State Library and Archives.

PVT. HILLIARD TODD
Compiled Service Records of Manigault's Battalion, South Carolina Artillery, National Archives.
Picture Credit: Dennis E. Todd, Cayce, S.C.

LT. ROBERT CUNNINGHAM
Compiled Service Records of the 4th Kentucky Cavalry, National Archives.
Picture Credit: Kentucky Military History.

JOHN ELIAS BOINEST
Compiled Service Records of the South Carolina Battalion of State Cadets, National Archives.
Picture Credit: Rev. and Mrs. James Edward Graham, Surfside Beach, S.C.

LT. COL. JAMES THOMAS WEAVER
Compiled Service Records of the 60th North Carolina Infantry, National Archives.
Ray, James M., "Sixtieth Regiment," *Histories of the Several Regiments and Battalions from North Carolina in the Great War, 1861–'65,* edited by Walter Clark. Goldsboro, North Carolina: Nash Brothers, 1901, p. 471–502.
Picture Credit: Library of Congress.

ALEXANDER MACKLIN
Compiled Service Records of the 9th Kentucky Cavalry, National Archives.
Picture Credit: Kentucky Military History.

PVT. JOHN SCOTT PICKLE
Compiled Service Records of the 18th Texas Cavalry, National Archives.
Picture Credit: Austin History Center, Austin Public Library.

COL. HENRY LAURENS BENBOW
Compiled Service Records of the 23rd South Carolina Infantry, National Archives.
Picture Credit: Gale H. Dixon, Florence, S.C.

PVT. ROBERT PATTERSON
Compiled Service Records of the 12th Tennessee Infantry, National Archives.
Picture Credit: Library of Congress.

"UNCLE BUD"
Photographs Collection: Museum of the History of Mobile.
Picture Credit: Museum of the History of Mobile.

Chapter 2. Johnny Reb in Camp and Field

"No Two Kept the Same Step."
Gordon, John B., *Reminiscences of the Civil War.* New York: Charles Scribner's Sons, 1903, pp. 4–11.
Picture Credit: U.S. Army Military History Institute.

"Every Day Is Very Much the Same."
James W. Morgan to Wife, August 28, 1861,
James W. Morgan Letters.
Manuscripts Section, Kentucky Building, Western Kentucky University.
Picture Credit: U.S. Army Military History Institute.

"Hugh Has Got the Measles."
D. C. Jones to Father, November 21–25, 1861,
Jones Family Papers, 1861–1862.
Joint Collection, Ellis Library, University of Missouri at Columbia.
Picture Credit: U.S. Army Military History Institute.

"Went Off Laughing."
"The Diary of Samuel Edward Burges, 1860–1862," edited by Thomas W. Chadwick, *The South Carolina Historical and Genealogical Magazine,* Vol. XLVIII, no. 4 (October 1947), p. 216.
Picture Credit: John W. Harris, Jr., Myrtle Beach, S.C.; Sgt. Sharon Harris, Washington, D.C.

"We'll Proudly Bear This Banner."
Manuscript of Speech by Mississippi College Rifles, Charles Viele Papers, Civil War Miscellaneous Collection, Archives Branch, U.S. Army Military History Institute.
Picture Credit: *Battles and Leaders of the Civil War.*

"We Must Reconcile Ourselves to His Will."
T. J. Rankin to Sarah, November 27, 1861,
Thomas J. Rankin Letters, Manuscript Collection,

McCain Library and Archives, University of Southern Mississippi.
Picture Credit: U.S. Army Military History Institute.

"From Civilian to Soldier."
Compiled Service Records of the 60th Regiment of North Carolina Infantry, National Archives.
Picture Credit: Mrs. James K. ("Bud") Chandler, Weaverville, N.C.

"No Soldiers Ever Marched with Less."
McCarthy, Carlton, "Detailed Minutiae of Soldier Life," *Southern Historical Society Papers,* Vol. VI, no. 1 (July 1878), pp. 1–9.
Picture Credit: *Scribner's Monthly Magazine.*

"Marching Along at a Brisk Rate."
Worsham, John H., *One of Jackson's Foot Cavalry.* New York: The Neale Publishing Company, 1912, pp. 155–158.
Picture Credit: *Battles and Leaders of the Civil War.*

"This Horde of Ragamuffins."
Hunter, Alexander, "A High Private's Account of the Battle of Sharpsburg," *Southern Historical Society Papers,* Vol. X, nos. 10–11 (October–November 1882), pp. 508–509.
Picture Credit: Library of Congress.

"The Incentives to Piety Were Abundant."
Goodloe, Albert Theodore, *Some Rebel Relics from the Seat of War.* Nashville: Publishing House of the Methodist Episcopal Church, South, 1893. pp. 235–51.
Picture Credit: Jones, J. William. *Christ in the Camp.*

"The Grayback Was an Undisputed Success."
Goodloe, Albert Theodore, *Some Rebel Relics from the Seat of War.* Nashville: Publishing House of the Methodist Episcopal Church, South, 1893, pp. 154–161.
Picture Credit: *Scribner's Monthly Magazine.*

"I Assure You I Am Lonely and Sad."
Patrick A. McGriff to Susan, July 1, 1864,
Patrick A. McGriff Papers, Manuscripts Collection, Florida State Archives.
Picture Credit: Florida State Archives.

"Both Men Were Cool."
Diary Entry of November 24, 1864, The Diary of Colonel William Lamb, October 24, 1864–January 14, 1865,
William Lamb Papers, Manuscripts Collection, Earl Greg Swem Library, The College of William and Mary.
Picture Credit: Library of Congress.

"The Young Ladies Were Looking Their Prettiest."

O'Ferrall, Charles T., *Forty Years of Active Service.* New York: The Neale Publishing Company, 1904, pp. 116–118.
Picture Credit: Johnston, Mary. *The Long Roll.*

"Give My Love to All the Children."
A. M. Glazener to Son and Daughter, July 31, 1863,
W. P. Glazener to Sister, September 10, 1913,
Abram Glazener Papers, *Civil War Times Illustrated* Collection, Archives Branch, U.S. Army Military History Institute.
Picture Credit: U.S. Army Military History Institute.

"A Soldier's View of Army Life."
"Pencil Sketches of Val C. Giles," Annie B. Giles Papers, John Barker Texas History Center, University of Texas at Austin.

"One Day Without Anything to Eat Was Common."
McCarthy, Carlton, "Detailed Minutiae of Soldier Life," *Southern Historical Society Papers,* Vol. VI, no. 1 (July 1878), pp. 1–9.
Picture Credit: Austin History Center, Austin Public Library.

"The Lady Wept and the Children Sobbed."
"A Moving Story of Privation," *Confederate Veteran,* Vol. VI, no. 3 (March 1898), p. 135.
Picture Credit: *Camp Fires of the Confederacy.*

"We Uns Calls It Stone Soup."
Hunter, Alexander, "A High Private's Sketch of Sharpsburg," *Southern Historical Society Papers,* Vol. XI, no. 1 (January 1883), pp. 10–13.
Picture Credit: Well, Edward, *Hampton and His Cavalry in '64.*

"We Stood There Within a Few Minutes of Eternity."
T. J. Rankin to Sarah, January 5, 1862,
Thomas J. Rankin Letters, Manuscript Collection, McCain Library of Archives, University of Southern Mississippi.
Hardcastle, C. L., "The Tragedy of Buck Island," *Confederate Veteran,* Vol. VI, no. 10 (October 1898), p. 523.
Picture Credit: Library of Congress.

"I Was in Bed with a Dead Man."
Killie, E. I., "Why I Got in Bed with a Corpse," *Confederate Veteran,* Vol XIV, no. 8 (August 1906), pp. 361–62.
Picture Credit: Library of Congress.

"That Banner Was Conquered."
"Origin of 'The Conquered Banner,' " *Confederate Veteran,* Vol. V, no. 8 (August 1897), pp. 436–37.
Picture Credit: Library of Congress.

Chapter 3. Down Home in Dixie

"Mr. Davis Came Forward Amid a Storm of Applause."
Capers, Henry D., *Recollections of the Civil Service of the Confederate Government.* N.p.n.d., pp. 4–6.
Picture Credit: National Archives.

"There Was No Sleep in Richmond."
DeLeon, T. C., *Four Years in Rebel Capitals.* Mobile: The Gossip Printing Company, 1890, pp. 124–27.
Picture Credit: *Battles and Leaders of the Civil War.*

"There Is No End to These Horrors."
Cumming, Kate, *A Journal of Hospital Life in the Confederate Army of Tennessee.* Louisville: John P. Morton and Company, 1866, pp. 13–19.
Picture Credit: Wells, Edward, *Hampton and His Cavalry in '64.*

"I Wish You Could Have Seen Ma."
Mary A. Brantly to Brothers, July 20, 1863,
John Fiser Papers, *Civil War Times Illustrated Collection,* Archives Branch, U.S. Army Military History Institute.
Picture Credit: South Carolina Confederate Relic Room and Museum.

"I Want to See You . . . the Worst I Ever Did."
Harvey Bailey to Wife and Children, June 20, 1864,
Harvey Bailey Papers, Civil War Miscellaneous Collection, Archives Branch, U.S. Army Military History Institute.
Picture Credit: Library of Congress.

"Our Circle Has Been Broken."
Albert Milton Walls to Pa and Ma, August 19, 1864,
Albert Milton Walls Papers, *Civil War Times Illustrated* Collection, Archives Branch, U.S. Army Military History Institute.
Picture Credit: *Battles and Leaders of the Civil War.*

"We Bore Bravely Every Reverse of Fortune."
Frye, Rose W., "The Way We Lived Then," *Our Women in the War.* Charleston: The News & Courier Book Presses, 1885, pp. 426–29.
Picture Credit: Library of Congress.

"We Expected to Make Our Dash."
Morgan, James Morris, *Recollections of a Rebel Reefer.* Boston: Houghton Mifflin Company, 1917, pp. 191–95.
Picture Credit: *The Illustrated London News.*

"An Indian Grabbed Little Betty."
Ramsey, Lucille, "Comanche's Attack on Brown Family in 1863," *The* (Weatherford, Texas) *Weekly Herald,* February 25, 1937.
Picture Credit: Library of Congress.

"Each Bomb Called Forth Wails and Shrieks of Terror."
Ripley, Elliza McHatton, *From Flag to Flag,* New York: D. Appleton and Company, 1889. pp. 32–52.
Picture Credit: Library of Congress.

"Sister Dealt Him a Severe Stroke with the Corn Knife."
Ridley, Bromfield, *Battles and Sketches of the Army of Tennessee.* Mexico, Missouri: Missouri Printing and Publishing Company, 1906, pp 498–500.
Picture Credit: Library of Congress.

"Young Gentleman, You Seem to Be a Little Excited."
Stiles, Robert, *Four Years Under Marse Robert.* New York: The Neale Publishing Company, 1904, pp. 132–33.
Picture Credit: Library of Congress.

"Terror Stricken, We Remained Crouched in the Cave."
Loughborough, Mrs. James M., *My Cave Life in Vicksburg.* Little Rock: Kellogg Print Company, 1882, pp. 56–92.
Picture Credit: *Howard Pyle's Book of the American Spirit.*

"Marster Was Good an' Kind, But I Like to Be Free."
WPA Slave Narratives. St. Clair Shores, Michigan: Scholarly Press, Inc., 1976. Part 1, p. 248–53; Part 3, pp. 288–93.
Picture Credit: Library of Congress.

"The Manly and Upright Will Brand Your Name Infamy."
"Mrs. Henrietta E. Lee's Letter to General David Hunter on the Burning of Her House," *Southern Historical Society Papers,* Vol. VIII, no. 5 (May 1880), pp. 215–16,
Andrews, Matthew Page, *The Women of the South in Wartimes.* Baltimore: The Norman, Remington Company, 1927, pp. 201–204.
Picture Credit: Library of Congress.

"The Rooms Swarmed with Armed Men."
Clifford, Helen, "Three Days and Nights of Terror," *Our Women in the War.* Charleston: News & Courier Book Presses, 1885. pp. 54–60.
Picture Credit: *Camp Fires of the Confederacy.*

"Hain't Ye Goin' to Wait fer Yer Dodgers?"
Holmes, Florence L., "Rebel Bees and Union Foragers," *Camp Fires of the Confederacy,* edited by Ben

LaBree. Louisville: Courier-Journal Job Printing Company, 1899, pp. 267–70.
Picture Credit: *Camp Fires of the Confederacy.*

"Oh! Miss Lucy, De Town's Burnin' Up!"
Dade, Virginia E., "The Fall of Richmond," *Our Women in the War.* Charleston: News & Courier Book Presses, 1885, pp. 99–108.
Picture Credit: Ellis, Edward. *The History of Our Country.*

Chapter 4. The Flame of Battle

"The Ball Was Opened."
John H. Hines to Ma and G. Pa, April 22, 1862, John H. Hines Letters, 1862–65, Manuscripts Section, Kentucky Building, Western Kentucky University.
Picture Credit: Library of Congress.

"The Battle Roared in Front."
Blackford, William W., *War Years with Jeb Stuart.* New York: Charles Scribner's Sons, 1945, pp. 28–31.
Picture Credit: *Harper's Weekly.*

"Battle Is Terrible and Fearful."
Barziza, Decimus et Ultimus, *The Adventures of a Prisoner of War 1863–1864.* Austin: University of Texas Press, 1964, pp. 47–49.
Picture Credit: Library of Congress.

"Desperation Seemed to Seize Me."
McKinstry, J. A., "With Col. Rogers When He Fell," *Confederate Veteran,* Vol. IV, no. 6 (June 1896), pp. 220–22.
Picture Credit: Library of Congress.

"The Order Was Given to Charge."
Watkins, Samuel R., *"Co. Aytch."* Jackson, Tennessee: McCowat-Mercer Press, 1952, pp. 183–85.
Picture Credit: *Battles and Leaders of the Civil War.*

"Steady Men! Steady! They Are Coming."
Hunter, Alexander, "A High Private's Account of the Battle of Sharpsburg," *Southern Historical Society Papers,* Vol. XI, no. 1 (January 1883), pp. 10–21.
Picture Credit: Library of Congress.

"I Saw That He Was Breathing His Last."
C. H. Gray to Father, December 12, 1862, C. H. Gray Papers, Manuscripts Collection, Prairie Grove State Park.
Beth Rider. Muskogee, Oklahoma.
Picture Credit: Library of Congress.

"The Earth Is Red with Blood."
Worsham, John H., *One of Jackson's Foot Cavalry.* New York: The Neale Publishing Company, 1912. pp. 129–30.
Watkins, Samuel R., *"Co. Aytch."* Jackson, Tennessee: McCowat-Mercer Press, 1952, pp. 233–35.
Picture Credit: Library of Congress.

"I Wish We Could All Go Home in Peace."
Neese, George M., *Three Years in the Confederate Horse Artillery.* New York: The Neale Publishing Company, 1911, pp. 83–88.
Picture Credit: *Century Magazine.*

"I Was Shot Just as We Reached the Top."
Fontaine, Lamar, *My Life and My Lectures.* New York: The Neale Publishing Company, 1908, pp. 68–75.
Picture Credit: *Scribner's Monthly Magazine.*

"He Fell Almost as Soon as They Started."
Fleming, Francis P., *Memoir of Capt. C. Seton Fleming.* Jacksonville, Florida: Times-Union Publishing House, 1881, pp. 96–97, 100–102.
Picture Credit: Florida State Archives.

"Another Hero Takes the Falling Standard."
"Story of Five Privates," *Confederate Veteran,* Vol. I, no. 5 (May 1893), p. 152.
Compiled Service Records of the 1st South Carolina Infantry, National Archives.
Picture Credit: South Carolina Confederate Relic Room and Museum.

"An Enthusiasm I Will Never Forget."
Twiggs, H. D. D., "Perilous Adventure at Battery Wagner," *Confederate Veteran,* Vol. XII, no. 3 (March 1904), pp. 104–106.
Picture Credit: U.S. Army Military History Institute.

"The Torpedo Struck the Vessel and Exploded."
Glassell, W. T., "Reminiscences of Torpedo Service in Charleston Harbor," *Southern Historical Society Papers,* Vol. IV, no. 5 (November 1877), pp. 225–35.
Picture Credit: Library of Congress.

"I Lunged My Bayonet at His Side."
Bernard, George S., "The Battle of the Crater," An Address Delivered Before the A. P. Hill Camp of Confederate Veterans of Petersburg, Virginia, June 24, 1890, *Civil War Times Illustrated* Collection, Archives Branch, U.S. Army Military History Institute

Picture Credit: Library of Congress.

"Woh-Who-Ey! Who-Ey! Who-Ey!"
"The Rebel Yell," *Confederate Veteran,* Vol. I, no. 4 (April 1893), p. 106.

"Open Letters." *Century Magazine,* Vol. XLIII, no. 6 (April 1892), pp. 954–55.
Picture Credit: Johnston, Mary, *The Long Roll.*

"We Have Surrendered."
McCarthy, Carlton, *Detailed Minutiae of Soldier Life in the Army of Northern Virginia 1861–1865.* Richmond: Carlton McCarthy and Company, 1882, pp. 148–52.
Picture Credit: *Howard Pyle's Book of the American Spirit.*

"In Proud Humiliation Stood the Embodiment of Manhood."
Chamberlain, Joshua L., *The Passing of the Armies.* New York: G. P. Putnam's Sons, 1915, pp. 260–65.
Picture Credit: Library of Congress.

Chapter 5. In Yankee Prisons

"Our Gloomy Journey."
King, John H., *Three Hundred Days in a Yankee Prison: Reminiscences of War Life, Captivity, Imprisonment at Camp Chase, Ohio.* Atlanta: J. P. Daves, 1904, pp. 55–72.
Picture Credit: U.S. Army Military History Institute.

"Twenty-Five Degrees Below Zero."
Carpenter, H., "Plain Living at Johnson's Island," *Century Magazine,* Vol. XLI (November 1891–April 1892), pp. 705–18.

Wyeth, John A., "Cold Cheer at Camp Morton," *Century Magazine,* Vol. XLI (November 1891–April 1892), p. 847.
Picture Credit: *Century Magazine.*

"Hungry, Hungry, Hungry All the Time."
Moffett, George H., "War Prison Experiences," *Confederate Veteran,* Vol. XIII, no. 3 (March 1905), pp. 105–10.

"Treatment of Prisoners During the War." *Southern History Society Papers,* Vol. I, no. 4 (April 1876), p. 254.
Milton A. Ryan Diary, Milton Ryan Papers, *Civil War Times Illustrated* Collection, Archives Branch, U.S. Army Military History Institute.
Picture Credit: *Century Magazine.*

"Much Sickness Prevailed."
King, John H., *My Experience in the Confederate Army and in Northern Prisons.* Clarksburg, West Virginia: Stonewall Jackson Chapter of the United Daughters of the Confederacy, 1917, pp. 38–44.
Picture Credit: U.S. Army Military History Institute.

"A Lamentable Affair."
"Treatment of Prisoners During the War," *Southern Historical Society Papers,* Vol. I, no. 4 (April 1876), pp. 272–73.
Picture Credit: Ohio Historical Society.

"Then Commenced a Race."
Seward, Simon, " Perilous Escape from Point Lookout," *Confederate Veteran,* Vol. XVI, no. 1 (January 1908), pp. 42–44.
Picture Credit: *Confederate Veteran.*

"Charlie Became an Object of Strictest Surveillance."
Johnson, W. Gart, "Prison Life at Harper's Ferry and on Johnson's Island," *Confederate Veteran,* Vol. II, no. 8 (August 1894), pp. 242–43.

McNamara, M. "Lieutenant Charlie Pierce's Daring Attempts to Escape from Johnson's Island," *Southern Historical Society Papers,* Vol. VIII, no. 2 (February 1880), pp. 61–67.
Picture Credit: Library of Congress.

"We Had Cut Through Forty-two Brick Walls."
Murray, J. Ogden, *The Immortal Six Hundred.* Winchester, Virginia: The Eddy Press Corporation, 1905, pp. 165–80.
Picture Credit: U.S. Army Military History Institute.

"Now for Canada."
Knauss, William H., *The Story of Camp Chase.* Nashville: Publishing House of the Methodist Episcopal Church, South, 1906. pp. 226–33.
Picture Credit: *Century Magazine.*

"I Was Arrested as a Spy."
Ridley, Bromfield, *Battles and Sketches of the Army of Tennessee.* Mexico, Missouri: Missouri Printing and Publishing Company, 1906, pp. 274–76, 280.
Picture Credit: *Confederate Veteran.*

"The Happiest Man in the Southern Confederacy."
Null, J. M., "Thrilling and Amusing Events," *Confederate Veteran,* Vol. II, no. 9 (September 1894), pp. 276–77.
Picture Credit: *Battles and Leaders of the Civil War.*

"We Longed for Death."
Fuzzlebug, Fritz (Pseudonym of John J. Dunkle),

Prison Life During the Rebellion. Singer's Glen, Virginia: Joseph Funk's Sons, Printers, 1869, pp. 19–37.

Picture Credit: Major Emanuel—B. F. Emanuel, Lancaster, S.C.; Rest—Murray, J. Ogden, *The Immortal Six Hundred.*

"He Is of This World No More."

Mrs. M. E. Jackson to Mrs. David Gaston, September 12, 1863,

David Gaston Papers, Harrisburg Civil War Roundtable Collection, Archives Branch, U.S. Army Military History Institute.

Picture Credit: Carl Hill, Jr., Florence, S.C.

"Father Ran to Meet Me."

John Malachi Bowden Manuscript, John Bowden Papers, *Civil War Times Illustrated* Collection, Archives Branch, U.S. Army Military History Institute, pp. 29–31.

Picture Credit: Library of Congress.

Chapter 6. In Sherman's Path

"Dear, Dear Atlanta!"

Mary Rawson Diary, Manuscripts Collection, Atlanta Historical Society.

Picture Credit: Library of Congress.

"The Heart Was Burning out of Beautiful Atlanta."

Conyngham, David P., *Sherman's March Through the South.* New York: Sheldon & Company, 1865, pp. 236–38.

Picture Credit: Library of Congress.

"The Vandals Left Suffering and Desolation."

The Journal of a Milledgeville Girl, 1861–1867, edited by James C. Bonner. Athens: University of Georgia Press, 1964, pp. 60–63.

Picture Credit: Library of Congress.

"We Looked out upon a Scene of Desolation and Ruin."

Canning, Nora M., "Sherman in Georgia," *Our Women in the War.* Charleston: News & Courier Book Presses, 1885, pp. 77–85.

Picture Credit: *Harper's Weekly.*

"Made to Feed the Flames."

Trowbridge, John Townsend, *A Picture of the Desolated States; and the Work of Restoration 1865–1868.* Hartford, Conn.: L. Stebbins, 1868, pp. 546–52.

Picture Credit: Library of Congress.

"A Visit from the Fire Fiends."

Steele, Mrs. E. A., "A Brave Colored Woman," *Our Women in the War.* Charleston: News & Courier Book Presses, 1885, pp. 309–11.

Picture Credit: U.S. Army Military History Institute.

"The Beds Were on Fire."

Quattlebaum, Paul, "When the Yankees Come to Pinarea," *South Carolina Magazine,* Vol. 26, no. 2 (February 1962), pp. 4–6.

Picture Credit: Laura J. Quattlebaum Jordan, Conway, S.C.

"Your City Is Doomed."

Trowbridge, John Townsend, *A Picture of the Desolated States; and the Work of Restoration, 1861–1868.* Hartford, Conn.: L. Stebbins, 1868, pp. 556–64.

Picture Credit: U.S. Army Military History Institute.

"Hell on Earth."

Mother to Gracia, March 3, 1865, Anonymous Manuscript, 3 March 1865, South Caroliniana Library, University of South Carolina.

Picture Credit: Richard Wearn Photographs, South Caroliniana Library, University of South Carolina.

"Aunt Penny Raided the Yankees."

Marlowe, Alexia, "The Rumor Became a Reality," Alexia Marlowe Papers, Waccamaw Room Collection, Kimbel Library, Coastal Carolina College.

Picture Credit: Alexia Marlowe Conway, S.C.

"A Reckless Demon . . . Ready for Any Atrocity."

Daniel Heyward Trezevant Papers, Ms. Vol. 1865, South Caroliniana Library, University of South Carolina.

MacLean, Clara D., "The Last Raid," *Southern Historical Society Papers,* Vol. XIII (January– December 1885), pp. 466–76.

Picture Credit: Library of Congress.

Chapter 7. Legends in Gray

NATHAN BEDFORD FORREST

"Lieutenant General N. B. Forrest," *Southern Historical Society Papers,* Vol. XX (January–December 1892), p. 329.

Lytle, Andrew, *Bedford Forrest and His Critter Company.* New York: Minton, Balch & Company, 1931, pp. 372–74.

Picture Credit: Library of Congress.

J. E. B. STUART

"The Death of Major-General J. E. B. Stuart," *Southern Historical Society Papers,* Vol. VII, no. 2

Picture Credit: Library of Congress.

PATRICK R. CLEBURNE

"Anecdotes of General Cleburne," *Southern Historical Society Papers,* Vol. XXI (January–December 1893), pp. 299–301

Buck, Irving A. *Cleburne and His Command.* Jackson, Tennessee: McCowat-Mercer Press, 1959, pp. 280–81, 289–94.
Picture Credit: Library of Congress.

RAPHAEL SEMMES

Official Records of the Union and Confederate Navies in the War of the Rebellion. Washington: U.S. Government Printing Office, 1880–1927. Series I, Vol. III, pp. 649–51.
Picture Credit: Library of Congress.

JOHN SINGLETON MOSBY

Mosby, John S., *The Memoirs of Colonel John S. Mosby.* Bloomington: Indiana University Press, 1959, pp. 172–81.
Picture Credit: Library of Congress.

JOHN HUNT MORGAN

Wyeth, John A., "Trials with Gen. John H. Morgan," *Confederate Veteran,* Vol XIX, no. 3 (March 1911), pp. 118–22; Vol. XIX, no. 4 (April 1911), pp. 161–164.
Picture Credit: Library of Congress.

JAMES LONGSTREET

The War of the Rebellion: A Compilation of the Official Records of the Union and Confederate Armies. Washington: U.S. Government Printing Office, 1880–1901. Series I, Vol. XXVII, Pt. 2, pp. 357–63.
Picture Credit: Library of Congress.

STONEWALL JACKSON

Jones, J. William, *Christ in the Camp.* Atlanta: The Martin & Hoyt Company, 1887, pp. 82–87.
Picture Credit: South Caroliniana Library, University of South Carolina.

JEFFERSON DAVIS

Duke, Basil W., "Last Days of the Confederacy," *Battles and Leaders of the Civil War,* edited by Robert Underwood Johnson and Clarence Clough Buel. New York: The Century Company, 1884. Vol. IV, pp. 764–65

Dictionary of American Biography, edited by Allen Johnson and Dumas Malone. New York: Charles Scribner's Sons, 1928–1936. Vol. III, p. 126.

Miller, Walter L. "The Last Meeting of the Confederate Cabinet," *The Southern Magazine,* Vol. I, no. 3, pp. 137–50.
Picture Credit: Library of Congress.

ROBERT E. LEE

"General Lee to the Rear," *Southern Historical Society Papers,* Vol. VIII, no. 3 (March 1880), pp. 108–109.
Picture Credit: Library of Congress.

Chapter 8. The Wages of War

Richmond Photographs: U.S. Army Military History Institute.
Fredericksburg Photograph: U.S. Army Military History Institute.
Hampton Photograph: Library of Congress.
Vicksburg Photograph: U.S. Army Military History Institute.
Knoxville Photograph: Library of Congress.
Bridgeport Photograph: U.S. Army Military History Institute.
Atlanta Photographs: Library of Congress.
Charleston Photographs: U.S. Army Military History Institute.
Columbia Photographs: South Caroliniana Library.
Sharpsburg Photograph: U.S. Army Military History Institute.
Spotsylvania Photograph: U.S. Army Military History Institute.
Hollywood Cemetery Photograph: U.S. Army Military History Institute.

Chapter 9. The Thin Gray Line

Richmond Photograph: U.S. Army Military History Institute.
Texas Veterans Photogaph: Texas State Library.
Atlanta Photograph: Atlanta Historical Society.
Charleston Photograph: Library of Congress.
Fredericksburg Photograph: Library of Congress.
Fort Monroe Photograph: Casemate Museum, Fort Monroe, Virginia.
Lookout Mountain Photograph: Library of Congress.
Jackson Monument Photograph: Library of Congress.
Starry Cross Photograph: U.S. Army Military History Institute.
West Virginia Veterans: West Virginia Department of Culture and History.
Columbia Photograph: South Carolina Confederate Relic Room and Museum.
Davis Funeral: Library of Congress.

LaGrange Photograph: U.S. Military History Institute.

Veterans Parade: Library of Congress.

Johnny Reb and Billy Yank: Library of Congress.

Gettysburg Photograph: Pennsylvania State Archives.

Longstreet Group: Library of Congress.

Jamestown Exposition Photograph: Library of Congress.

Richmond Reunion: U.S. Army Military History Institute.

Lake City Reunion: Stan and Anne Collins, Conway, South Carolina.

Morgan Monument Photographs: Library of Congress.

Birmingham Parade: Birmingham Public Library.

Forrest's Veterans: Birmingham Public Library.

Missouri Veterans' Home: Confederate Memorial State Historic Site and the State Historical Society of Missouri.

Mosby Veterans: Library of Congress.

Handshaking Veterans: Birmingham Public Library.

Elderly Veteran and Flag: Library of Congress.

Selected Bibliography

Books, Articles, and Government Publications

"A Boy in Gray," *Scribner's Monthly Magazine,* Vol. XXII, no. 5 (September 1881).

The American Heritage Picture History of the Civil War, edited by Richard M. Ketchum. New York: American Heritage Publishing Co., 1960.

"A Moving Story of Privation," *Confederate Veteran,* Vol. VI, no. 3 (March 1898), p. 135.

Andrews, Matthew Page, *The Women of the South in Wartime.* Baltimore: The Norman, Remington Company, 1927.

"Anecdotes of General Cleburne," *Southern Historical Society Papers,* Vol. XXI (January–December 1893), pp. 299–301.

As They Saw Forrest, edited by Robert Selph Henry. Jackson, Tenn. McCowat-Mercer Press, Inc, 1956.

Barbiere, Joe, *Scraps from the Prison Table at Camp Chase and Johnson's Island.* Doylestown, Pa.: W. W. H. Davis, Printer, 1868.

Barrett, John G., *Sherman's March Through the Carolinas.* Chapel Hill: The University of North Carolina Press, 1956.

Barziza, Decimus et Ultimus, *The Adventures of a Prisoner of War 1863–1864,* edited by R. Henderson Shuffler. Austin: University of Texas Press, 1964.

Battles and Leaders of the Civil War, edited by Robert Underwood Johnson and Clarence Clough Buel. 4 vols. New York: The Century Company, 1884.

Beale, R. L. T., *History of the Ninth Virginia Cavalry in the War Between the States.* Richmond: B. F. Johnson Publishing Company, 1899.

Beers, Fannie A., *Memories: A Record of Personal Experience During Four Years of War.* Philadelphia: J. B. Lippincott Co., 1888.

Bird, W. H., *Stories of the Civil War.* Columbiana, Ala. Advocate Printing, n.d.

Blackford, William H., *War Years with Jeb Stuart.* New York: Charles Scribner's Sons, 1945.

Boatner, Mark Mayo, III, *The Civil War Dictionary.* New York: David McKay and Company, 1959.

Boyd, Belle, *Belle Boyd in Camp and Prison.* New York: Blealock and Company, 1866.

Boykin, Edward M., *The Falling Flag: Evacuation of Richmond, Retreat and Surrender at Appomattox.* New York: E. J. Hale and Sons, Publishers, 1874.

Brokenburn: The Journal of Kate Stone 1861–1868, edited by John Q. Anderson. Baton Rouge: LSU Press, 1955.

Buck, Irving A., *Cleburne and His Command.* Jackson, Tenn. McCowat-Mercer Press, Inc., 1959.

Camp Fires of the Confederacy, edited by Ben LaBree. Louisville: Courier-Journal Job Printing Company, 1899.

Capers, H. D., *Recollections of the Civil Service of the Confederate Government.* N.p.n.d.

Carpenter, H., "Plain Living at Johnson's Island," *Century Magazine,* Vol. XLI (November 1891–April 1892), pp. 705–18.

Chamberlain, Joshua L., *The Passing of the Armies.* New York: G. P. Putnam's Sons, 1915.

Cochran, Hamilton, *Blockade Runners of the Confederacy.* New York: The Bobbs-Merrill Company, Inc., 1958.

Coggins, Jack, *Arms and Equipment of the Civil War*. Garden City, N.Y.: Doubleday & Company, 1962.

Connelly, Thomas L., and Barbara L. Bellows, *God and General Longstreet: The Lost Cause and the Southern Mind*. Baton Rouge: Louisiana State University Press, 1982.

Conyngham, David, *Sherman's March Through The South*. New York: Sheldon & Company, 1865.

Cooke, John Esten, *Wearing of the Gray*. Bloomington: Indiana University Press, 1959.

Copley, John M., *A Sketch of the Battle of Franklin, Tennessee; with Reminiscences of Camp Douglas*. Austin, Tex.: Eugene Von Boeckman, Printer, 1893.

Cumming, Kate, *A Journal of Hospital Life in the Confederate Army of Tennessee*. Louisville: John P. Morton and Company, 1866.

Dabney, Virginius, *The Last Review: The Confederate Reunion, Richmond, 1932*. Chapel Hill, N.C.: Algonquin Books, 1984.

Davis, Burke, *The Long Surrender*. New York: Random House, 1985.

————. *Sherman's March*. New York: Random House, 1980.

"The Death of Major-General J. E. B. Stuart," *Southern Historical Society Papers*, Vol. VII, no. 2 (February 1879), pp. 107–10.

DeLeon, T. C., *Four Years in Rebel Capitals: An Inside View of Life in the Southern Confederacy from Birth to Death*. Mobile, Ala.: The Gossip Printing Company, 1890.

DeSaussure, Mrs. N. B., *Old Plantation Days*. New York: Duffield and Company, 1909.

D'Hamel, E. B., *The Adventures of a Tenderfoot*, reprint ed. Waco, Tex.: W. M. Morrison, n.d.

"The Diary of Samuel Edward Burges, 1860–1862," edited by Thomas W. Chadwick, *The Southern Historical and Genealogical Magazine*, Vol. XLVIII, no. 4 (October 1947), p. 216.

Dictionary of American Biography, edited by Allen Johnson and Dumas Malone. 20 vols. New York: Charles Scribner's Sons, 1928–1936.

Dinkins, James, *The Balaclava of America: Reminiscences of the Battle of Franklin*. New Orleans: The New Orleans Picayune, 1903.

Douglas, Henry Kyd, *I Rode with Stonewall*. Chapel Hill: The University of North Carolina Press, 1940.

Dowdey, Clifford, *Lee*. Boston: Little, Brown and Company, 1965.

Eaton, Clement, *Jefferson Davis*. New York: The Free Press, 1977.

Eckenrode, H. J., and Bryan, Conrad. *James Longstreet: Lee's War Horse*. Chapel Hill: The University of North Carolina Press, 1936.

Eggleston, George Cary, *A Rebel's Recollections*. Bloomington: Indiana University Press, 1959.

Ellis, Edward S., *The History of Our Country*. New York: Henry W. Knight Company, 1899.

Fishwick, Marshall W., *Lee After the War*. New York: Dodd, Mead and Company, 1963.

Fleming, Francis P., *Memoir of Capt. C. Seton Fleming*. Jacksonville, Fla. Times-Union Publishing House, 1881.

Flood, Charles Bracelen, *Lee: The Last Years*. Boston: Houghton Mifflin Company, 1981.

Fontaine, Lamar, *My Life and My Lectures*. New York: Neale Publishing Company, 1908.

Foote, Shelby, *The Civil War: A Narrative*. 3 vols. New York: Random House, 1958, 1963, and 1974.

Freeman, Douglas Southall, *Lee's Lieutenants*. 3 vols. New York: Charles Scribner's Sons, 1942.

————, *R. E. Lee*. New York: Charles Scribner's Sons, 1934.

————, *The South to Posterity*. New York: Charles Scribner's Sons, 1951.

Fuzzlebug, Fritz (pseud. of John J. Dunkle), *Prison Life During the Rebellion*. Singer's Glen, Virginia: Joseph Funk's Sons, Printers, 1869.

"General Lee to the Rear," *South Historical Society Papers*, Vol. VIII, no. 3 (March 1880), pp. 108–109.

General Robert E. Lee: Soldier, Citizen and Christian Patriot, edited by R. A. Brock. Atlanta: H. C. Hudgins and Company, 1897.

Gibbons, A. R., *The Recollections of an Old Confederate Soldier*. Shelbyville, Mo.: Herald Print. n.d.

Gibson, John M., *Those 163 Days*. New York: Coward-McCann, Inc., 1961.

Giles, Valerius Cincinnatus, *Rags and Hope: The Recollections of Val C. Giles, Four Years with Hood's Brigade*, edited by Mary Lasswell. New York: Coward-McCann, 1961.

Glassel, W. T., "Reminiscences of Torpedo Service in Charleston Harbor," *Southern Historical Society Papers*, Vol. IV, no. 5 (November 1877), pp. 225–35.

Goodloe, Albert Theodore, *Some Rebel Relics from the Seat of War*. Nashville: Publishing House of the Methodist Episcopal Church, South, 1893.

Gordon, John B., *Reminiscences of the Civil War*. New York: Charles Scribner's Sons, 1903.

Gragg, Rod, *The Civil War Quiz and Fact Book*. New York: Harper & Row, Publishers, 1985.

Greenhow, Rose O'Neal, *My Imprisonment and the First Year of Abolition Rule at Washington*. London: Richard Bentley, 1863.

Hagood, Johnson C., *Memoirs of the War of Secession*. Columbia, S.C.: The State Company, 1910.

Hague, Parthenia Antoinette, *A Blockaded Family*. Boston:

Houghton, Mifflin & Company, 1888.

Hardcastle, C. L., "The Tragedy of Buck Island," *Confederate Veteran*. Vol. VI, no. 10 (October 1898), p. 523.

Headley, John W., *Confederate Operations in Canada and New York*. New York: The Neale Publishing Company, 1906.

Hesseltine, William Best, *Civil War Prisons: A Study in War Psychology*. Columbus, Ohio: Ohio State University Press, 1930.

Heth, Henry, *The Memoirs of Henry Heth*, edited by James L. Morrison, Jr. Westport, Conn.: Greenwood Press, 1974.

Histories of the Several Regiments and Battalions from North Carolina in the Great War, 1861–1865, edited by Walter Clark. 5 vols. Goldsboro, N.C.: Nash Brothers, 1901.

Historical Times Illustrated Encyclopedia of the Civil War, edited by Patricia L. Faust. New York: Harper & Row, Publishers, 1986.

Hopley, Catherine Cooper, *Life in the South: From the Commencement of the War*. 2 vols. London: Chapman & Hall, 1863.

Howard Pyle's Book of the American Spirit, edited by Francis J. Dowd. New York: Harper & Brothers, Publishers, 1923.

Howard, Robert M., *Reminiscences*. Columbus, Ga.: Gilbert Printing Company, 1912.

Hull, Susan R., *Boy Soldiers of the Confederacy*. New York: The Neale Publishing Company, 1905.

Hunter, Alexander, "A High Private's Account of the Battle of Sharpsburg," *Southern Historical Society Papers,* Vol. X, nos. 10–11 (October–November 1882), pp. 508–509; Vol. XI, no. 1 (January 1883), pp. 10–21.

The Image of War 1861–1865, edited by William C. Davis. 6 vols. Garden City, N.Y.: Doubleday & Company, 1983–84.

Johnson, W. Gart, "Prison Life at Harper's Ferry and on Johnson's Island," *Confederate Veteran*, Vol. II, no. 8 (August 1894), pp. 242–43.

Johnston, Mary, *The Long Roll*. Boston: Houghton Mifflin Company, 1911.

Jones, Katharine M., *Heroines of Dixie: Confederate Women Tell Their Story of the War*. Indianapolis: The Bobbs-Merrill Company, Inc., 1955.

Jones, G. W., *In Prison at Point Lookout*. Martinsville, Va.: The Bulletin Printing & Publishing Company, n.d.

Jones, J. William, *Christ in the Camp: Religion in the Confederate Army*. Atlanta: The Martin & Hoyt Company, 1887.

Jones, J. William, *Personal Reminiscences, Anecdotes and Letters of General Robert E. Lee*. New York: D. Appleton & Company, 1875.

The Journal of a Milledgeville Girl, 1861–1867, edited by James C. Bonner. Athens: University of Georgia Press, 1964.

Keiley, A. M., *In Vinculis; The Prisoner of War*. New York: Blelock and Company, 1866.

Kell, John McIntosh, *Recollections of a Naval Life*. Washington, D.C.: The Neale Company, 1900.

Killie, E. I., "Why I got in Bed with a Corpse," *Confederate Veteran,* Vol. XIV, no. 8 (August 1906), pp. 361–62.

King, John H., *Three Hundred Days in a Yankee Prison: Reminiscenses [sic] of War Life, Captivity, Imprisonment at Camp Chase, Ohio*. Atlanta: J. P. Daves, 1904.

———, *My Experience in the Confederate Army and in Northern Prisons*. Clarksburg: W.V.: Stonewall Jackson Chapter of the United Daughters of the Confederacy, 1917.

Knauss, William H., *The Story of Camp Chase*. Nashville: Publishing House of the Methodist Episcopal Church, South, 1906.

Lee, Robert E., Jr., *Recollections and Letters of General Robert E. Lee*. Garden City, N.Y.: Doubleday, Page and Company, 1904.

Lee, Susan P., *Memoirs of William Nelson Pendleton*. Philadelphia: J. B. Lippincott Company, 1893.

"Lieutenant General N. B. Forrest," *Southern Historical Society Papers,* Vol. XX (January–December 1892), p. 329.

Longstreet, James, *From Manassas to Appomattox*. Philadelphia: J. P. Lippincott, 1896.

Loughborough, Mrs. James M., *My Cave Life in Vicksburg*. Little Rock: Kellogg Print Co., 1882.

Lord, Francis A., *Civil War Collector's Encyclopedia,* Vol. I. New York: Castle Books, 1965.

Lucas, Marion Brunson, *Sherman and the Burning of Columbia*. College Station, Tex.: Texas A & M University Press, 1976.

Lytle, Andrew, *Bedford Forrest and His Critter Company*. New York: Minton, Balch & Company, 1931.

MacLean, Clara D., "The Last Raid," *Southern Historical Society Papers,* Vol. XIII (January–December 1885), pp. 466–76.

McCarthy, Carlton, "Detailed Minutiae of Soldier Life," *Southern Historical Society Papers,* Vol. VI, no. 1 (July 1878), pp. 1–9.

———, *Detailed Minutiae of Soldier Life in the Army of Northern Virginia 1861–1865*. Richmond: Carlton McCarthy and Company, 1882.

McDonough, James Lee, *Shiloh: In Hell Before Night*. Knoxville: University of Tennessee Press, 1977.

McDonough, James Lee, and Thomas L. Connelly, *Five Tragic Hours: The Battle of Franklin*. Knoxville: The University of Tennessee Press, 1983.

McKinstry, J. A., "With Col. Rogers When He Fell," *Confederate Veteran*, Vol. IV, no. 6 (June 1896), pp. 220–22.

McMurray, Richard M., *John Bell Hood: and the War for Southern Independence*. Lexington: University Press of Kentucky, 1982.

McNamara, M., "Lieutenant Charlie Pierce's Daring Attempts to Escape from Johnson's Island," *Southern Historical Society Papers*, Vol. VIII, no. 2 (February 1880), pp. 61–67.

McPherson, James M., *Ordeal by Fire: The Civil War and Reconstruction*. New York: Alfred A. Knopf, 1982.

Marshall, John A., *American Bastille: A History of Illegal Arrests and Imprisonment of American Citizens During the Late Civil War*. Philadelphia: Thomas W. Hartley, 1869.

Miller, Walter L., "The Last Meeting of the Confederate Cabinet," *The Southern Magazine*, Vol. I, no. 3, pp. 137–50.

Moffett, George H., "War Prison Experiences," *Confederate Veteran*, Vol. XIII, no. 3 (March 1905), pp. 105–10.

Morgan, James Morris, *Recollections of a Rebel Reefer*. Boston: Houghton Mifflin Company, 1917.

Mosby, John S., *The Memoirs of Colonel John S. Mosby*. Bloomington: Indiana University Press, 1959.

"Mrs. Henrietta E. Lee's Letter to General David Hunter on the Burning of Her House," *Southern Historical Society Papers*, Vol. VIII, no. 5 (May 1880), pp. 215–16.

Murray, J. Ogden, *The Immortal Six Hundred*. Winchester, Va.: The Eddy Press Corporation, 1905.

Neese, George M., *The Years in the Confederate Horse Artillery*. New York: The Neale Publishing Company, 1911.

Nichols, G. W. (Pvt.), *A Soldier's Story of His Regiment (61st Georgia)*. Kennesaw, Ga.: Continental Book Company, n.d.

Null, J. M., "Thrilling and Amusing Events." *Confederate Veteran*, Vol. II, no. 9 (September 1894), pp. 276–77.

O'Ferrall, Charles T., *Forty Years of Active Service*. New York: The Neale Publishing Company, 1904.

Official Portfolio of the War and Nation, edited by Marcus F. Wright. Washington, D.C.: War Department, 1907.

The Official Records of the Union and Confederate Navies in the War of the Rebellion. Washington, D.C.: U.S. Government Printing Office, 1880–1927.

"Open Letters," *Century Magazine*, Vol. XLII, no. 6 (April 1892), pp. 954–55.

"Origin of 'The Conquered Banner,'" *Confederate Veteran*, Vol. V, no. 8 (August 1897), pp. 436–37.

Our Women in the War. Charleston: The News & Courier Book Presses, 1885.

Pasha, Hobart, *Sketches from My Life*. New York: D. Appleton and Company, 1887.

Pember, Phoebe Yates, *A Southern Woman's Story: Life in Confederate Richmond*. Jackson, Tenn.: McCowat-Mercer Press, Inc., 1959.

Polley, J. B., *Hood's Texas Brigade*. New York and Washington: The Neale Publishing Company, 1910.

Quattlebaum, Paul, "When the Yankees Came to Pinarea," *South Carolina Magazine*, Vol. 26, no. 2 (February 1962), pp. 4–6.

Ramsey, Lucille, "Commanche's Attack on Brown Family in 1863," *The* (Weatherford, Tex.) *Weekly Herald*, February 25, 1937.

Randall, J. G. and David, Donald. *The Civil War and Reconstruction*. Boston: D. C. Heath and Company, 1961.

"The Rebel Yell," *Confederate Magazine*, Vol. I, no. 4 (April 1893), p. 106.

The Reports of the Committees of the House of Representatives. First Session of Thirty-ninth Congress. 1865–66. 3 vols. Washington, D.C.: U.S. Government Printing Office, 1866.

Richmond During the War, by a Richmond Lady. New York: G. W. Carleton & Company, Publishers, 1867.

Ridley, Bromfield, *Battles and Sketches of the Army of Tennessee*. Mexico, Mo.: Missouri Printing and Publishing Company, 1906.

Ripley, Eliza McHatton, *From Flag to Flag*. New York: D. Appleton & Company, 1889.

Roy, Paul L., *The Last Reunion of the Blue and Gray*. Gettysburg: The Bookmart, 1950.

Saint-Amand, Mary Scott, *A Balcony in Charleston*. Richmond: Garrett & Massie, Inc., 1941.

Sears, Stephen W., *Landscape Turned Red: The Battle of Antietam*. New Haven: Ticknor & Fields, 1983.

Semmes, Raphael, *Memoirs of Service Afloat*. Baltimore: Kelly, Piet & Company, 1869.

Seward, Simon, "Perilous Escape from Point Lookout," *Confederate Veteran*, Vol. XVI, no. 1 (January 1908), pp. 42–44.

Sinkins, Francis B. and James W. Patton, "The Work of Southern Women Among the Sick and Wounded of the Confederate Armies," *The Journal of Southern History*, Vol. I, no. 4 (November 1935).

Simpson, Harold B., *Hood's Texas Brigade, A Compendium*. Hillsboro, Tex.: Hill Junior College Press, 1977.

Sommers, Richard J., *Richmond Redeemed: The Siege at Petersburg*. Garden City, N.Y.: Doubleday and Company, 1981.

Sorrel, G. Moxley, *Recollections of a Confederate Staff Officer*, edited by Bell I. Wiley. Jackson, Tenn.: McCowat-Mercer Press, 1958.

Southwood, Marion, *"Beauty and Booty": The Watch-*

word of New Orleans. New York: M. Doolady, 1867.

Sprunt, James, Tales of the Cape Fear Blockade. Wilmington, N.C.: Charles Towne Preservation Trust, 1960.

Stephens, Alexander H., A Constitutional View of the Late War Between the States: Its Causes, Character, Conduct and Results. 2 vols. Philadelphia: National Publishing Company, 1868.

Stern, Philip Van Doren, The Confederate Navy. New York: Crown Publishers, Inc., 1962.

Stiles, Robert, Four Years Under Marse Robert. New York: Neale Publishing Company, 1904.

"Story of Five Privates," Confederate Veteran, Vol. I, no. 5 (May 1893), p. 152.

Summersell, Charles Grayson, CSS Alabama: Builder, Captain and Plans. University, Ala.: University of Alabama Press, 1985.

Taylor, Thomas E., Running the Blockade. London: John Murray, 1897.

Taylor, Walter H., Four Years with General Lee. New York: D. Appleton & Company, 1878.

Thomas, Emory M., Bold Dragon: The Life of J. E. B. Stuart. New York: Harper & Row, Publishers, 1986.

"To Markie": The Letters of Robert E. Lee to Martha Custis Williams, edited by Avery Craven. Cambridge, Mass.: Harvard University Press, 1933.

"Treatment of Prisoners During the War," Southern Historical Society Papers, Vol. I, no. 4 (April 1876), p. 254.

Trezevant, D. H., The Burning of Columbia, S.C. Columbia: South Carolina Press, 1866.

The Tribute Book, Illustrated by Frank B. Goodrich. New York: Derby & Miller, 1865.

Trowbridge, John Townsend, A Picture of the Desolated States; and the Work of Restoration 1865–1868. Hartford, Conn.: L. Stebbins, 1868.

Twiggs, H. D. D., "Perilous Adventure at Battery Wagner," Confederate Veteran, Vol. XII, No. 3 (March 1904), pp. 104–106.

Underwood, J. L., The Women of the Confederacy. New York: The Neale Publishing Company, 1906.

The War of the Rebellion: A Compilation of the Official Records of the Union and Confederate Armies. 128 Volumes. Washington, D.C.: U.S. Government Printing Office, 1880–1901.

Warner, Ezra J., Generals in Blue: Lives of the Union Commanders. Baton Rouge: LSU Press, 1964.

Warner, Ezra J., Generals in Gray: Lives of the Confederate Commanders. Baton Rouge: LSU Press, 1959.

Watkins, Samuel R., "Co. Aytch." Jackson, Tenn.: McCowat-Mercer Press, 1952.

Welch, Spencer Glascow, A Confederate Surgeon's Letters to His Wife. New York: The Neale Publishing Company, 1911.

Wells, Edward, Hampton and His Cavalry in '64. Richmond: B. F. Johnson Publishing Company, 1899.

Wheeler, Richard, Sherman's March. New York: Thomas Y. Crowell, 1978.

Wiley, Bell Irvin, The Life of Johnny Reb. Baton Rouge: LSU Press, 1970.

Williamson, James J., Prison Life in the Old Capitol. West Orange, N.J.: n.p., 1911.

Woodward, C. Vann, Mary Chesnut's Civil War. New Haven: Yale University Press, 1981.

Worsham, John H., One of Jackson's Foot Cavalry. New York: The Neale Publishing Company, 1912.

WPA Slave Narratives. St. Clair Shores, Mich.: Scholarly Press, Inc., 1976.

Wyeth, John A., "Cold Cheer at Camp Morton," Century Magazine. Vol. XLI (November 1891–April 1892), p. 847.

———. That Devil Forrest: Life of General Nathan Bedford Forrest. New York: Harper & Row, 1959.

———. "Trials with General John H. Morgan," Confederate Veteran, Vol. XIX, no. 3 (March 1911), pp. 118–22; Vol. XIX, no. 4 (April 1911), pp. 161–64.

Manuscripts and Picture Sources

Atlanta Historical Society, Atlanta, Georgia.
Manuscripts Collection. Mary Rawson Diary.
Photographs Collection.

Austin Public Library, Austin History Center, Austin, Texas.
Photographs Collection.
John Scott Pickle Papers.

Birmingham Public Library, Birmingham, Alabama.
Photographs Collection.

Casemate Museum, Fort Monroe, Virginia.
Photographs Collection.

Century Magazine.

Mrs. James K. ("Bud") Chandler, Weaverville, North Carolina.

Coastal Carolina College, Waccamaw Room, Conway, South Carolina.
Alexia Marlowe Papers.

The College of William and Mary, Earl Greg Swem Library, Williamsburg, Virginia.
Manuscripts Collection.
William Lamb Papers.

Dr. Stan and Mrs. Anne Collins, Conway, South Carolina.

Confederate Memorial State Historic Site, Higginsville, Missouri.
Photographs Collection.

Confederate Research Center, Hill Junior College, Hillsboro, Texas.

Confederate Veterans.
Gale H. Dixon, Florence, South Carolina.
B. F. Emanuel, Lancaster, South Carolina.
Florida State Archives, Tallahassee, Florida.
    Laurie M. Anderson Papers.
    C. Seton Fleming Papers.
    Benjamin G. Liddon Papers.
    Thomas R. Love Papers.
    Patrick A. McGriff Papers.
    Photographic Collections.
    Amos Whitehead Papers.
Frank Leslie's Illustrated Newspaper.
Mr. and Mrs. James Edward Graham, Surfside Beach,
    South Carolina.
Harper's Weekly.
John W. Harris, Jr., Myrtle Beach, South Carolina.
Sharon Harris, Washington, D.C.
Carl Hill, Jr., Florence, South Carolina.
Laura J. Quattlebaum Jordan, Conway, South Carolina.
Kentucky Military History Museum, Frankfort, Kentucky.
    Robert Cunningham Papers.
    Alexander Macklin Papers.
    John Washington Payne Papers.
Library of Congress, Washington, D.C., Prints and Photo-
    graphs Division.
The London Illustrated News.
Alexia Marlowe, Conway, South Carolina.
Gwynn Meroney, Mocksville, North Carolina.
Museum of the History of Mobile, Mobile Alabama.
    Photographs Collection.
National Archives, Washington, D.C.
    Compiled Service Records of the 1st Florida Infantry.
    Compiled Service Records of the 2nd Florida Infantry.
    Compiled Service Records of the 8th Florida Infantry.
    Compiled Service Records of the 3rd Georgia Infantry.
    Compiled Service Records of the 4th Kentucky
        Cavalry.
    Compiled Service Records of the 9th Kentucky
        Cavalry.
    Compiled Service Records of the 2nd Kentucky
        Mounted Infantry.
    Compiled Service Records of the 14th North Carolina
        Infantry.
    Compiled Service Records of the 60th North Carolina
        Infantry.
    Compiled Service Records of Mannigault's Battalion
        of South Carolina Artillery.
    Compiled Service Records of the 3rd South Carolina
        Light Artillery.
    Compiled Service Records of the South Carolina
        Battalion of State Cadets.
    Compiled Service Records of the 7th South Carolina
        Cavalry.
    Compiled Service Records of the 23rd South Carolina
        Infantry.
    Compiled Service Records of the 1st South Carolina
        Rifles.
    Compiled Service Records of the 1st Tennessee
        Infantry.
    Compiled Service Records of the 12th Tennessee
        Infantry.
    Compiled Service Records of the 18th Texas Cavalry.
    Compiled Service Records of the 1st Texas Infantry.
    Compiled Service Records of the 5th Virginia Infantry.
    Compiled Service Records of the 6th Virginia Infantry.
    Compiled Service Records of the 17th Virginia
        Infantry.
    Compiled Service Records of the 51st Virginia Militia.
    Still Photographs Section.
Ohio Historical Society, Columbus, Ohio.
    Photographs Collection.
J. Keith Parker, Charlotte, North Carolina.
Pennsylvania State Archives, Harrisburg, Pennsylvania.
    Records of the Special Commission on the 50th
        Anniversary of Gettysburg.
Prairie Grove State Park, Prairie Grove, Arkansas.
    C. H. Gray Papers.
Beth Rider, Muskogee, Oklahoma.
Scribner's Monthly Magazine.
South Carolina Confederate Relic Room and Museum,
    War Memorial Building, Columbia, South Carolina.
    Photographs Collection.
Tennessee State Library and Archives, Nashville,
    Tennessee.
    Ferdinand Berry Papers.
Texas State Library, Austin, Texas.
    Photographs Collection.
Barbara Thomas, Myrtle Beach, South Carolina.
Dennis E. Todd, Cayce, South Carolina.
United States Army Military History Institute, Archives
    Branch, Carlisle Barracks, Pennsylvania.
    Harvey Bailey Papers.
    George S. Bernard Papers.
    John Bowden Papers.
    John Fiser Papers.
    David Gaston Papers.
    Abram Glazener Papers.
    Photographic Collection.
    Milton A. Ryan Papers.
    Charles Viele Papers.
    Albert Milton Walls Papers.
West Virginia Department of Culture and History,
    Charleston, West Virginia.
    Photographs Collection.
Western Kentucky University, Kentucky Building,
    Manuscripts Section, Bowling Green, Kentucky.

John H. Hines Letters, 1862–65.
James W. Morgan Letters.
University of Missouri. Ellis Library, Columbia, Missouri.
  Jones Family Papers, 1861–1862.
University of South Carolina, South Caroliniana Library,
  Columbia, South Carolina.
    Anonymous Manuscript 3023, March 3, 1865.
    Richard Bacot Papers.
    Katherine Heyward Album.

Daniel Heyward Trezevant Papers.
Richard Wearn Photographs.
University of Southern Mississippi, McCain Library and
  Archives, Hattiesburg, Mississippi.
    Thomas J. Rankin Letters.
University of Texas at Austin, John Barker Texas History
  Center, Austin, Texas.
    Annie B. Giles Papers.

Acknowledgments

Throughout the South, a detailed record of the Confederate experience has been carefully preserved. It awaits examination, piecemeal, at major universities, in expertly catalogued state archives, in the collections of numerous historical societies, at small colleges, in modest county libraries, at both notable and obscure museums, and in countless private collections. Fragile letters, faded *cartes de visite*, aging diaries, original and microfilmed military records, manuscript memoirs, and a century of published works collectively reveal a fascinating and often personal history of the Southern people in a war for independence. Studying these literal links with the past has been both a challenge and a pleasure. The pleasure has been the adventure of the search and the excitement of discovery. The challenge has been selecting a collection of accounts that faithfully reflects a reasonably full and accurate image of mid-nineteenth-century Southerners in their vain struggle for nationhood.

Researching *The Illustrated Confederate Reader* led me to manuscript and photographic collections throughout the South and elsewhere in the nation. Without exception, my personal contacts with repository staff members were pleasant and rewarding. In fact, dealing with the staffs of the one hundred–plus archival collections I contacted was probably the most enjoyable task in producing this work. Equally pleasant were my contacts with the many private citizens who responded to my public appeals for unpublished materials by coming forward with family photographs, letters, documents, and other historical sources.

The idea for *The Illustrated Confederate Reader* originated with M. S. Wyeth, Jr., my editor at Harper & Row. I hope I have developed the work in a manner that is complimentary to his original concept. His advice and suggestions throughout the production of this volume have been invaluable, and he has been my friend as well as my editor. Harper & Row's Florence Goldstein, always pleasantly efficient, has been a great help. I also appreciate the valuable counsel provided by Daniel Bial and Jim Armstrong in Harper & Row's New York office. Copy editor Ann Finlayson offered advice that improved the book's style and content.

I'm especially indebted to the staff of Kimbel Library at USC–Coastal Carolina College. Public Service Librarian Mary Bull graciously remained patient while I set a record for interlibrary loan requests. Reference Librarian Margaret Fain gracefully tolerated the flood of paperwork I sent her way, and Serials Assistant Paul Fowler provided expert advice and knowledgeable insight into the historiography of the war. Other Kimbel Library staff members who aided this project are David Wilkie, Charmaine Tomczyk, Joan Caldwell, Janice Schuster, and Peggy Bates.

Dr. Richard J. Sommers, archivist-historian at the U.S. Army Military History Institute, provided expert direction into research on a broad range of topics related to the Confederacy. Randy Hackenburg provided invaluable assistance in my survey of USAMHI's superb photographic collection. Other USAMHI staff members who aided my research were Michael J. Winey, John Crowe, John Spangle, Pamela A. Cheney, David A. Keough, and Lt. Col. Martin W. Andresen. My research in the Prints and Photographs Division of the Library of Congress was aided by the capable advice of Reference Librarian Leroy Bellamy and staff members Jerry Kearns, Beverly Brannon, Sam Daniel, and Mary Ison. My thanks also to those staff members who assisted my research at the National Archives.

I'm especially grateful for the valuable contributions made to this work by these individuals and institutions: Joan Morris at the Florida State Archives in Tallahassee; Jane Keeton at the Birmingham Public Library in Birmingham, Alabama; Sandra E. Boyd and Terry Latour at the University of Southern Mississippi's McCain Library and Archives; Bill Erquitt at the Atlanta Historical Society; Patricia M. Hodges at the Department of Library of Western Kentucky University; Col. Harold B. Simpson at the Confederate Research Center in Hillsboro, Texas; Caldwell Delaney at the Museum of the History of Mobile in Mobile, Alabama; Michael A. Comer at the Confederate Memorial State Historic Site in Higginsville, Missouri; Eleanor M. Richardson, Herbert Hartsook, and Charles Gay at the South Caroliniana Library in Columbia, South Carolina; Nancy Sandleback at the University of Missouri's Western Historical Manuscript Collection; Thomas W. Fugate at the Kentucky Military History Museum in Frankfort; Dotsy Boineau and John A. Martin, Jr., at the South Carolina Confederate Relic Room and Museum in Columbia, South Carolina; Ralph L. Elder and John Slate of the Eugene C. Barker Texas History Center at the University of Texas in Austin; James J. Holmberg and Mary Jean Kinsman at the Filson Club in Louisville, Kentucky; Wayne C. Moore at the Tennessee State Library and Archives in Nashville; Charles L. Sullivan at Mississippi Gulf Coast Junior College; and John Anderson at the Texas State Library in Austin.

I'm grateful, too, for the assistance I received from these institutions: The Casemate Museum in Fort Monroe, Virginia; Prairie Grove State Park in Prairie Grove, Arkansas; the West Virginia Department of Culture and History; Wilson's Creek National Battleground in Republic, Missouri; Fort Pulaski National Monument; Thomas Cooper Library at the University of South Carolina; Ohio Historical Society; Wilson Library at the University of North Carolina; Chemung County Historical Society in Elmira, New York; the Historic New Orleans Collection; Greensboro Historical Museum in Greensboro, North Carolina; Ina Dillard Russell Library at Georgia College in Milledgeville; Shiloh National Military Park; Grand Gulf Monument Commission in Port Gibson, Mississippi; South Carolina Department of Archives and History; William R. Perkins Library at Duke University; Pensacola Historical Museum in Pensacola, Florida; Lower Cape Fear Historical Society in Wilmington, North Carolina; Hargrett Rare Book and Manuscript Library at the University of Georgia; Virginia Historical Society; Knox County Public Library in Knoxville, Tennessee; Beauvoir in Biloxi, Mississippi; Petersburg National Battlefield; North Carolina Division of Archives and History; the Rosenberg Library in Galveston, Texas; Mississippi Department of Archives and History; Vicksburg National Military Park; DuPont Library at the University of

the South in Sewanee, Tennessee; Maryland Historical Society; Richland County Public Library in Columbia, South Carolina; Fredericksburg and Spotsylvania National Military Park; Middle Georgia Archives in Macon; Fairfield County Library in Winnsboro, South Carolina; State Historical Society of Missouri; Winchester-Frederick County Historical Society; Syms-Eaton Museum in Hampton, Virginia; John C. Pace Library at the University of West Florida; Alabama Department of Archives and History; Charlie Gragg Homestead in Globe, North Carolina; the Handley Library in Winchester, Virginia; Andrews Public Library in Andrews, North Carolina; South Carolina Historical Society; War Memorial Museum of Virginia in Newport News; The Citadel: The Military College of South Carolina; Central Rappahannock Regional Library in Fredericksburg, Virginia; Augusta-Richmond County Library in Augusta, Georgia; Massachusetts Historical Society; Rutherford B. Hayes Presidential Center in Fremont, Ohio; Chester County Library in Chester, South Carolina; Eggleston Library at Hampden-Sydney College; Alexandria Library in Alexandria, Virginia; Jacksonville Public Libraries in Jacksonville, Florida; Rockbridge Regional Library in Lexington, Virginia; The Mariner's Museum of Newport News; Delaware State Archives in Dover, Delaware; Museum of the Ozarks in Springfield, Missouri; Indiana Historical Society; Petersburg Public Library in Petersburg, Virginia; the Museum of the Confederacy in Richmond, Va.; the American Military Institute of Washington, D.C.; Gettysburg National Military Park; Andersonville National Historic Site; Maryland State Archives; Earl Greg Swem Library of The College of William and Mary; Ellis Library at the University of Missouri; Florence County Library in Florence, South Carolina; Pennsylvania State Archives; and the Horry County Memorial Library in Conway, South Carolina.

Numerous individuals shared graciously from their private collections and provided meaningful and previously unpublished materials for this work. My special thanks go to Barbara Thomas of Myrtle Beach, South Carolina; J. Keith Parker and Clint Johnson of Charlotte, North Carolina; Mr. and Mrs. James Edward Graham of Surfside Beach, South Carolina; Dr. Stan and Anne Collins, Floyd Goodwin, Laura J. Quattlebaum Jordan, and Alexia Marlowe of Conway, South Carolina; Beth Rider of Muskogee, Oklahoma; Gale H. Dixon and Carl Hill, Jr., of Florence, South Carolina; Mrs. James K. ("Bud") Chandler of Weaverville, North Carolina; Gwynn Meroney of Mocksville, North Carolina; Dennis E. Todd of Cayce, South Carolina; Tom Herring of Eldorado, Arkansas; David Ruth of Charleston, South Carolina; Perry Outlaw of Spanish Fort, Alabama; Dr. B. F. Emanuel of Lancaster, South Carolina; James Troy Massey of Harrison, Arkansas; Dr. Frank Lord, Dr. Clyde Wilson, Dr. Tom Connelly and Ed

Crosby of Columbia, South Carolina; Thomasine Haynes of Wilmington, North Carolina; Geoffrey R. Walden of New Baltimore, Michigan; Mrs. Thomas D. Caldwell of Lexington, Virginia; John W. Harris, Jr. of Myrtle Beach, South Carolina; Sharon Harris of Washington, D.C.; Erma Dennis of Verbena, Alabama; Jean Stevens of Pauline, South Carolina; Kathy Gantt Widner of Montmorenci, South Carolina; Ralph Ford, Jr., of Georgetown, South Carolina; and Dr. Sandra Garrett of Austin, Texas. I'm also grateful to various members of the United Daughters of the Confederacy, the Military Order of the Stars and Bars, and the Sons of Confederate Veterans for their assistance with this work.

Primary credit for reproducing much of the photography in this work must be given to Bill Edmonds, David Parker, Lisa Harrington, Lisa Moore, Jim Enos, and the staff at KPC Photography.

I'm especially grateful to Newt Outlaw of Washington, D.C., for his timely, valuable research in the Library of Congress.

Donna Williams, who spent many hours entering manuscript materials in a word processor, was an invaluable source of assistance on this project. My thanks also goes to Brenda Cox for her help with manuscript.

Essential elements in the content of this work were developed while my father and I fished John's River and ambled around Globe Valley under the shadow of Grandfather Mountain. Other inspiration came from Lib's Kitchen on Long Avenue. I'm thankful to my parents, L. W. and Elizabeth Gragg, for their constant support and encouragement, and I value the support I received from these: Bill and Margaret Outlaw, Doug and Jackie Rutt, Jimmy, Gail, John, and Joe Outlaw, Ted and Connie Gragg, the Rev. Randy Riddle and my friends at Grace Presbyterian Church, P.C.A.

More than anyone else, my wife, Cindy, and my children—Faith, Rachel, Elizabeth, Joni, and Penny—helped me produce this book. They sacrificed time, endured my preoccupation with the past, and were always there, happily, to remind me not to put the urgent before the important. For them and for the truth of Romans 5:8–9, I'm eternally grateful.

Index

Page numbers in *italics* refer to illustrations.

279